Cigarettes Are Sublime

Cigarettes Are Sublime

Richard Klein

Duke University Press   Durham and London 1993

This book has been published with the aid of

a grant from the Hull Memorial Publication

Fund of Cornell University.

© 1993 Duke University Press   All rights reserved

Printed in the United States of America

on acid-free paper ∞

Typeset in Joanna by Tseng Information Systems

Library of Congress Cataloging-in-Publication Data

and permissions for quoted material appear on the

last printed page of this book.

For M.-A. D.

Contents

Preface

My motives for writing this book are complex. They certainly had their origin in my urgent desire to stop smoking. In order not to do it any more, I felt I needed above all to understand the specific nature and determine the general conditions of my habit. That need, in turn, led me to the question that shaped this book's conception: What prompts nearly a billion people in the world, every day, to light up and inhale, when they know it is bad for their health? It is no longer seriously credible, if it ever was, to suppose they are ignorant of the dangers. Every day new studies demonstrate the more and more extensive potential harm that cigarettes do to ever-widening categories of people exposed to their noxious effects. It is not enough to say that people who smoke are addicted to tobacco. The fact of addiction in itself explains nothing; after all, millions choose to stop, or never start. Becoming addicted and continuing to smoke implies a persistent disposition to find some benefit or pleasure in the drug—but, in the present climate, it is hard even to imagine what they might be. What possible benefits or advantages accrue to anyone using a substance so extensively and deservedly reviled for the injury it does to your health? What conceivable pleasures could derive from an activity so distasteful that it makes everyone sick the first time they do it and frequently later on—as often as every day? I wanted to write a book that, in the present climate, would seek to discover the nature of the advantages and the conditions of the satisfaction that cigarettes deliver, in order to acquire another perspective on smoking, as a first, perhaps an indispensable, step toward giving it up.

It has been pointed out that the word *drug* is being used so loosely these days to characterize so many different things with such diverse effects that it has come to be affixed to repetitive behavior that is not even harmful, but actually beneficial—like exercise.* Using the word *drug* to describe an activity like exercise may be a sign that it has begun to lose its conventional meaning and maybe even its pejorative connotation. Another term may eventually be needed to designate more accurately the exciting cause of what one calls addiction. But before coining a new word, it will be necessary to distinguish more carefully one kind of drug from another, to specify the mode and analyze the mechanisms of their specific habituating power. Only when we know much more about the multiple and complicated ways in which different substances or activities lend themselves, privately or socially, to abuse, will we start to glimpse the outline of some overarching explanation of their role in society and culture. And it is probably only after acquiring a new notion or a more general concept for what we lump together today as drugs that successful policies and therapies to combat them can be devised.

In my own struggles with the habit, the decisive encounter came through reading Italo Svevo's novel *The Confessions of Zeno*, considered by many to be one of the great novels of the twentieth century. These are the fictional memoirs of a man who spends his entire life trying to stop smoking, and who finally succeeds only late in life, when, very old, he at last concludes that continuously giving up smoking is itself a way of life, no better or worse than any other. At that moment, neither smoking nor giving it up has any interest for him anymore. I was strangely moved by the dandyism of this existence that consisted in doing little else but repeatedly trying and failing to give up a futile habit. I began thinking about the way that smoking, and renouncing it, is a form of meditation, a sort of mandala spun at the end of the fingers—a discipline of breathing, as well as a sacrament consumed.

I further became interested in the heroism of what Théodore de Banville in the nineteenth century called a cigarette dandy—an aristocratic type who devoted himself to rolling and smoking more than sixty a day. It led me to reflect with sympathy on the compulsive smoking of great men and women whose lives have been tragically cut short by their inability to renounce their habit. The head-wagging their example

*Cf. Eve Sedgwick, "Epidemics of the Will."

provokes, the humiliating disapproval their smoking elicits in a culture for which longevity is an absolute value, overlooks the possibility that cigarettes may have contributed, in ways we do not fully grasp, to fostering the greatness we admire. For these people, smoking cigarettes was a kind of sacrifice, perhaps, for which we might honor them. After all, cigarettes are honored in wartime—a condition in which longevity hardly seems an option and cigarette smoking is not only tolerated but approved as a remarkably effective tool for relieving tension and mitigating anxiety. In part because of their specific physiological effects, cigarettes are often the indispensable companions of soldiers in combat, relied upon to sustain their courage and endurance in the face of intolerably stressful circumstances.

But in the end, I concluded, it is not the utility of cigarettes, however significantly useful they may be, that explains their power to attract the undying allegiance of billions of people dying from their habit. Rather, the quality that explains their enormous power of seduction is linked to the specific forms of beauty they foster. That beauty has never been understood or represented as unequivocally positive; the smoking of cigarettes, from its inception in the nineteenth century, has always been associated with distaste, transgression, and death. Kant calls "sublime" that aesthetic satisfaction which includes as one of its moments a negative experience, a shock, a blockage, an intimation of mortality. It is in this very strict sense that Kant gives the term that the beauty of cigarettes may be considered to be sublime. This conclusion allowed me to think that I better understood some of the puzzling anomalies or paradoxes surrounding the private use and social reception of cigarettes. The sublimity of cigarettes explains why people love what tastes nasty and makes them sick; it elucidates the conflicting policy of governments like ours that campaign against smoking while they provide large subsidies to tobacco growers.

Finally, I became absorbed by the culture that surrounds cigarettes and to which they gave rise—that is, by the remarkable wealth and richness of cigarettes as an example or a theme, a topic, or even a character in a great many major modern works of philosophy, poetry, fiction, and cinema. I became persuaded that cigarettes are a crucial integer of our modernity and that their cultural significance is about to be forgotten in the face of the ferocious, often fanatic or superstitious, and frequently suspect attacks upon them that are often, but not always, conducted by well-meaning people. Some of the attacks are redolent of strains of American Puritanism directed against any form of pleasure, and particularly the pleasure that women increasingly find in cigarettes, after generations of their having been surrounded by taboos. In some cases, the attacks seem to serve the interest of politicians, who are happy to denounce private smoking but are less interested in addressing the more pervasive, public sources of pollution over which they have greater direct authority.

Under the coordinated assault by the enormous power invested in the so-called health industry and its allies in government, the whole beautiful culture of cigarettes may well vanish—for some, not soon enough. "Soon," wrote Banville at the end of the nineteenth century, "there will be no more real cigarette smokers left" (233). He was, of course, absolutely wrong; in the twentieth century, smoking cigarettes became universal. But a hundred years later, his prophecy may be on the point of being realized. The question then, as cigarettes, the most combustible sort of smokes, may be on the point of disappearing, is this: Will anything have been lost? Is there any reason at all to mourn the passing of the culture of cigarettes?

This book aims to be simultaneously a piece of literary criticism, an analysis of popular culture, a political harangue, a theoretical exercise, and an ode to cigarettes. It seeks, without wanting to seem eclectic, to avoid conventional genre categories, with the aim of producing a more spirited kind of critical writing than one is accustomed to reading. This book may sin on the side of irresponsibility, slip on the slope of fatuity, or slide into fiction or provocation in order to avoid being boring. Intending to situate itself theoretically somewhere between literary criticism and political argument, what follows may fall and fail on both sides, disqualified from ever successfully being one by virtue of its participation in the other. Nevertheless it aspires to be both, and something else more illegitimate—a good example of a bad example of critical writing, one that brings literary criticism to bear, with a certain frivolity, on urgent social issues.

The cigarette is located here somewhere between popular and high culture, taken as an object of both literary and so-called cultural criticism. Its consummation is assumed to depend on its mythic identifications no less than its social uses, on its aesthetic properties no less than the conditions of its trade. This book attributes to the cigarette a certain philosophical dignity that derives from its being considered a symbolic instrument, and lends it the poetic qualities of a sacred object or an erotic one, endowed with magical properties and seductive charms, surrounded by taboos and an air of danger—a repository of illicit pleasure, a conduit to the transcendental, and a spur to repression. Six chapters recall the cultural history of cigarettes, their representation in philosophy and fiction, poetry and novels, cinema and photography, in order, in conclusion, to speculate on the reasons for their current demonization.

The reader may observe a certain repetition or echo effect in these pages, which speak only about cigarettes—about everything from the perspective of cigarettes. But the indifferent reiteration of pure number belongs to their essential nature; each cigarette is the recapitulation of all the identical ones smoked before and after. Taken as an object of reflection, cigarettes invite the return of the same, like smoke rings circling round before vanishing. The recurrence is a signal that what is being written here is smoke, or jazz—the effluently chatty story that cigarettes mutely unroll as they timelessly go up in smoke.

Acknowledgments

In relation to many of my contemporaries in the academy, I am already quite old to be publishing a first book. Being closer to the end of my career than to the beginning, this work is long overdue. In order to have been able to stay in the university, and to attain the comfortable position I occupy, I have had to have the support of many colleagues and friends who were repeatedly put in the uncomfortable position of having to recommend for promotion someone who had not even fulfilled what is everywhere considered these days the minimum condition for advancement. And yet over the years they not only wrote long, explanatory letters but were frequently called upon to defend, on the basis of slender evidence, their confidence in my value to the institution. There is no way I can thank them for that. And I fear this book may cause them more embarrassment than reason to feel justified. But I wish to acknowledge with gratitude the generous help and unfailing friendship of Philip Lewis, Jonathan Culler, and Neil Hertz. I owe very much to other friends and colleagues at Cornell and elsewhere: to Emoretta Yang, Cynthia Chase, Catherine Porter, Anne Berger, Jim Siegel, Pietro Pucci. Naomi Schor and Eve Sedgwick sponsored this book. Anne Dubuisson and Tamara Parker took great pains with it. I would like to thank Magnum Photos, and especially Melissa Dehnke, for their generous help. My debt to Jacques Derrida, to his work and his friendship, is everywhere visible in these pages. I owe my life to Muriel—not just a cigar. Judith lent me taste; Ellen wit. I owe my survival to Billie-Jean, my highs to Michelle. This book to Marie-Anne.

Cigarettes Are Sublime

Introduction

La vida es un cigarillo
Hierno, ceniza y candela
Unos la fuman de prisa
Y algunos la saborean.
—Manuel Machado, "Chants andalous"

My aim in this book is to praise cigarettes, but certainly not to encourage smoking—not at all. But I am not trying to discourage it, either. If I had wanted to do that, I would not have come out and said so directly (i.e., have discouraged in a way so as to mention I was discouraging), on the principle, which is one of the conclusions of this book, that openly condemning cigarette smoking frequently fails to have the desired effect—often accomplishes the opposite of what it intends, sometimes inures the habit, and perhaps initiates it. For many, where cigarettes are concerned, discouraging is a form of ensuring their continuing to smoke. For some, it may cause them to start.

A corollary of this conclusion asserts that it is not enough to know that cigarettes are bad for your health in order to decide not to smoke. The noxious effects of tobacco have been observed since the moment of its introduction into Europe at the end of the sixteenth century. Since the early nineteenth century, it has been recognized that the alkaloid of nicotine, administered to rats in pure form in minute doses, instantly produces death. No one who smokes fails eventually to get the signals that the body, with increasing urgency, sends as it ages; in fact, every smoker probably intuits the poison from the instant of experiencing the first violent effects of lighting up, and probably confirms this understanding every day with the first puffs of the first cigarette. But understanding the noxious effects of cigarettes is not usually sufficient reason to cause anyone to stop smoking or resist starting; rather, knowing it is bad seems an absolute precondition of acquiring and confirming the cigarette habit. Indeed, it could be argued that few people would smoke if cigarettes were actually good for you, assuming such a thing were possible; the corollary affirms that if cigarettes were good for you, they would not be sublime.

Cigarettes are not positively beautiful, but they are sublime by virtue of their charming power to propose what Kant would call "a negative pleasure": a darkly beautiful, inevitably painful pleasure that arises from some intimation of eternity; the taste of infinity in a cigarette resides precisely in the "bad" taste the smoker quickly learns to love. Being sublime, cigarettes, in principle, resist all arguments directed against them from the perspective of health and utility. Warning smokers or neophytes of the dangers entices them more powerfully to the edge of the abyss, where, like travelers in a Swiss landscape, they can be thrilled by the subtle grandeur of the perspectives on mortality opened by the little terrors in every puff. Cigarettes are bad. That is why they are good—not good, not beautiful, but sublime.

Alcoholics Anonymous long ago discovered the limits of assuming that a simple act of will, performed in response to an imperious injunction issuing from the self or some external authority, would cause alcoholics to stop drinking. The suggestion that one can "Just say No" entertains the very illusion that motivates the habituated person. Any habit carries with it the endlessly repeated belief that one has sufficient self-control to stop, abruptly, at any moment: believing one can stop is the preeminent condition of continuing.[1]

Just saying No, over and over again, while continuing to smoke, becomes the motivating aim, the consuming pleasure pain, of Italo Svevo's hero in the novel The Confessions of Zeno. His whole life is spent in enacting the illusory belief that he can smoke "The Last Cigarette." But the last one always turns out to be just one more cigarette, another in the series of last cigarettes; taken together, they form the narrative of Zeno's paradoxical existence, serving as milestones marking the passage of time and the progressive stages of his unheroic but strangely gallant life. Endlessly trying to stop smoking leads to a life of doing nothing but smoking (until, in the final chapter, as an old man, Zeno discovers the ingenious means to a cure).

To intervene in this conundrum, an altered—more paradoxical, more hypocritical—strategy is necessary: not aiming to discourage smoking, in order to discourage it. Not wanting to condemn smoking, this book may actually have a positive—that is, a negative—effect. It may happen that smokers, from simply reading this book that praises cigarettes for their social and cultural benefits, for their contribution to work and freedom, for the consolation they offer, the efficiency they promote, the dark beauty they bring to the lives of smokers, will acquire a new perspective on their habit. A change of point of view sometimes prompts the initial step—perhaps forms the absolute precondition—of making a decisive break.

But more than a change of viewpoint may be required to stop smoking. Something else is called for, something like an active engagement with it, an admission of love. Perhaps one stops smoking only when one starts to love cigarettes, becoming so enamored of their charms and so grateful for their benefits that one at last begins to grasp how much is lost by giving them up, how urgent it is to find substitutes for some of the seductions and powers that cigarettes so magnificently combine.

It is the premise of this book that cigarettes, though harmful to health, are a great and beautiful civilizing tool and one of America's proudest contributions to the world. Seen in this light, the act of giving up cigarettes should perhaps be approached not only as an affirmation of life but, because life is not merely existing, as an occasion for mourning. Stopping smoking, one must lament the loss to one's life of something—or someone!—immensely, intensely beautiful, must grieve for the passing of a star. Writing this book in praise of cigarettes was the strategy I devised for stopping smoking, which I have—definitively; it is therefore both an ode and an elegy to cigarettes.

It is no easy task to praise cigarettes at this time in America. We are in the midst of one of those periodic moments of repression, when the culture, descended from Puritans, imposes its hysterical visions and enforces its guilty constraints on society, legislating moral judgments under the guise of public health, all the while enlarging the power of surveillance and the reach of censorship to achieve a general restriction of freedom. The present hysteria concerning cigarettes bears comparison with other moments of violent antitabagism [2] in this country; it contrasts starkly with times in America's history when great mobilizations of the people were called for—during wars, for example, when cigarettes were deemed to be necessary not only to survive (General Pershing wrote that they were as vital to his troops as food), but to live while surviving, because survival might be brief. Cigarette smoking during wartime and depressions was not merely approved as a pleasure but viewed almost as a duty that owed to the principle of camaraderie and to the requirements of consolation in the face of tragedy. It was also recognized as an index of one's adult reliability. In those periods, smoking was admired, praised, and encouraged. Whenever the society needed more soldiers (civilian as well as military, men as well as women), smoking cigarettes changed its value and became not only laudatory but patriotic. In 1920, just after World War I, when some antitobacco people bravely reemerged in Indiana to renew their campaign (the same groups whose triumphs in the 1890s had led twenty-six states to ban public smoking), they were indicted on charges of . . . Treason!

The history of America's great love affair with cigarettes is being neglected, perhaps even erased, in the present climate. The contributions tobacco has made to this continent, since well before Columbus brought it to the avid Europeans, gave rise to the formerly often-cited celebratory slogan, which Americans are in danger of being the first to forget: "Tobacco is American." And it was America, in the person of James B. Duke of Durham, that made cigarette smoking universal, giving to the entire world what at first had been a class privilege and what Pierre Louÿs, writing in 1896, called "une volupté nouvelle"—the only decisive advance in the knowledge of pleasure that modern European culture had achieved over antiquity.[3]

Intellectual honesty, at the very least, requires that we seek to explore the sources of what Jean Cocteau calls the "powerful charms" of a pack of cigarettes. Cocteau, himself an illusionist, writes, in the wavy parataxis of a smoky preface: "Il ne faut pas oublier que le paquet de cigarettes, le cérémonial qui les en sort, allume le briquet, et cet étrange nuage qui nous pénètre et que soufflent nos narines, c'est par des charmes puissants qu'ils ont fait la conquête du monde" [One must not forget that the pack of cigarettes, the ceremony that extracts them, lights the lighter,[4] and that strange cloud which penetrates us and which our nostrils puff, have with powerful charms seduced and conquered the world] (Cocteau i).[5] Cocteau alludes here to the universally seductive magic that cigarettes exercise everywhere, among every class, in every milieu; there is no society, however fanatic its values and exotic its customs, that has not succumbed to the dangerous attractiveness of cigarettes, the alluring, fiery risk their beauty engenders. There is nowhere in the world where people do not smoke if they are allowed to.

It is tempting to suppose that America, which gave tobacco and cigarettes to the world, may be the first country to ban them, although not the first to try. At the end of the last century, however, people were predicting the imminent end of cigarette smoking, so it may be premature to foresee its disappearance now. It is rather more likely that we are at an apogee in one of the cyclical movements of encouragement and prohibition of smoking, with which America enacts repression and its return—a cycle already repeated several times in the twentieth century. That would

Jean Cocteau
Photo © Herbert List. By permission of Magnum Photos, Inc.

suggest that we are due for a swing in the other direction; the sharp rise of smoking among certain sectors of the population, in the face of a generally slowing decline, leaves one to wonder what fate awaits the antismoking movement under conditions of economic or social crisis.

But suppose, which is highly unlikely, that cigarette smoking were to vanish from America. Would anything be lost? If billions of people during nearly a hundred years have been taking uncounted puffs from trillions of cigarettes, there must be some advantage—at least a perceived one—in smoking. If smoking were to cease tomorrow, not only might something of utility be lost (although compensated by the enormous gain to general health), but a certain quality of experience that smoking made possible would be extinguished as well. Perhaps it is only at the moment that cigarette smoking vanishes that we can discover the place it occupies in our social imaginary—in the myths and the dreams, the consolation and the intensification, the intuitions and the charms to which it has given rise. Suppose one were to write an adieu to cigarettes?

In Cocteau's formula, the ritual charms of smoking "have conquered the world." This military metaphor connoting seduction implicitly combines the two principal poles of cigarette smoking, whose permanent alliance is directly illustrated by the two most popular brands of cigarettes in France, Gauloises and Gitanes: emblems of risk and beauty, exerting "powerful charms," are embodied on those packs in the figures of the Soldier and the Gypsy. The expression "charmes puissants" recalls unmistakably in a French ear the "puissant dictame," rolled out by the pipe in Charles Baudelaire's famous poem "La Pipe," which "charms the heart [of the smoker] and cures his spirit of its fatigues" (Baudelaire, vol. 1, 67). Baudelaire endowed smoking with the beauty of his women, whose fascination and seduction held poetic charms: consoling and delighting the heart, they also revive the spirit, giving it courage. The French poet Paul Valéry called a volume of his poems Charmes, wishing to endow them with magical powers—to produce material effects of transformation at a distance by the manipulation of texts. He also wanted to evoke carmen, the Latin word for poem, particularly a sung poem. Valéry, a man in love with cigarettes, who smoked sixty a day, may have also been thinking of the seduction of the Gypsy Carmen, who is the first figure in literature to be identified with cigarettes.

When Georges Bizet's Gypsy heroine encounters her soldier lover Don José, she is one of the cigarières who work rolling cigarettes in the tobacco factory in Seville, from which they emerge upon the scene in the first act of the opera. Carmen's Seville, it is no accident, was in the nineteenth century

the principal center and probable origin of cigarette making in Europe—
a city famous for its immense factory where thousands of women, many
young and barely dressed, languorously rolled cigars and manufactured
cigarettes in dense heat and the poisoned air of tobacco smells and human
sweat, intoxicated by the thick effluvia arising from leaves and bodies and
by their own continuous smoking; their skin was dyed to ravishing or
ravished shades of nut-brown color by the stain of nicotine.

In Prosper Mérimée's *Carmen*, the novella on which Bizet's libretto is
based, Don José begins his narration of his encounter with Carmen by
describing the factory in Seville:

> You must know, sir, that there are easily four or five hundred women
> employed at the factory. It is they who roll cigars in a great hall, where
> men may not enter without permission of the Twenty-four, because
> they are half-undressed [elles se mettent à leur aise], especially the
> young, when the weather is warm. At the hour when the workers re-
> turn, after their dinner, many young men go to see them pass, and tell
> them every manner of story. There are few of these young ladies who
> refuse a mantilla of taffeta, and the lovers of this kind of fishing need
> only bend over to take the fish. (Mérimée 367)

In the first act of the opera, the *cigarières*, leaving work, "appear, smoking
cigarettes, and come slowly into the square" (Bizet 10). Their chorus celebrates the amorous evocations that perfumed smoke, gently rising, continuously scribbles in the intricate syntax of its swirling articulations. The
cigarette becomes a love poem that they ceaselessly write and that writes
itself throughout the day—whose correlative is the dreamy melody they
sing:

> Le doux parler des amants
>   c'est fumée!
> Leurs transports, leurs transports et leurs serments
>   c'est fumée!
> Dans l'air nous suivons des yeux
>   La fumée
>   La fumée
>   La fumée
>   La fumée
>
> Sweet talk, sweet talk of lovers
>   it's all smoke!

Their raptures, their raptures, and their vows,
   it's all smoke!
We watch the smoke drifting into the air
(Bizet 11)

One of the first appearances in French literature of the word *cigarette* is in Baudelaire's "Les Salons de 1848." The suffix *-ette* adds a belittling feminine connotation to the masculine noun, le cigare. The word, like the object, makes its appearance in Baudelaire's text between the slack fingers of *lorettes*, the lower-class prostitutes associated with the quartier around the Church of Our Lady in the Ninth Arrondissement—women whom Baudelaire, slumming, observes assuming poses of cynical, languorous, distressed beauty: "Prostrate they display themselves in desperate attitudes of boredom . . . smoking cigarettes to kill time" (vol. 2, 721). The cigarette kills time, chronometric time, the stark, mechanical measure of mortality whose relentless ticktock terrifies Baudelaire in the poem "L'horloge" with its whispered intimations of mortality. The series of moments the clock records is not only a succession of "nows" but a memento mori diminishing the number of seconds that remain before death. But the cigarette interrupts and reverses the decline, accomplishes a little revolution in time, by seeming to install, however briefly, a time outside itself. In the June days of 1848 Baudelaire reports seeing revolutionaries (he might have been one of them) going through the streets of Paris with rifles, shooting all the clocks. Smoking cigarettes, as subsequent chapters will demonstrate, is permanently linked to the idea of suspending the passage of ordinary time and instituting some other, more penetrating one, in conditions of luxuriating indifference and resignation toward which a poetic sensibility feels irresistible attraction.

A cigarette bespeaks the smoker, as the poem the poet. Reading it, one overhears the smoker engaged in a lyrical conversation with the cigarette, within the limits of the syntax and lexicon determined by a widely recognized cultural code of smoking. With a cigarette, the smoker enacts a subtle dance or enters a dialogue that accompanies every gesture and word. Extracted from its pack and smoked, the cigarette writes a poem, sings an aria, or choreographs a dance, narrating a story in signs that are written hieroglyphically in space and breath. Dressed in its neat paper suit, the cigarette is more subtle, demure, and cool than the naked cigar fancied by rough, exuberant men and psychoanalysts. The smoker enacts an unconscious tango with the body of the cigarette, whose beauty makes the smoker beautiful and whose power she (he?) absorbs. The cigarette is analogous to what linguists call a shifter, like the word I; this device for expressing the irreducible particularity of my innermost self is universally available to every speaker and is thus the least particular thing in the world. The smoker manipulates the cigarette, like the word I, to tell stories to herself about herself—or to an other.

Many authors have understood the uses to which cigarettes are put as instruments of what is frequently called communication. Smoking cigarettes bodies forth an implicit language of gestures and acts that we have all learned subliminally to translate and that movie directors have used with conscious cunning, with the explicit intention of defining character and advancing plot. Careful viewers have long observed that in the movies, one can not only watch but read cigarettes like subtitles—translating the action on the screen into another language which the camera registers but rarely foregrounds, a part of the thickness of the medium which is almost never brought into focus. It is the sign of everything the camera sees without announcing that it sees it. The cigarette in the scene serves as a subtext, a mute caption or subtitle, sometimes accompanying, sometimes contradicting or diverting the explicit premises of the action or the open meaning of signs. Its appearance in film may be even more complex if one assumes that the cigarette is not merely a prop but a character on the scene, and not merely a character but at times the principal actor. In some films, cigarettes are so prevalent and insistent that they assume a role of their own, even a leading role, with a pose and a personality, even a voice. The demonstration of that possibility for cigaretticism will be left to the chapter analyzing the cigarettes in *Casablanca*—a film in which everybody, except Ingrid Bergman, constantly, passionately, significantly smokes.

In the still photography of Jacques-Henri Lartigue, in the 1980 collection of photographs called *Les femmes aux cigarettes*, the dialogue between the subject and her cigarette is the ostensible focus of the camera's eye. The witty, touching, beautiful language of cigarettes is linked to the way they organize the woman's pose, the "air" she assumes. The little, invisible cinder, the fire in the cinder beneath the ash at the end of the cigarette, is the invisible other spirit or soul in the photo, the other point of life in relation to which the woman posing composes her pose—speaking to the cigarette, so to speak, with the language that her body speaks in the process of arranging itself, holding itself, in relation to the point of fire at the end of the cigarette. The stories a cigarette tells may be in considerable harmony with those the person smoking is otherwise telling, but they may also become a mask of the smoker, or betray her, revealing narratives and motives that she hardly suspects. In his collection of photographs, Lartigue may be the first to have defined the parameters of a repertoire of gestures that accompany women smoking, an idiom and syntax that determine an implicit but well-understood code for communicating what in the last chapter I call "l'air du temps."

But the cigarette is more than a mirror reflecting the smoker's subjectivity. Not just an object one holds in one's hand, it must be considered a subject, a creature alive with a body and spirit of its own. Not merely a poem, the cigarette is a poet, -esse or -ette: the fiery cinder ash is the heart of a living being, an effemin-ette, perhaps even a feminine being, endowed with abundant resources of seduction and diverse powers to focus the mind. There is nothing extravagant about considering the cigarette to be a daemon, a little divinity, a minor déesse (dé-ette), if one recalls that American Indians, from the Iroquois to the Aztecs, universally considered tobacco a god. The Romans, with their enormous pantheon, would have made a little goddess of the first cigarette of the morning, speculates Valéry: "They would have called it, had they known it, 'Fumata Matutina'" (Valéry quoted in Alyn 86). Alas for them, "tobacco is the only pleasure [volupté] that the Romans did not know" (Louÿs quoted in Alyn 54).

How does one reconcile the divinity of the cigarette with its demonization by the forces arrayed against smoking? "Lady Nicotine" is not a lady but "a little white Devil" made from "the demon plant," wrote the Reverend George Trask, founder of the Anti-tobacco League in Massachusetts, who succeeded before the Civil War in having public smoking banned in Boston (Rival 210). Indeed, how, one might ask, can one insist on the beauty of cigarettes, when former Surgeon General Everett Koop denounces their sale abroad as equivalent to "exporting disease, disability, and death" (International Herald Tribune, August 8, 1989)? It is well known that no one has ever liked cigarettes the first time they tried them, and no one has ever said tobacco was good for you—at least not since the sixteenth century, when doctors, as ever faddish, held it briefly to be the panacea, the pharmaceutical equivalent of the philosopher's stone.

Historians of tobacco frequently observe that antitabagism arose simultaneously with tobacco's introduction to the West and has accompanied its universalization. But of course, the earliest objections to tobacco were moral rather than medical; the clergy knew in an instant that they were dealing with a mind-altering drug, a potent source of pleasure and consolation that threatened competition with their own opiated nostrums.

Whereas tobacco was a god to the Indians who brought it to the Span-
iards, to the Christian mind it immediately appeared as another devilish
animism.

Bartholomé de Las Casas, who accompanied Columbus in 1498 and 1502,
was one of the earliest pious observers of tobacco and its effects. In his *Historia de las Indias*, he provides the first recorded evidence of the existence of
cigarettes and with remarkable prescience succinctly anticipates the major
moral themes of the next four hundred years of public hygiene. He writes:

> They are dried weeds that are enveloped in certain leaves, also dried,
> in the form of those paper firecrackers [*pétards*] that boys make at Pen-
> tecost. Lit at one end, it is sucked at the other end or they inhale it or
> receive it with their breath into their interior, this smoke with which
> they put flesh to sleep and almost get drunk. So that they say they
> feel no fatigue. These firecrackers, or whatever we call them, they call
> tobaccos [*tabacs*]. I have known Spaniards in Española [Santo Domingo/
> Haiti] who had become accustomed to taking them and who, after I
> had reprimanded them, saying that it was a vice, answered that they
> were unable to stop taking it. I do not know what savor or taste they
> find in it. (Quoted in Rival 11)

Not having acquired the habit of smoking, it is no wonder de Las Casas
failed to appreciate its charms. The moralist jumps to conclude that
smoking, like any activity compulsively performed, irresistible in its grip,
dispensing narcosis and intoxication, magically dissipating the pain and
fatigue of work, must be, perforce, demonic. But being a philosopher, he
tries it, and, having indulged the new vice, attests that it does not even taste
good. Ned Rival, the great modern historian of tobacco, confirms the absence of texts praising the taste of cigarettes. He writes: "It is remarkable,
in effect, to observe that in the prehistory of tobacco, smoking is rarely
evoked as a pleasure or a relaxation. At most, chroniclers insist on the fact
that tobacco calms hunger, soothes fatigue, and procures intoxication . . .
but they nowhere write that it is agreeable to the taste or smell" (Rival 36).

King James I wrote, in Latin, *Misocapnus, sive De abusu tobacci* (Counterblast
to Tobacco) in 1604, directing sharp thrusts against the despicable habit
his subjects were eagerly taking up. "The habit of smoking," writes the
king, "is disgusting to sight, repulsive to smell, dangerous to the brain,
noxious to the lung, spreading its fumes around the smoker as foul as
those that come from Hell" (James I 27). The King was also honing edges

here against the neck of Sir Walter Raleigh, whom he had beheaded under unwarranted suspicion of treason—that noble privateer who plagued the Spanish Main, the man who introduced Virginia tobacco to England, the gallant favorite of James's hated predecessor, a symbol of the new pleasures and perspectives that the Elizabethan age had brought to the dour religious perspectives of sixteenth-century England.[6] Sir Walter, however, refused to abandon his pipe and kept it in his mouth until his head fell. Indeed, it has been written: "No man could die more splendidly than did Raleigh. He smilingly picked up the axe on the way to the block, and running his finger over the edge of it said: 'This is sharp medicine, but it will cure all disease' " (Blair quoted in Rival 33). The philosophy of health that is implicit in Raleigh's witticism, and its relation to smoking, is the focus of chapter 3, which restates and reinterprets that philosophy through the work of Italo Svevo.

Like other tyrants such as Louis XIV, Napoleon, and Hitler, James I despised smoking and demonized tobacco. The relation between tyranny and the repression of the right to grow, sell, use, or smoke tobacco can be seen most clearly in the way movements of liberation, revolutions both political and cultural, have always placed those rights at the center of their political demands. The history of the struggle against tyrants has been frequently inseparable from that of the struggle on behalf of the freedom to smoke, and at no time was this more the case than during the French and American revolutions. The earliest political history of this country, from the time of the first English settlers in Virginia, who survived on the commerce of tobacco, to the revolutionary struggle against English taxes, was forged in the name of the right and freedom to grow and use tobacco— free from the impositions of the state. Governments have always sought to control the use of tobacco, for reasons that have to do with what Napoleon, the first to create a state monopoly of tobacco, called its eminent taxability: it is a habituating luxury that even the poorest will pay for. But the reasons may also have to do with these tyrants' moralizing tendency and their allergic reaction to individual acts of expressive freedom. Napoleon, like Louis XIV and Hitler, was violently, personally disgusted by smoking. Hitler was a fanatically superstitious hater of tobacco smoke; he is known to have granted to Mussolini the only exception to his refusal to permit it in his presence. Signs everywhere in the Third Reich, and throughout the war, proclaimed: "Deutschen Weiben rauchen nicht" [German women do not smoke]; yet, in fact, the opposite was massively true. There is nowhere in the world where people do not smoke if they are allowed to.

Vaclav Havel
Photo © Milon Novotny. By permission of Magnum Photos, Inc.

The most recent evidence of the link between smoking and liberation is visible in the struggle women have waged in this century for their freedom. It is probably no accident that in April 1945 women received the right to vote in France, two weeks after they had received cigarette rations for the first time since the war. They were allotted, however, only one-third of the rations men received—"a long way, baby," but not yet there. In the Conclusion, I will review the results of a European Community health investigation showing that European women are much more likely to smoke in those countries where they are the most liberated from traditional places and roles. This fact lends credence to the suspicion that some of the current impetus for the wave of antitabagism derives from its concealed misogyny, or antifeminism.

Americans today, as always forgetting their own history, aroused to paroxysms of antismoking sentiment, think they invented it. At the turn of this century, as well as in the 1920s and 1930s, powerful political forces combated the "demon weed." Then, as now, protests on behalf of the health of the citizenry masked moral objections, just as censors always defend their interdictions by adducing the harm that some form of expression or pleasure may inflict on society as a whole.

The beauty and benefits of cigarettes have been repressed and forgotten in America, where the climate of opinion ranges in abstractness from implicit forms of social disapproval to laws banning smoking on all domestic flights. The last is a sign of the dangerous lengths to which antismoking impulses will go to deny others the freedom to enjoy the consolation and the mastery cigarettes provide in moments of stress or fear. Many people who do not normally smoke take up smoking during times of personal or public crisis, at moments of great anxiety when self-control and concentration are required. Nowhere these days does one hear voices lifted to praise cigarettes, as one often does in wartime, for their multiple psychological and social benefits, for their cultural value, or for their aesthetic power. But as time goes by, the circle turns. This book proceeds on the hunch that the present climate may change, perhaps gently as the result of something like fashion—an effect of the turning of an obscure process of cyclical historical development—perhaps violently, under the pressure of widespread social tensions. The United States does not need to await a vast calamity in order to rediscover the social benefits of cigarettes or to appreciate their remarkable contribution to modernity—and to resume its love affair with cigarettes, America's gift to the world. It could come suddenly, with a vengeance, in a moment when the society needs all the collective control over anxiety that it can muster.

To evoke a climate of opinion other than the current one, we need only recall the value that was assigned to a carton of cigarettes, for example in Europe in 1945. Cigarettes served then, as tobacco had for the earliest settlers in Virginia, and later for Lewis and Clark, as a universal token of exchange—the "Gold Token," as good as gold. George Washington wrote to the Continental Congress: "If you can't send money—send tobacco" (Rival 188). Lewis and Clark used it as their principal token of exchange with the Indians. In Drancy, the French concentration camp, on the eve of departures a puff on a cigarette was worth 10 francs; 100 francs bought two whole ones.

The world can only be grateful for the precision and insistence with which doctors remind it of the dangers of smoking poison; that is their job. But the suspicion here is that the passions and the uses to which that information is being put are wildly disproportionate to the danger that tobacco poses—particularly other people's smoke. For the moment, cigarettes have become the focus or fetish of puritanical prohibitions like those that, in the past, periodically constrained freedom and censored pleasure in the name of protecting the collective well-being from harm, but always under the darker suspicion of wishing to increase state control or to conceal other interests. Not long ago, the secretary of health castigated cigarette marketing during the very week that the White House chief of staff weakened the clean air bill. The passionate excess of zeal with which cigarettes are everywhere stigmatized may signal that some more pervasive, subterranean, and dangerous passions are loose that directly threaten our freedom. The freedom to smoke ought to be understood as a significant token of the class of freedoms, and when it is threatened one should look instantly for what other controls are being tightened, for what other checks on freedom are being administered. The attitude of a society toward the freedom to smoke is a test of the way it understands the rights of people at large, for at any time, all the time, a quarter to a half of all the adults in the world are puffing away at cigarettes. The question of the connection between the freedom to smoke and general freedoms in the society is hard to prove, but this book will suggest that it ought never to be disimplicated.

It is one of the many paradoxes surrounding smoking that this double-dosed drug, both calming and exciting, is both combated and subsidized by the federal government. At the very moment that Jimmy Carter, with tears in his eyes, was swearing to a group of tobacco growers in North Carolina that he would never sanction cutting their subsidies, Joseph Califano, the head of the Department of Health, Education, and Welfare, was launching a $50 million campaign, the largest in history, to combat smoking. This book aims to reveal the coherence beneath this apparent contradiction—a deeper logic that the concept of the "sublime" allows us to perceive.

In 1856 a journal devoted to smoking, called Paris fumeur, had as its motto "Qui fume prie": Smoking is praying. For many modern writers, notably Annie Leclerc in Au feu du jour, "La cigarette est la prière de notre temps" (49). The moment of taking a cigarette allows one to open a parenthesis in the time of ordinary experience, a space and a time of heightened attention that give rise to a feeling of transcendence, evoked through the ritual of fire, smoke, cinder connecting hand, lungs, breath, and mouth. It procures a little rush of infinity that alters perspectives, however slightly, and permits, albeit briefly, an ecstatic standing outside of oneself.

Laws are passed against cigarette smoking on statehouse grounds where three hundred years before sat Indians, smoking, for whom tobacco was part of a ritual that unified the individual with the tribe and with the collective memory of its ancestor gods, the guardians of the myths of its identity. When the religious dignity of smoking is completely obscured, we have lost a right to pray in public. The freedom to smoke may not be protected by the constitutional protection of religion. But there is much about the ritual act of taking a cigarette that this book wishes to explore.

Forces arrayed against smoking have little feeling for the historical irony of their position. They are unable to see that their movement belongs to the permanent, parallel alliance between smoking tobacco and antitabagism, which has persisted throughout the history of tobacco's universalization. It is as if not only the censors but also the censored, not only antismokers but smokers, require each other's permanent hostility as the condition of their continuing existence.

Antismoking forces in this country have not yet succeeded in banning cigarettes, only in changing the value of the signs that surround them. This book recalls to mind the other, secret side of cigarettes, the side that has been all but suppressed in the current climate of public disapproval. For a moment it wants to reverse the reversal of judgment and, instead of decrying cigarettes, to celebrate them—not in order to recommend them or to minimize the harm they do to the body, but to recall that, despite their many disadvantages, which have always been known and widely proclaimed, they present benefits, universally acknowledged by society.

Those benefits are connected with the nature of the release and consolation that cigarettes provide, with the mechanism they offer for regulating
anxiety and for mediating social interaction. They serve as well to spur concentration and, consequently, to permit the efficient production of many
different kinds of work.

Nevertheless, this book does not aim to praise cigarettes chiefly for
their utility, but rather for what Théodore de Banville calls their "futility."
It is their uselessness that ensures the aesthetic appeal of cigarettes—the
sublimely, darkly beautiful pleasure that cigarettes bring to the lives of
smokers. It is a pleasure that is democratic, popular, and universal; it is a
form of beauty that the world of high as well as popular culture has for
more than a century recognized and explicitly celebrated, in prose and
poetry, in images both still and moving. So widespread is this understanding of the beauty of cigarettes that this book can seem to argue in favor of
taking them seriously, as among the most interesting and significant cultural artifacts produced by modernity. That is the position, we will see,
at which the heroine of Pierre Louÿs arrives, in "La volupté nouvelle":
Louÿs seduces the reader into exploring the life of beauty that cigarettes
inspire under even the humblest and most suffering conditions, not to
mention the most sophisticated and refined.[7] The complex functions they
perform in the lives of individuals and in social intercourse have been
so repressed beneath the negative value they are currently assigned, as to
shame smokers, encouraging them to postpone gratification and, increasingly, to conceal the habit. Whereas smoking cigarettes was once an act of
defiance, it is now largely an occasion for guilt, although defiance and guilt
have always belonged to the psychology of cigarette smoking—forms of
the violence of transgressing the interdiction of a taboo. Cigarettes have
always been identified with the illicit; many of the texts considered in
this book refer to the conditions surrounding beginning to smoke, which
traditionally arises in connection with theft or the breaking of other rules.

If one wanted to celebrate cigarettes, one would find it difficult to adopt
a convincing rhetorical tone. Cigarettes are trivial, nasty things, unsuited
for elegiac purposes. In the present climate they have been so denigrated,
so demonized, that it is hardly possible to give a measured argument about
their virtues and disadvantages; their very mention evokes fiercely negative connotations. In these circumstances, hyperbole is called for, the rhetorical figure that raises its objects up, excessively, way above their actual
merit: it is not to deceive by exaggeration that one overshoots the mark,
but to allow the true value, the truth of what is insufficiently valued, to

appear.[8] The validity of hyperbole, the truth that exaggeration may often convey, depends on a principle well recognized by marksmen: there are times when aiming to overshoot the mark is the condition of hitting it. One cannot praise cigarettes these days without seeming perverse; one can only overpraise them, hoping that the reader, hearing the excessiveness of the hyperbole, will not dismiss the extravagance but will restore what has been immoderately debased to something more approaching its actual worth. The effort of imagination required to praise cigarettes way beyond their value allows one to measure the depths to which their value has fallen. To say that cigarettes are sublime installs a ratio that allows one to conclude that they are not simply abysmal. Erasmus invented the rhetorical problem when he sat down to write In Praise of Folly.

To accomplish this task, a writer would have need of a muse, for nothing he can invent will dictate the tone required to sing the praise of what all around is being condemned and despised. Zeno, the narrator of Svevo's novel, facing the same dilemma, begins his journal with an invocation: "Non so come cominciare et invoco l'assistenza delle sigarette tutte tanto somiglianti a quelle che ho in mano" [Not knowing how to begin, I invoke the aid of all the cigarettes similar to the one I am holding in my hand] (Svevo 4).

The muse of smoking cigarettes frequently accompanies writing. Authors, like Svevo's Zeno, often hold both pen and fag in hand, spilling ink and taking drags interchangeably. Ned Rival in Tabac, miroir du temps reproduces old valentines of men with cigarettes sitting writing at desks, while a bubble of smoke over their heads contains an image of their beloved. The cigarette gives the writer, inhaling, the inspiration that permits him to summon the beloved image, bodied forth in a lyric effusion—a recent muse in the tradition dating back to Petrarch. The cigarette is itself a woman—the word, the concept, and the thing being identified, from its origins, with a certain feminine—and poets have not been lacking who have written sonnets and odes to praise its darkly modern beauty.

An ode to cigarettes is hard to imagine today, although Jules Laforgue wrote one in 1861 titled "La cigarette" that reiterates one of the earliest identifications of cigarettes with beautiful, dangerous women, with lorettes, or grisettes, or Bohémiennes.[9] Praising cigarettes is like composing a bouquet of Fleurs du mal, where the beauty one celebrates gives rise not to the usual aesthetic feelings of satisfaction and repose but to troubled, menacing pleasures. It raises up what ought not to be exalted (if to praise must always mean to laud what is good, what is worthy of praise). It is inevitably a hypocritical gesture designed to circumvent the hypocrisy of the reader whose public good conscience masks the truth that he already knows too well, the perverse enchantment of what is risky, ugly, shameful. In the first chapter of this book, "What Is a Cigarette?" something like the concept or notion of cigarette is defined, with help from a philosopher and a poet. The definition emerges from Sartre's reflection on cigarettes in L'être et le néant and from "Cigarettes," by Théodore de Banville, one of the pieces the poet collected (at the end of a life devoted to the Parnassian ideal of pure poetry) in a volume published, at the end of the century, under the title L'âme de Paris. In my second chapter, "Cigarettes Are Sublime," the nature of their beauty is evoked through reading poems in which their sublimity is celebrated and described in terms echoing those one finds in the analytic of the sublime, in Kant's Critique of Judgment.

The third chapter, "Zeno's Paradox," proposes a close reading of the opening chapter of Italo Svevo's great novel, the standard English translation of which is always called "The Last Cigarette," but which in Italian is simply entitled "Il fumo." Written in the guise of a therapeutic memoir, the novel presents itself as a smoker's case history written by the smoker himself on the model of a self-psychoanalysis. But instead of recalling his earliest memories of childhood, the narrator, Zeno, begins with his first cigarette, giving birth to what he calls a "fumo-analysis." Zeno's writing-cure of smoking raises in a surprisingly rigorous fashion the question of the concept of health, the meaning of a word that is so much taken for granted that its seeming self-evidence disposes in advance our society's understanding of the uses and abuses of cigarettes. Zeno makes us rethink the relation of smoking to health by reexamining a life enthralled by the leisurely business of stopping smoking. Not life, he discovers, but death is the condition of true health—a conclusion that leads him to reinterpret the value of bad habits, parasites, and disease.

A woman can be beautiful; a Gypsy woman is sublime. For Nietzsche, the Gitane, whose apotheosis is Bizet's Carmen, is the fatal embodiment of Mediterranean passions, superior to the frigid spirits of Richard Wagner's northern mists. Nietzsche writes about Bizet's music as if he were describing Carmen herself: "This music of Bizet seems to me to be perfect. It approaches with a delicate allure, supple and polished. It is amiable, it raises no sweat. Everything that is good is light, what is divine runs on delicate feet: first principle in my Aesthetic. This music is irreverent, refined, fatalistic: it remains however that of a race not an individual. It is rich. It is precise" (letter from Turin, May 1888). Nietzsche's reading of Bizet's music is rendered in language that immediately recalls the qualities the narrator assigns to the character of Carmen in the original story by Prosper Mérimée, from which the opera libretto was taken. The first time Carmen appears, endowed with ominously fabled beauty, is also the first time in literature that a woman is represented as accepting a cigarette and smoking. It is one of the aims of this book to suggest that the fascination of the myth surrounding Carmen is linked to her association with the beauty inherent in cigarettes, which were being introduced into Bohemian France around the time she was invented.

In chapter 4, "The Devil in Carmen," after considering Mérimée's story in conjunction with Bizet's opera, we turn to another figure of demonic femininity, Thérèse Desqueyroux, the sublime witch of François Mauriac's somber novel who feeds poison to her bourgeois husband for the purpose of once rousing him from his irremediably complacent self-righteousness. Mauriac calls her Sainte Locuste, a holy version of Nero's venomous apothecary, to mark the negative transcendence she is supposed to represent (a bit too patly, Sartre notes); she smokes three packs a day, and hardly a page of the novel does not contain reference to a cigarette being taken or offered, smoked or extinguished, loved or hated. Every cigarette in a novel—perhaps not always in life—is significant; reading *Thérèse Desqueyroux* will lend insight into the literary code of cigarette smoking, understood as an organized discourse with its own conventions, rules, and syntax.

The passion and the risk associated with cigarettes are emblematized by the two figures that compose the tragic couple of Carmen and Don José, the Gypsy and the Soldier. Together they serve as the elliptical double focus of the fourth and fifth chapters. Their mythical connection is preserved most vividly today by the two most popular brands of French cigarettes, Gitanes and Gauloises. Both brands were created in 1910, on the eve of the Great War. Gitanes were considered the first "modern" cigarette, lighter in flavor and elegantly boxed. Gauloises were called Hollandaises until a dispute involving a foreign brand by the same name obliged the French to change theirs. The pack was colored a patriotic blue, the color of the *poilu* or French foot soldier's uniform—"le bleu des Vosges." Later a Gallic helmet was placed on the pack surrounded by an unbroken ring of chain links. Chapter 5 explores the role of cigarettes in war through an analysis of their appearance in half a dozen great war novels from the First World War to the (imagined) Third. The cigarette is every soldier's best friend, for the solace it brings, for the relief from hunger and fatigue it provides, for the relaxation it encourages, for the courage it summons when the fighting gets thick and hard. Erich Maria Remarque's Im Westen nichts Neues is the model on which most war novels in the twentieth century have been written; for that reason, and because cigarettes play such a central role in it, it is the masterpiece through which the other novels will be read.

Cigarettes kill time. Baudelaire writes of women "fumant des cigarettes pour tuer le temps, avec la résignation du fatalisme orientale" [smoking cigarettes to kill time, with the resignation of oriental fatalism] (vol. 2, 721). The Orientalist slur (not all Orientals are fatalistic) may take its origin from the stereotypical comparison in French, "to smoke like a Turk"; it has its hyperbolic overcompensation in the exalted value Baudelaire assigns to the "resignation" these women practice. In his system of values, it is the condition of a kind of dandified heroism, a triumph over vulgar forms of egotism, a sort of elevation above the pressing crowd of desires and fears. For Théodore de Banville, the resignation cigarettes promote, being the opposite of ambition, is closely linked to the conditions of poetic expression. My sixth chapter, "L'air du temps," could also be called "But I Didn't Inhale." It evokes the obscure utopian ambition of every smoker to have all the pleasures of the cigarette with none of its noxious consequences— like watching smokers in a film or through a lens.

Nothing, it appears, is simple where cigarettes are concerned; they are in multiple respects contradictorily double. They both raise the pulse and lower it, they calm as well as excite, they are the occasion for reverie and a tool of concentration, they are superficial and profound, soldier and Gypsy, hateful and delicious. Cigarettes are a cruel, beautiful mistress; they are also a loyal companion. The conflicting nature of the pleasure they provide, both sensual and aesthetic, and the duplicity of their social, cultural value are consequences of their physiological effects, which are surprisingly contrary. Svevo's Zeno is the modern master of the abundant paradoxes that arise from considering cigarettes.

Machado's little poem (used above as an epigraph) asserts that life is a cigarette. One of the principal aims of this book is to reflect on the possibilities concealed within that metaphor. Metaphors classically illuminate the unknown by giving us the known for comparison. If we take seriously Machado's metaphor, we quickly realize that for anything to be a metaphor for life it must itself be vast, profound, and mysterious—however trivial, superficial, and familiar it might normally seem. To know that life is a cigarette may answer only some of life's questions, but it opens up the issue of the cigarette to practically infinite consideration. The answer that the metaphor is supposed to provide conceals a new mystery that this book aims to explore. I therefore look with the greatest attention at those conditions that allow us to reverse Machado's proposition, those moments when it seems, not that life is a cigarette, but that a cigarette is bigger than life. Banville is full of fascinated admiration for the absolutism of the "true smoker," a kind of "dandy" of the cigarette, devoting every waking moment, with great elegance and discipline, all but exclusively to its consumption—smoking, for example, between every spoonful of soup, or even, he says (imagine!), in lieu of making love.

Banville admires the absolute futility of the habit, even though he does not wish to pay its price; but he nevertheless recognizes, in the elevated indifference it promotes, a figure of the highest form of artistic life. It is he, after all, who gave the century the phrase "L'art pour l'art" that Baudelaire, while qualifying it, wields as a weapon against cultural utilitarianism. The tautological self-sufficiency of the formulation, no less than the aesthetic ideology it proclaims, bespeaks the cold and polished surface of the dandy who lives, says Baudelaire, forever in front of a mirror, and whose perfect self-mastery results from an infinitely inward reflection on the self ("Le peintre de la vie moderne," "Le dandy," vol. 2, 709–12). The "true smoker" for Banville belongs to the happy few of the "others" Machado evokes who, savoring their cigarettes, lend to life its aesthetic justification:

> Life is a cigarette,
> Cinder, ash, and fire,
> Some smoke it in a hurry,
> Others savor it.

1 What Is a Cigarette?

Only smoking distinguishes humans from
the rest of the animals. —Anonymous

A photographic self-portrait from the 1930s, reproduced in *Le Monde* (December 17, 1987), pictures the popular French photographer Brassaï, standing on the rue Saint-Jacques, shooting the streets of Paris at night.[1] Posed against the intermittent shadows of the cobblestones, he is seen in profile, peering through the glass of his bellowed Rolleiflex. The camera is supported at his eye level by a tripod, one foot of which is barely visible in the gutter; the camera could be peering back at him. He wears a long, shadowy overcoat, distinctly well-worn, whose loose folds, like the dark cloth of a portrait camera, completely obscure his body; from beneath a broad fedora emerge, barely, his face and neck, straining to see through the glass. He is hunched against the rawness of one of those cold Paris nights, when the wet wind, sweeping in from the Atlantic uninterrupted by the plains to the west, blows down into the city streets, banishing cobwebs. Half his face is illuminated by the oblique ray of a street lamp that is the apparent but invisible source of the pool of light at his feet. The light, coming from above at an angle, lends a theatrical air to the prominence of his face in the photograph, a face that features a large aquiline nose and, jutting out and down, a cigarette—long, inordinately thick, and very white against the darkness. His craning neck bespeaks his avid wish to see through the lens something that lies improbably beyond the frame in the gloom—something his camera, haloed by light for its role in another photograph, probably could not record. Photographed photographing, he may in fact see nothing in the lens, standing, as he is, beneath the harsh glare whose function is to illuminate him and his camera for us, for the camera we do not see that gives us to see (in) this self-portrait. Seeming, with the angle of his neck, to form the leg of another tripod, the cigarette may be another index of avidity, sticking out from his lip like a sign of incipient arousal. Not merely a prop, although also that, like everything else in this self-portrait, the cigarette is an index—not a symbol but an entity that is what it is, while at the same time being a sign for the general category of things it is. The index of the cigarette points to itself to indicate that it is an instrument of the photographer's trade. In fact, the cigarette in the photo is a timer for determining, roughly, the long duration of the film's nighttime exposure. Brassaï explains: "Une gauloise pour une certaine lumière, une boyard s'il faisait plus sombre" [A Gauloise for a certain light, a Boyard if it was darker]. The Boyard is a cigarette first introduced into commerce in 1896 on the occasion of the visit to Paris of Czar Nicolas II; the word translates as seigneur, or lord, and designates the landed aristocracy of czarist Russia. What matters for Brassaï's purposes is that the diameter of the cigarette (10.5 mm for a Boyard versus the normal 8.7 mm for a Gauloise) determines the time it takes to smoke.

This cigarette is not a cigarette but a clock, as every smoker knows intuitively, and as many literary and cinematographic representations attest. It is an intimate counter that the photographer uses to divine the moment when enough light has done its magic on the emulsion. The photographic image takes time to form, but the image we see all at once, in the time of a look, is of a photographer smoking a clock, measuring the time needed to produce this image. Brassaï has in fact taken a photograph of the timer that may be timing the exposure, not of the picture he appears in the photo to be taking, but of the one we are observing, the self-portrait taken through the lens of the other camera we do not see. The peculiar and rather amusing centrality that is lent to the photographer's cigarette—a wink at the phallic intrusiveness of the camera's "eye"—is intended therefore to put light on the time of the photograph's exposure to the light and, more particularly, on the difference between the time of the image's production and the instantaneity of its consumption by a look. Every photo seems to represent the snapping off of a single frozen moment, the stereotypical time of a camera's click (or cliché, in French), even if, in fact, the exposure took the time it took to smoke a Boyard. No event is ever instantaneous, of course; the punctual unity that seems to define it is always an idealized fiction or a technically persuasive illusion. Frequently the illusion of instantaneity is ideologically motivated by the desire to erase from the appearance of what appears the multiple, heterogeneous labor times that went into its presentation as a single coherent occurrence. But how can one represent that difference in a photograph—the difference that is constitutive of its production and consumption—except by a little allegory of that difference in the person of the cigarette? It becomes the focus of this photographer's self-portrait. For all its apparent insignificance (the result of the ubiquity and the mechanical stereotyping of cigarettes), it speaks of what the photograph before us occults; it is a kind of hermeneutic hole in the surface of the image that opens onto a dimension of time—the time of its production—which the photograph itself cannot represent but must obscure in the stillness of its image.

One of the ironies of this photographic self-portrait is that its star is not the photographer but the production of the photograph, represented by its timer, a cigarette. The rare importance Brassaï lends to the cigarette contrasts with the way cigarettes are usually photographed or painted, depicted or indicated, in prose as well as images, always marginally—propping a gesture, sketching a pose, but rarely the direct focus of attention. The cigarette is usually considered to be merely an accessory to the face of the portrait, to the scene of whatever activity may be being observed. Its role is inessential or nugatory, its utility—if it has any—belongs to the realm of leisure or distraction, its function is decorative and incidental.

The caption in Le Monde accompanying the photograph of Brassaï is not misled by the modesty of cigarettes. After identifying the brand, it suggests, half seriously, that the subject of the Boyard, like the one Brassaï is smoking, "deserves a whole Sorbonne thesis in itself"; after all, Le Monde impeccably informs us, the boyard is also the "fat number" [gros module] Sartre used to "pop" [brûler] when he was writing Being and Nothingness. It is not true, as the myth has it, that Sartre wrote his masterpiece sitting in the Café Flore, on the Boulevard St. Germain, drinking small cups of coffee and filling ashtrays with innumerable ends of cigarettes, which had hung so long untouched on his Frenchman's lip that nothing remained but the barest butt. But it is true that, while writing, he smoked like a Turk. It will, therefore, be easy to show that any Sorbonne thesis on the Boyard would be bound to contrast the capital role played by cigarettes in the physical writing of Sartre's book with the depreciated value and insignificant functions they are assigned in the moral hierarchies of Being and Nothingness. But before getting too deep in anticipation of the putative thesis, the reader must remember that Le Monde's suggestion is only half-serious; such a thesis is impossible. Calling Sartre's cigarette a gros module in French has burlesque, bordering on obscene, connotations analogous to those in English surrounding a "fat number," referring to a large, thickly rolled joint. The mechanical impersonality of *module*, like the slangy word *number*, makes it antiphrastic, intimating the opposite of what it designates—the least indifferent, the most highly personal component of pleasure and taste the cigarette affords ("Who is that cute number?"). The joke of proposing that the fat number Sartre used to pop become the object of a Sorbonne thesis points up the inherent futility, the irredeemable triviality of cigarettes, all-too-ironically "worthy," like so many academic subjects, of being treated, out of all proportion to their actual value or significance, with the misplaced gravity of a weighty academic tome. Only a fool or an academic would undertake to write a thesis on the Boyard—to write a book on cigarettes!

But imagine for a moment that you were both an academic and a fool, like the author, and you took seriously *Le Monde*'s suggestion. For a moment, try to imagine the shape of such a thesis. It would doubtless present some very peculiar anomalies. In the first place, the cigarette does not lend itself to the sort of Aristotelian definitions with which every Sorbonne thesis inaugurates its investigation. One has difficulty asking the question, the Aristotelian philosophical question, "Ti estin [What is] a cigarette?" The cigarette seems, by nature, to be so ancillary, so insignificant and inessential, so trifling and disparaged, that it hardly has any proper identity or nature, any function or role of its own—it is at most a vanishing being, one least likely to acquire the status of a cultural artifact, of a poised, positioned thing in the world, deserving of being interrogated, philosophically, as to its being. The cigarette not only has little being of its own, it is hardly ever singular, rather always myriad, multiple, proliferating. Every single cigarette numerically implies all the other cigarettes, exactly alike, that the smoker consumes in series; each cigarette immediately calls forth its inevitable successor and rejoins the preceding one in a chain of smoking more fervently forged than that of any other form of tobacco.

Cigarettes, in fact, may never be what they appear to be, may always have their identity and their function elsewhere than where they appear—always requiring interpretation. In that respect they are like all signs, whose intelligible meanings are elsewhere than their sensible, material embodiment: the path through the forest is signaled by the cross on the tree. Cigarettes are frequently signs, but especially ambiguous ones, difficult to read. The difficulty is linked to the multiplicity of meanings and intentions that cigarettes bespeak and betray; they speak in volumes, rather than in brief emblematic legends. The cigarette is itself a volume, a book or scroll that unfolds its multiple, heterogeneous, disparate associations around the central, governing line of a generally murderous intrigue. The cigarette is a thyrsus, the wand of Dionysus, which Baudelaire took to be the emblem of all poetic language, whose vine leaves are the poet's fantasy and invention swirling around a rigid, central hop-pole that stands for poetic intention and creative purpose. Smoking there at the end of two delicately poised fingers or emerging from its pack at the end of an offer to smoke, the cigarette may convey worlds of meaning that no thesis could begin to unpack, that require armies of novelists, moviemakers, songwriters, and poets to evoke.

There are other, more contingent reasons why Aristotle could not ask, "What is a cigarette?" Tobacco was unknown to antiquity, and not even Aristotle, who knew every damn plant, knew anything about it, botanically or experientially. But a more subtle ignorance may be involved here: Aristotle did not know the experience of tobacco, which, to some, may be equivalent to saying that he, an ancient, was uninformed about modernity. The introduction of tobacco into Europe in the sixteenth century corresponded with the arrival of the Age of Anxiety, the beginning of modern consciousness that accompanied the invention and universalization of printed books, the discovery of the New World, the development of rational, scientific methods, and the concurrent loss of medieval theological assurances. The Age of Anxiety gave itself an incomparable and probably indispensable remedy in the form of tobacco; it was an antidote brought by Columbus from the New World against the anxiety that his discoveries occasioned in the Eurocentered consciousness of Western culture, confronted by the unsuspected countenance of a great unknown world contiguous with its own.[2] The paradoxical experience of smoking tobacco, with its contradictory physical effects, its poisonous taste and unpleasant pleasure, was enthusiastically taken up by modernity as a drug for easing the anxiety arising from the shock of successive assaults on old certainties and the prospect of greater unknowns. It is tempting to think that Aristotle could not have known tobacco even if he knew it. Tobacco, the avid enjoyment of which quickly spread to every corner of the Continent and promptly beyond to Asia, defines modernity; its use is an index of whatever revolution in consciousness may have occurred to transform the culture and the mores, the ethics and principles, of antiquity. Aristotle could not define the cigarette because, resisting the Aristotelian definition, the cigarette defines him and his age: the cigarette asks Aristotle, "What's this, the question: 'What is'?" Such an argument was advanced by Pierre Louÿs, the

French classicist and pornographer, in a short story written in 1896, "Une volupté nouvelle." Cigarettes, he suggests through his heroine Callistô, are the only new pleasure that modern man has invented in eighteen hundred years, and perhaps his sole originality with respect not only to the pleasures but to the wisdom of antiquity. For Louÿs they thus define the difference between modern man and antiquity and therefore become the most important thing to study, the one most worthy to occupy the attention of the historian of culture. History, in fact, should be nothing else, in a way, than the history of cigarettes.

However impossible it may be to ask the Aristotelian question of the cigarette, we cannot pretend to ignore that the question "Qu'est-ce que la Cigarette?" has already literally been asked, in French, in an essay written at the end of the nineteenth century by Théodore de Banville. For the moment we will put off consideration of the answer he proposes and assume that the question cannot be asked at all.

We can be certain, however, that no thesis could fail to include a chapter titled "Le Boyard in L'être et le néant." It would not only narrate what could be learned of Sartre's smoking habits, which were compulsive (Simone de Beauvoir, for example, attests that "he smoked two packs of Boyards a day" [8]), but it would contrast the importance of the role cigarettes played in the material production of the work with the insignificance they are implicitly assigned within it, whenever they serve as an exemplary, thematically explicit topic of philosophical reflection. For Sartre makes frequent reference in those pages to smoking. It is one of the charms of L'être et le néant [Being and nothingness] that its abstract formulations are illustrated with an abundance of concrete examples drawn from the writer's immediate surroundings—examples whose deictic formulations, such as "this inkwell," "this table," "these cigarettes," recall the style of Descartes's Meditations much more than, say, Heidegger's austere and rarely illustrated Sein und Zeit, to which Sartre constantly refers. It is instructive to contrast Sartre's constant cigarette smoking while writing L'être et le néant with his systematic devaluation of them in the work itself, particularly compared to his beloved pipe. Among the many references to cigarettes (but no cigars: wrong class) and pipes (to which we may assimilate the examples of matches and tobacco pouches), the latter are assigned to the side of Being while cigarettes belong to Nothingness.

What is a cigarette, philosophically speaking? A Sorbonne thesis such as the one Le Monde proposes might have less difficulty addressing the narrower question: "What exactly is a Boyard?" It would perforce begin by

Jean-Paul Sartre
Photo © Marc Riboud. By permission of Magnum Photos, Inc.

noting the circumstances surrounding the Boyard's introduction to France in 1896 on the occasion of an official visit to Paris of the ill-fated Czar Nicolas II, a heavy smoker whose habit was not what killed him. The name Boyard was chosen no doubt to honor the imperial guest, but it resembles many other names of cigarettes intended to lend an air of aristocratic luxury to the most democratic, popular form of tobacco; the putative thesis would not likely miss the irony that the cigarette named for the czar was adopted by the proletarian class that in Russia overthrew him.

Cigarettes first appear in L'être et le néant when Sartre wants to exemplify the existence of attributes that are objective properties of things but not inherent in them. He writes: "If I count the cigarettes in this cigarette case, I have the impression that I am uncovering an objective property of this group of cigarettes: *they are twelve*. This property appears to my consciousness as a property existing in the world. . . . an excellent refutation of Alain's formula: 'To know is to know one knows.' And yet, at the moment in which these cigarettes are revealed to me as being twelve, I have a nonthetic consciousness of my act of addition" (19). Sartre at this moment is distinguishing between reflexive consciousness and immediate consciousness of things. The former consists in judgments that consciousness passes on itself and therefore implies the "thetic" positioning of consciousness by itself—explicitly, nominally, self-reflexively posing itself as its own object, knowing that it knows. Immediate consciousness, perception or counting, attributes objective properties to things (the number twelve to cigarettes, for example) without posing its operation as an object of consciousness: one may count without knowing that one counts, or how. One can know, contrary to Alain, without knowing that one knows. What is of interest here is the way cigarettes lend themselves to the illustration of this philosophical distinction. It is not that "these cigarettes" actually themselves possess the "objective property" of being twelve; they only appear to do so at the moment they are counted. Nevertheless, they lend themselves better to this appearance than other things might (pipes or tobacco pouches, for example) by virtue of their eminent countability.

The distinctive character of cigarettes compared to other forms of tobacco is their indistinctness; one cannot distinguish one smoke from another. Each cigarette is exactly, mechanically, indifferently like every previous cigarette one has smoked, perhaps hundreds of thousands of them. Each individual cigarette has its identity insofar as it is like every other one, mere interchangeable tokens. There is no existential, Kierkegaardian uniqueness in the individual cigarette, only an abstract Hegelian generality under which every individual is subsumed. Deprived of any irreducible specificity or distinguishing characteristics, the cigarette has only a collective identity, not an individual one. The one is the many; number seems to belong to its identity. In that respect cigarettes are radically different from, say, a pipe, whose value is a direct function of its "character," the accidental or crafted features that lend it the aura of an irreplaceable object—uniquely itself. Neither are tobacco pouches easy to count; their function is rather to hold what is countable, frequently a form of money, with a calculable value. Like the prior material condition of counting, they keep together whatever lends itself to receiving the objective attributes of number—money or smokes. That is why a tobacco pouch is called, in French, une bourse.

A cigarette lends itself much less readily, by contrast, to the self-asserting appropriation that for Sartre, following Hegel (cf. chapter 4 of The Phenomenology of the Mind), is the motive for the ownership of things. Sartre writes, for example: "Thus, to the extent that I appear to myself as creating objects simply by virtue of appropriation, these objects are me. The pen and the pipe, the clothing, the desk, the house, is me. The totality of my possessions reflects the totality of my being. I am what I have" (652). Cigarettes cannot be Sartrean objects of appropriation; rather, they are abstract, unindividuated entities that can be offered and accepted indiscriminately. Having few qualitative determinations, they frustrate efforts to foster the illusion of being a kind of surrogate self, an exteriorization of one's most intimate identity. But to whom does one offer a pipe? If I am what I have, since I have nothing so completely as my pipe, la pipe, c'est moi. One would never dream of asserting "I am my cigarette" unless one were seized by a Mallarméan rage to vanish.

Of course, Sartre's ethical aim is to discredit this bourgeois conception of property, whose whole ideology is based on the premise that I am what I have. But even if, as he argues, the pipe resists appropriation, having been smoked, it nevertheless remains, before me on the table, a substantial, independent, palpable object—very different from the cigarette, whose destiny is to disappear in consumption. Sartre writes: "The pipe is there, on the table, independent, indifferent. I take it in my hands, I feel it, I contemplate it, in order to achieve this appropriation; but precisely because these gestures are destined to give me the enjoyment [jouissance] of this appropriation, they misfire, I have nothing but a piece of inert wood between my fingers" (652). The pipe seduces its owner with the illusion that it can be appropriated by virtue of its palpable presence; but the more I manipulate it in view of enjoying its possession, imagining it to be an extension of myself, the more surely those gestures misfire. The bloody thing, for example, keeps going out, shattering the illusion that it can perfectly fulfill my appropriative desire; it remains there, in itself, independent, an inert piece of wood.

Mallarmé seems to make the same distinction between cigarettes and pipes in a remarkable passage in which they are distributed—like the two great poems on which he worked for most of his adult life, "L'après-midi d'un faune" and "Hérodiade"—between summer and winter activities:

> Hier j'ai trouvé ma pipe en rêvant une longue soirée de beau travail d'hiver. Jetées les cigarettes avec toutes les joies enfantines de l'été dans le passé qu'illuminent les feuilles bleues de soleil, les mousselines et reprise ma grave pipe par un homme sérieux qui veut fumer longtemps sans se déranger, afin de mieux travailler. (275)
> Yesterday I found my pipe while dreaming a long evening of work, of beautiful winter work. Discarded were cigarettes with all the childlike joys of summer in the past illuminated by the blue leaves of sun, flimsy veils [mousselines], and taken up was my grave pipe by a serious man who wants to smoke a long time, without being disturbed, in order better to work.

Smoking cigarettes engenders the gauzy pleasure of ephemera; it promotes the dissolving of the I, the movement of depersonalization that is the condition of the Mallarméan poetic experience. Conversely, the pipe accompanies the labor of the negative, dreams of a more heroic sort, like the grave undertaking of pure poetry: Mallarmé at "beautiful winter work." Pipes are adult, serious, grave, while cigarettes are childish, irresponsible, flimsy veils.

Whenever Sartre speaks about cigarettes, it is never as things-in-themselves, but always as things traversed toward something other than themselves; fleeting, they are always signs or mediators for something else that unveils itself in the moment they vanish: "It is only in lighting this cigarette that I discover my concrete possibility or, if one prefers, my desire to smoke" (72). Precisely because the cigarette resists the illusion that it can be appropriated through smoking, that its mere enjoyment can lend substantial being to the nothingness of the self's radical freedom, the bourgeois smoker invents a more ingenious strategy to possess it. Artistic creation, doubling enjoyment, adds a more refined means of appropriation to the process by which one makes the cigarette into "my cigarette." Sartre writes: "Thus, those who prefer to surround themselves with objects of daily use that they have created themselves have more refined ways of appropriation. They unite, in a single object, in a simultaneous moment, appropriation through enjoyment and appropriation through creation. We everywhere find the same projected unity, from the case of artistic creation to that of the cigarette, which is supposed to be 'better when you roll it yourself'" (638). For Sartre, the idea that a cigarette tastes better when you roll it yourself has nothing to do with any intrinsic quality of the object; rather, it has to do with the appropriative-creative act that produces it. Its taste lies more in my hands than on my tongue.

Curiously, in L'être et le néant, the match appears to fall somewhere between a cigarette and a pipe, insofar as its ontological status is concerned. Like the pipe, it offers the resistance of a dense piece of matter, but like the cigarette its being is exterior to itself, other than what it is when it lies on the table before me:

> The same can be said for this piece of wood, for this match which is what it is, but whose meaning as a match is exterior to it, which certainly can ignite, but which, for the moment is just a piece of wood with a black head. The potentiality inherent in this, while rigorously connected to it, appears as belonging to the thing itself in a state of entire indifference to its being. . . . To conceive the match as a piece of white wood with a black head, is not to strip it of all potentiality but simply to give it new ones (a new permanence—a new essence). (237)

Like the cigarette, the match's essence is exterior to itself in a state that is different from its form as a little piece of white wood with a black head. The way Sartre repeats the formula, "little piece of white wood with a black head" [bout de bois blanc avec une tête noire], lends to the match the substantial, repeatable identity of matter itself (in Greek, the word for matter is hylé, which means "wood"). But the catachresis of the match "head" prosopopoeically turns the little white piece of wood into a tiny surrogate for Sartre himself, whose mode of being, like that of the match propped against his cups, is never limited to what it appears to be. Like the match, Sartre at every moment enjoys the possibility of being other than what he may seem, leaning there on the table at the Café Flore. The tranquil scribbler, gazing myopically across the Boulevard St. Germain in the direction of Lipp, is permanently endowed with the existential freedom to project

himself into a situation other than the one in which he presently abides—
to burst, for example, into radical flame when the time for revolutionary
action has come.

The denigrated ontological status of cigarettes, when compared with the
pipe, corresponds to their ethical position within other binary opposi-
tions that are central to Sartre's existential morality. Cigarette smoking, for
example, proposes itself to Sartre in the course of an important philosophical argument concerning the difference between an authentic and an inauthentic act: "It is in fact appropriate to note first that an act is in principle
intentional. The clumsy smoker who, by inadvertence, exploded a powder
dump has not acted. Conversely, the worker assigned to dynamite a quarry
and who obeyed his given orders acted when he provoked the expected
explosion: he intentionally accomplished a conscious project" (487).

This illustration appears at the beginning of the fourth section of L'être et
le néant, in the crucial chapter on the concept of freedom and the act. Even
though the throwaway gesture of the cigarette smoker might have political
or military consequences more important than that of the bomb thrower,
the latter, unlike the former, accomplishes an act, according to Sartre, because the gesture of dynamiting comprises an intention, an enactment,
and a result that is in some appropriate relation to the intention. Tossing a
cigarette, however explosive its result, is not an act, properly speaking in
existential terms; its consequence has no relation to the presumed intention that surrounded its enactment. No choice, no freedom was entailed
in its performance; its consequences were determined purely by chance.

Sartre's attachment to these brief, seemingly casual philosophical examples is demonstrated dramatically in a crucial scene in his play Les mains
sales, written not long after L'être et le néant. In the "Second tableau, first
scene," the (anti)hero Hugo is seen sitting at a typewriter composing the
Communist party newspaper. The noise of the machine disturbs Ivan, who
is waiting to leave on a clandestine mission; he has been ordered by the
party to blow up a bridge. "What's your name?" he asks Hugo. "Raskol-
nikoff," comes the reply, "he's a character in a novel." Hugo, smoking,
expresses his sense of impotence at having to serve the party in the passive role of journalist-writer. Ivan tries to assure him that writing well for
the party newspaper is also a form of action. For most of the play, Hugo
remains unconvinced. Philosophically, Hugo is the cigarette thrower, or
thinks he is, and Ivan is the worker taking orders to blow up the bridge;
one is an authentic actor (in a play on a stage where no act is authentic)
and the other is not.

Smoking a cigarette is usually considered doing nothing; it is not usually defined as an act. It is an activity—a gesture—that may accompany action but cannot be considered to *be* action. It has no utility, like eating or sleeping; it either belongs to leisure, a time that is out of the time of work, or at best may be a supplementary accompaniment to work. And yet one has to wonder how many drags on his Boyard Sartre was obliged to take before he finished sketching out this description of the man smoking and committing—what? a non-act, like blowing up an arsenal by mistake or writing a book of philosophy. The philosopher's example, like most stereotypical representations of the cigarette, systematically discounts its usefulness, even if, as here, it may have played a determining role in the production of the very philosophical discourse that predicates its inessentiality.

The connection between smoking and writing will come up throughout these pages. Like writing, smoking belongs to that category of action that falls in between the states of activity and passivity—a somewhat embarrassed, embarrassing condition, unclean, unproductive, a mere gesture. The distinction between an authentic and an inauthentic act seems to have, for Sartre, its equivalent in the distinction he makes between two kinds of language: the language of prose, which represents reality—interior or exterior—and the language of poetry, which refers only to itself. In *Situations I*, in the essay "Qu'est-ce que la littérature," that distinction underlies a fundamental ethical, political difference between prose and poetry that closely corresponds to the distinction in *L'être et le néant* between an act that transparently translates an intention into an appropriate result and one that is a gratuitous gesture, neither motivated nor consequential, self-contained, opaque to any significance. The distinction between the two kinds of writing corresponds in Sartre to the difference between the political and the aesthetic. Smoking a cigarette is closer to writing poetry than writing prose; writing prose is more like a conscious act of terrorism than smoking and tossing a cigarette—even if the consequences of the latter may, unintentionally, be explosive. But what about *L'être et le néant*, Sartre's own philosophical writing? Does it more closely approximate Hugo's journalism or the act of taking an order and blowing up a bridge? It is hard not to think that writing philosophy, like smoking cigarettes, lies somewhere between action and nonaction, between the activity of doing something and the futility of a beautiful *far niente*.

The strongest justification for taking Sartre's Boyard as a crucial element in the elaboration of his existentialist philosophy may be found in an extraordinary page, toward the end of the tome, in which Sartre, uncharacteristically, makes an explicit reference to his own biography. Like many biographies of smokers, it tells the story of a successful attempt to stop. And like many stories of success, the happy ending leaves unspoken tobacco's eventual revenge. Sartre's serene account of his philosophical triumph over cigarettes is belied, in reality, by the brevity of that triumph; he continued to smoke for the next forty years—an outcome that should make us view his philosophical conclusions with some skepticism. The significance here of this lengthy passage warrants quoting it in its entirety:

> Each object possessed, raised up against the background of the world, manifests the entire world, the way a beloved woman [for Stendhal] manifests the sky, the beach, the sea that surrounded her when she appeared. To appropriate this object to oneself is thus to appropriate the world, symbolically. Each person can recognize it with reference to his own experience; in my case I will cite a personal experience, not to prove anything but to guide the reader's inquiry.
>
> A few years ago, I was led to decide to stop smoking. The beginning was rough, and in truth, I did not so much care for the taste of tobacco that I was going to lose, as for the meaning [le sens] of the act of smoking. A whole crystallization had taken place. I used to smoke at performances, mornings at work, evenings after dinner, and it seemed to me that in ceasing to smoke I was going to subtract some of the interest of the performance, some of the evening dinner's savor, some of the fresh vivacity of the morning's work. Whatever unexpected event might have struck my eyes, it seemed to me that it was fundamentally impoverished as soon as I could no longer welcome it by smoking. To-be-susceptible-to-be-encountered-by-me-while-smoking: that was the concrete quality that had been universally spread over things. And it seemed to me that I was going to tear it away from them and that, in the midst of this universal impoverishment, life was a little less worth living. However, smoking is an appropriative destructive reaction. Tobacco is a symbolically "appropriated" being, since it is destroyed following the rhythm of my breath by a manner of "continuous destruction," since it passes in me and its changing into myself manifests itself symbolically by the transformation of the consumed solid into smoke. The bond (liaison) between the landscape seen while smoking and this little crematorial sacrifice was such, as we have just seen, that the latter was like a symbol of the former. It therefore signifies that the destructive appropriative action of tobacco was symbolically equiva-

lent to an appropriative destruction of the entire world. Through the tobacco I was smoking it was the world that was burning, that was being smoked, that reabsorbed itself in steam to reenter in me. To maintain my decision to stop, I had to achieve a sort of decrystallization—that is, without exactly realizing it, I reduced tobacco to being only itself: a leaf that burns; I cut the symbolic links with the world, I persuaded myself that I would take nothing away from the theater, from the landscape, from the book I was reading, if I considered them without my pipe; that is, it finally came down to my having other modes of possessing these objects than that sacrificial ceremony. As soon as I was persuaded of it, my regret was reduced to insignificance: I deplored not having to smell the odor of the smoke, the warmth of the little heater between my fingers, etc. But suddenly my regret was disarmed and quite bearable. (657)

The story Sartre tells is intended not to "prove" anything, he says, merely "to guide the reader's inquiry." The personal reflections are offered as a gently guided interlude in the inexorable march of argument, as if the philosopher, for a moment on vacation, had taken time out for a smoke; one may be permitted to suspect that the leisurely narrative conceals the force of the rhetorical pressure he means to apply to the reader's reluctant assent.

It is not just for Sartre, ever the philosopher, that smoking is motivated less by its taste than by its "meaning"; probably no one ever smokes cigarettes just for the taste of them. But the meaning he attributes to them is philosophical, goes to the heart of his political philosophy. Even though cigarettes are the least easily appropriated objects in the world (one has the greatest difficulty saying "my cigarette"), smoking them reveals the essence of appropriation—displays, in its most abstract form, the motive behind all desire to possess something, to own at all. For with cigarettes we do not appropriate the thing in itself but everything that it "crystallizes" for us. Sartre borrows the idea of crystallization from Stendhal's treatise De l'amour, and applies to every form of possession what Stendhal described only for the case of love. For Sartre, modifying and extending Stendhal's insight, "Each object possessed, raised up against the background of the world, manifests the entire world, the way a beloved woman [for Stendhal] manifests the sky, the beach, the sea that surrounded her when she appeared. To appropriate this object to oneself is thus to appropriate the world, symbolically" (657).

The cigarette, for Sartre, is an even more powerful instrument of crystallization, because it allows us, in a symbolic act, to take into ourselves the world around us, the whole landscape that smoking a cigarette accompanies. When we light up at a performance or a dinner, or at the sight of any new or unfamiliar experience, we perform an act of projection/identification/interiorization whose movement corresponds to the physical process of lighting up, drawing deeply, exhaling slowly into the space around. Sartre calls this act of appropriation, which makes the world mine, an "appropriative destructive reaction." We appropriate the world by "reducing" it to flame and smoke and ash, to the merest air we take into our lungs. We appropriate the world around us by destroying it, symbolically, in the same way that potlatch, the Kwakiutl Indian ceremony of tribal giving, consists in burning great quantities of the merchandise that is offered by one tribe as a "gift" to the other. Tobacco, says Sartre, is "the symbol of the appropriated object" because, as it is smoked, the solid thing is gradually turned into smoke which enters my body. Smoking mimes the desired transformation of an object into myself through an act of appropriative possession; the object becomes "mine" by a process of "continuous destruction," "the transformation of the consumed solid into smoke," whereby it passes into me and becomes (part of) myself. Smoking a cigarette is therefore a "sacrificial ceremony" in which the disappearance of something solid, tobacco, is infinitely compensated by the symbolic gain I acquire in appropriating to myself the world around me. To give up smoking, therefore, effects an impoverishment of the world and of the self one is naturally reluctant to tolerate. Life without cigarettes is not worth living.

The motive of appropriation, says Sartre, is never simply the desire to possess an object; one desires through that possession to possess the self as (if it were) an object. The thing we aim to possess or appropriate is a "concrete representative" of "l'être en-soi" (being-in-itself), which we wish to appropriate as the foundation and guarantee of our own being. The appropriated object never has value only in itself, for its individual qualities or uses—every singular thing also has "indefinite prolongations," insofar as it not only belongs to a general class of things but also symbolically represents our wish to ground our being with the stability and positivity that ontologically attach to things in themselves. Appropriation through crystallization is the paradigm that proves the aim of all appropriation and possession. It is, for Sartre, the mode in which we normally flee the implications of our radical freedom, the negativity in the possibility that belongs to us, the possibility of not being, of becoming other than what we are. All forms of appropriation, of making mine, aim to give the self the ontological stability and foundational positivity that we attribute to what Sartre, following Hegel, calls the en-soi: the thing insofar as it exists in itself, permanently identical to itself. For existentialism, the self has its authentic mode of existence in the possibility of its being pour-soi, of being able to project itself beyond what it is in any present moment, toward possibilities that reduce the present to insignificance, or nonbeing, what Sartre calls nothingness, néant.

Sartre claims to have found it easy to stop smoking once he "decrystallized" the experience—that is, once he found other ways of taking possession of the significant events in his daily life: the savor of a dinner, the pleasure of a performance, the act of early morning writing. He does not imply that he, or anyone, can renounce the appropriative desire that cigarette smoking so emblematically expresses, merely that he found other means to make symbolic appropriations. He no longer required the sacrificial ceremony of "grilling" a cigarette, as one says in French. Once he was "persuaded" that he did not require that particular mode of appropriation, he had no problem, he says, mastering the pain of missing the smell of smoke, the warmth of holding fire in his hand, "etc." The "etcetera" includes all the unstated insignificant charms of smoking that must have had some importance for Sartre, because he shortly took up smoking again, with a vengeance. Even at the end of his life, suffering from "grave disturbances in the circulation in the left hemisphere of his brain (the hemisphere that has to do with speech) and a narrowing of the blood vessels" (9), Sartre, defying his doctors' orders, "obstinately drank and smoked and we were horrified" (42), writes Simone de Beauvoir; "He found it difficult to hold a cigarette" (18), "his cigarette kept dropping from his lips" (18), the doctors "prescribed a powerful tension reducer and Valium to help him smoke less" (90), but "in spite of all this, he said, with an obstinate look, that he was going to go back to smoking" (90). One evening, in Montparnasse, on his way back from a Brazilian restaurant, his legs gave way and he nearly fell. In the hospital, the doctor spoke to him forcibly:

> Sartre could save his legs only by giving up tobacco. If he did not smoke anymore, his state could be much improved and he could be assured of a quiet old age and a normal death. Otherwise his toes would have to be cut off, then his feet, and then his legs. Sartre seemed impressed. Liliane and I took him home without too much difficulty. As for tobacco, he said he wanted to think it over. . . .
>
> We spent the evening reading and talking. He had made up his mind

to stop smoking the next day, Monday. I said, "Doesn't it make you sad to think you're smoking your last cigarette?" "No. To tell you the truth I find them rather disgusting now." (101–2)

Not altogether disgusting, for a little later he went back to smoking heavily. The reason for his persistent recidivism may be found, perhaps, in an interview he gave that year for the European edition of Newsweek. Asked, "What is the most important thing in your life at present?" he replied, "I don't know. Everything. Living. Smoking"; de Beauvoir translates, ignoring smoking: "He was fully conscious of the beauty of this blue and golden fall, and he rejoiced in it" (92). Against the philosopher's power of intellectual "persuasion," and despite the most imperious claims of health, the charms of smoking, the evocativeness of its perfumed smoke, the Promethean heat of its controlled flame, and its "etcetera" work their magic, seducing him back to performing the familiar sacrificial ceremony with his usual compulsive enthusiasm. De Beauvoir's translation of Sartre's response to the interviewer, evoking the beauty of the fall, lets us think that the "etcetera" must also include what Sartre alludes to implicitly in his reading of Stendhal ("the way a beloved woman manifests the sky, the beach, the sea that surrounded her when she appeared")—the whole realm of the aesthetic that has little place in the philosophy of freedom and in the imperatives to action that existentialism wishes to locate at the essence of life.

The founder and most distinguished exponent of the Parnassian school of "l'art pour l'art," Théodore de Banville, who was much admired by Baudelaire, wrote a piece on cigarettes at the end of his long life that begins with this paradoxical reflection: "There cannot be any longer—and in a short time there will no longer be at all—any cigarette smokers" (233). Banville's prophecy, made on the verge of the moment when James B. Duke, in 1895, put the Bonsak machine to work producing billions of cigarettes sold around the world, was instantly and colossally refuted. But he was not mistaken, if one grants him the right to his distinction between "les vrais fumeurs de cigarettes" and the others. "But what are the conditions," he asks, "that need to be joined to make a real smoker of cigarettes?" (235). Before he can answer that question, he feels an Aristotelian compulsion to define the thing itself: "D'abord et avant tout, car il faut définir, qu'est-ce que la Cigarette?" [First and foremost, because it must be defined, what is a cigarette?]; the answer comes immediately, all too succinctly: "It is a pinch of tobacco, rolled in a little leaf of tissue paper [papier de fil]" (235–36).

If a cigarette is defined as tobacco rolled into a leaf of something other than itself, its origins can be traced, as we have seen in the passage from Bartholomé de Las Casas, to the earliest moment of tobacco's introduction into the West, and beyond that to pre-Columbian practices. But if we take a narrower view, we must agree with Ned Rival, who wrote: "Tout le chic de la cigarette tient alors dans le papier" [The whole chic of the cigarette resides in the paper] (171). It would then appear that the cigarette arrived first in Spain, where it was introduced by Brazilians, according to Rival, sometime around the years 1825–30 (Rival 170–71). The Crimean War played the same role in popularizing cigarettes as the Thirty Years' War did in spreading tobacco throughout Europe: French soldiers encountered cigarettes for the first time when fighting Turks in the 1850s, and, with the enthusiasm that soldiers ever since have shown, took them up and brought them back to their admiring compatriots.

Cigarettes had an earlier, brief moment of vogue in 1843 when King Louis Philippe and his queen, Marie-Amélie, ordered the vicomte Siméon, head of the Régie, the royal tobacco monopoly, to manufacture twenty thousand gold-tipped cigarettes, rolled in lithographed paper, made up in packs of ten, to be sold at auction for sixty gold francs to benefit the survivors of the hurricane in Guadeloupe (Rival 173). Thereafter production in France fell off, before resuming abundantly in the revolutionary year 1848. It cannot be an accident that cigarette smoking always finds propitious conditions in times of political crisis or social stress. It was not, however, until the Second Empire that Louis Napoleon, a compulsive user of all kinds of tobacco, and a fifty-cigarettes-a-day man, legitimized their use by the aristocracy. James B. Duke and his machine made them democratic.

Rival's remark about the chic of paper and the hint provided by the mention of "papier lithographié" recall that smoking a cigarette has always meant, as well, sending up in smoke what has been printed—words or images, pressed or inked on the paper; the cigarette itself is stamped, stereotyped, printed out mechanically. The earliest attempts to mechanize the production of cigarettes, at first on an individual scale, gave rise to the little cigarette-rolling machines that were called "cigarettotypes," as if making a cigarette were understood from the first to be equivalent to pressing or printing one. In *Tras los montes*, Gautier, after describing the Spanish rolling a "papelito" between thumb and index finger yellowed by tobacco, adds: "A propos de *papel español para cigarittas*, notons en passant que je n'en ai pas vu encore un seul cahier: les naturels du pays se servent de papier à lettre ordinaire coupé en petits morceaux; ces cahiers teintés de réglisse,

bariolés de dessins grotesques et historiés de letrillas ou de romances bouf-
fonnes sont expédiés en France aux amateurs d'exotisme" [With respect
to papel español para cigarittas, let us note in passing that I have not seen here
a single little packet: the native inhabitants used ordinary letter-writing
paper cut up into little pieces; those packets flavored with licorice, wildly
colored with drawings and covered with letrillas or funny stories, are ex-
pedited to France to lovers of exoticism] (quoted in Rival 171). Not only
sparse words, like those written on packaged cigarettes, but whole little
fictions dreamily vanish in air as the paper, tinted with licorice, wildly
colored, and thick with writing, vanishes into smoke. Consuming cigarettes meant at the origin consuming romances, burning up in perfumed
smoke the words of dreams and fictions.

As one might expect, Banville's definition is only the beginning of the
frame he draws around an object not easily encompassed; for cigarettes,
defining only begins to tell the story. "It is a pinch of tobacco, rolled in a
little leaf of tissue paper. But once the tobacco has been placed and distributed equally, the leaf must be rolled elegantly, rapidly, with a rhythmic
harmony, with a rapid, confident gesture" (Banville 235–36).

It is already clear that for Banville, the cigarette is not only a product
but a production—a little work of art. Its existence depends on the exercise of a minor craft, whose technique is choreographed as rigorously as
a ballet, whose charm depends on qualities of poise, harmony, elegance,
rapidity, and confidence of gesture. Nor is that all—only the beginning of
the cigarette's production, enactment. Banville continues: "That finished,
has the cigarette been made? Not at all, for its shape must never be fixed
and defined; ceaselessly remolded, rolled again, according to the particular
genius of whoever is smoking it, it remains varied, diverse, impressionable,
sensitive, living; isn't that enough to prove how inartistic it is to smoke
packaged cigarettes, mechanically made?" (237).

The cigarette, between the fingers of the artistic smoker, becomes a
living, sensitive creature, brought to sentience the way the mute opacity of
marble comes to life beneath the sculptor's tools. The cigarette acquires an
existence all its own, an irreducible particularity that reflects the "genius"
of the one who made it, but that seems no longer to require the creator
to sustain its being in the world as an independent, living creature. Hence,
to smoke cigarettes rolled in advance, by machines yet, contradicts the
artistic vocation to which "real smokers" consecrate themselves with a
devotion and fervor resembling those of a priest or a soldier.

The figure in the nineteenth century who brings together the most intense spiritual concentration with the most rigorous personal discipline in the service of an aesthetic ideal is, of course, the dandy. And Banville does not hesitate to identify the "real smoker" with that Baudelairean figure of the artist. He writes about the nature of the concentration and single-mindedness of the real smoker in language that could have been lifted, that must have been inspired, by Baudelaire's reflections on dandyism in "Le peintre de la vie moderne." Cigarette smoking, a frivolous activity, becomes the whole end of life, which for Banville fulfills the definition of dandyism. The dandy carries aesthetic refinement to elegant lengths by beautifully performing activities that are absolutely not worth doing. Banville like Baudelaire appreciates the heroism of this aristocratic pose, in the midst of an industrial revolution that had dethroned both aristocracy and heroes. The uselessness of the activity the dandy refines permits the disinterestedness that, since Kant, has been seen to be inseparable from pure aesthetic judgments of taste. The dandy aims to be able to do what he does for its own sake, not for any profit with which it might enhance his personal interests. Smoking is such a worthless, unproductive activity that it lends itself to becoming the whole purpose of life—if life is to be justified aesthetically, and not according to some utilitarian principle.

Banville deplores the passing of dandyism in a society that has become utterly devoted to material possession and no longer thinks it worthy to renounce the world in favor of an exclusive obsession or preoccupation. He writes: "In a word, everyone wants everything; however the cigarette, which is the most imperious, the most engaging, the most demanding, the most loving, the most refined of mistresses, tolerates nothing which is not her, and compromises with nothing: it [elle] inspires a passion that is absolute, exclusive, ferocious like gambling or reading" (234). The cigarette is a woman, a terrible, ferocious, demanding, but absolutely, passionately desirable one, who allows no compromise and no alternative to her jealously required devotion.

In this respect, the cigarette, says Banville, may be distinguished from the pipe and the cigar. Smoking them, after a meal or at other carefully chosen moments, satisfies a need, and the need, once satisfied, for the moment disappears. But cigarettes obey another, more perverse logic of desire. "It is quite otherwise with the cigarette; it creates a delicious, voluptuous, cruel and soft excitation, which, the more one yields to it, the more it renews itself, and which never sleeps and is never extinguished" (234).

The pleasure of cigarette smoking is distinguished from that procured by other forms of tobacco consumption insofar as it defies the economy of

Cigarette Dandy, Marseille
Photo © Henri Cartier-Bresson. By permission of Magnum Photos, Inc.

what Freud calls the pleasure principle. According to that principle, which interprets pleasure on the model of need, the satisfaction of a desire results in the elimination of the desire, the way an infant's demand for milk and desire for the breast are perfectly gratified by the mother's nursing. Cigarettes, however, defy that economy of pleasure: they do not satisfy desire, they exasperate it. The more one yields to the excitation of smoking, the more deliciously, voluptuously, cruelly, and sweetly it awakens desire— it inflames what it presumes to extinguish. The perversity of this excitation consists in the fact that it never sleeps and is never extinguished; it is removed from the economy of utility in which the expenditure of energy can be calculated, according to an equation of profit and loss. Filling a lack hollows out an even greater lack that demands even more urgently to be filled.

In a strange reversal of the temporality of desire and fulfillment of desire, cigarette smoking seems to run desire backward—as if the fulfillment were even more the desire than the desire it fulfills, as if what normally comes after, comes upon desire, comes before. The logic of this desire, manifestly not utilitarian, is more nearly aesthetic. Cigarette smoking, like a Kantian work of art, does not serve any purpose, has no aim outside itself; Banville, the Parnassian poet, seems to be advancing a doctrine of "la cigarette pour la cigarette," in terms that bear the closest comparison with his aesthetic ideology. Banville recognizes how radically useless cigarette smoking must be: "This murderous pastime," he says, demands "more qualities, aptitudes, and marvelous gifts than all that is required to enchant, to dominate, to govern men and even women." He acknowledges explicitly that to give oneself to cigarettes is "to put one's unique concern into creating a desire that cannot be satisfied." And yet he concludes his "little study" with a question that is inescapably rhetorical: "However, is it not a pretty dandyism," he asks, "to give one's life to a cruel, inextinguishable, and completely useless desire?" (234).

Of course, the very existence of Banville's study implies that he himself is not this kind of dandy; the mere fact of his writing indicates, not that he has found prettier forms of dandyism (in his system, being a cigarette dandy is the highest form of artistic life), but that he has decided to settle for the less pure, more messy business of printing words on pages, with all its vagaries and accidents—its inevitable loss of control. The sacrifice of the poet is as nothing compared to that of the smoker, who abandons every material concern for the sake of the goddess: "The smoker of cigarettes must always, at each instant, have two hands free and lips also; he can therefore be neither someone ambitious, nor a worker, nor, with a very few exceptions, a poet or an artist; every task is forbidden him, even the ineffable pleasure of screwing [le baiser]" (234).

It is clear that smoking, if it is a form of aesthetic pleasure, the production of something like a work of art, is nevertheless—in theory—all but incompatible with the production of actual works of art, of poems, for example, such as those that Banville himself might write. Thus, while he excludes himself from the select company of the cigarette dandies, the highest class of artists, in order actually to produce art, he realizes that what he creates can only be a vulgar material version of the poetic purity that continuously smoking cigarettes exhales. It is manifest that Banville does not include himself among the real smokers, for to do so would be to exclude him from the possibility of artistically describing them.

Banville recognizes certain important exceptions to the rigid rule he lays down. He allows that although cigarettes may be considered to be absolutely useless, they can be said to lead somewhere, to give the smoker something: "But in the end this tyrannical cigarette that takes everything from you, chases you away from everything, exiles you from everything, doesn't it lead you anywhere and give you something? Yes, it gives a calm and virile resignation which does not exclude action, and it carries you away in inalterable mystic joy [l'inaltérable joie mystique]. All the great smokers of cigarettes are among the resigned [les résignés] and the mystics, never among the ambitious or the talkers" (236).

Unfazed by all the exceptions that spring to mind, Banville grants the exceptions but then uses them to prove his rule: "To tell the truth, reality seems to give me the lie. But it is only because it is ill understood" (237). He begins with George Sand, who "was one of the most terrible smokers of cigarettes that has ever existed" (237). After five minutes in the theater, at the rehearsal of her plays, she became entirely incapable of understanding a word of what she had written. If her opinion was required by the actors, she would light up a cigarette, which promptly invited the appearance of the "incorruptible fireman, who in the theater no more tolerates the conflagration of a cigarette than that of the building itself." Banville explains the seeming paradox of this "woman of action, never ceasing to create and to produce," who nevertheless never ceased to smoke. During the day she was a "bonne bourgeoise" who liked entomology and making jam, but at night she became "the prey of a daemon of genius, which invaded, dominated her thinking, and dictated to her sublime pages." Hence her creativity took place "outside herself," was accomplished "without her having to get involved," and she could smoke "as if she had nothing at all to do" (237). Since inspiration dictated her extraordinary productivity, it was as if she herself had nothing to do but be a mystically resigned spectator, actively passive, at the spectacle of her prodigious creation, passively active. The exception that Banville made for artists and poets has to do with the ambiguous status of the "act" of artistic creation, which is not exactly doing anything at all and yet may result in the most frenetic activity. Just as we saw in Sartre's *L'être et le néant*, the fact of smoking cigarettes has a privileged connection to this other kind of (non)activity that is the production of art.

Banville interrogates another seeming exception to his rule, that of the emperor Napoleon III, who was "one of the greatest, one of the most obstinate smokers of cigarettes." How does one explain that a man of such vaulting ambition should have been so in love with cigarettes, the passion of the mystically resigned? It was because he was entirely fatalistic, and considered that everything he did was in obedience to a preordained plan over which he had no control, which fulfilled itself without even his participation. "Thus he was resigned in the most unexpected good fortune and in the most terrible reverses, and when everything was finished [when he was deposed in 1870], as usual, he tranquilly lit a cigarette." This "visible daydream [*rêverie visible*]," this "smoke which carries the soul into paradises more immaterial than those of opium or hashish," provided the head of state with "a supreme calm" (237).

Finally, Banville considers the case of Victor Hugo, the most active, ambitious, epically prodigious writer of the century. Hugo execrated cigarettes and is not known to have ever tolerated tobacco around him—either in the 1830s and 1840s, when he was a peer of the realm, or later as an exile and a proscribed author. Only once, says Banville, did he allow people to smoke in his presence, and that was during the siege of Paris in 1870, when Banville saw national guard officers at Hugo's table smoking after dessert. But that, says Banville, was the "Terrible Year!" (239).

Even though he belonged approximately to the same illustrious era as Hugo, Alfred de Musset, dreamer, feminine, charmer, has always been a smoker of cigarettes. I see him still on the couch, having near at hand, on his table, a pack of Marylands, a packet of papers with the image of the smuggler, and a box of cylindrical matches, in wood painted red. As the poet exercises an art in which retouching is as impossible as in frescoes, and must always succeed at the first shot, alone, perhaps, among writers, he has the right to light a cigarette to reread the page he has just written. But a Titan like Hugo did not have to reread his pages, time being too precious to him. (239)

The difference between Musset and Hugo is that between a poet and a Titan; poets like Musset who practice an ephemeral lyric art depend on the inspiration of the moment and write their little poems in a single burst. There is no work to writing lyrical poetry, Banville seems to be saying, but only a burst of energetic exertion that takes no time and leaves plenty of time to do "nothing" like rereading, during which time cigarette smoking is possible. A giant worker like Hugo, on the other hand, does not smoke, but for obverse reasons: for him there is no inactive time when smoking is possible; every moment is preciously reserved for his ambitious, creative production. It is by such convoluted arguments that Banville seeks to prove, despite all the evidence to the contrary, that there is some fundamental incompatibility between active work and smoking; what he actually succeeds in demonstrating is the peculiar ambivalence that surrounds the "act" of writing and the curiously intimate relation it bears to the "act" of smoking cigarettes.

A calm and virile resignation, inalterable mystic joy—Banville does not explain why cigarettes, of all drugs, have the power to induce these particular states. They correspond perhaps to the two conditions we have already seen in Baudelaire: the double postulation of the artist, concentration and evaporation, the steeling of the self that comes from resignation and the loss of the self in mystical expansion. Understood in the absolute terms of these conditions, Banville's prediction was profoundly true: there can no longer be—and there are no longer—real smokers of the kind he describes, dandies of the cigarette who devote themselves with an exclusive, intolerant passion to something that is entirely useless. The aristocratic beauty of that pose flies in the face of a world that, as Banville says, no longer permits the renunciation of material well-being in favor of an "ideal" of beauty and pleasure like those the real smoker pursues, sacrificing everything for this absolutely demanding, cruel, imperious, but most adorable of "mistresses." Writing at a moment when cigarette smoking was on the brink of becoming a universal passion, Banville was no doubt right in asserting that there could no longer be—in a brief time there would be no longer—any real cigarette smokers left.

It may well seem, a century later, that there will shortly be no more cigarette smokers left at all, anywhere. What was once the unique prerogative of the most refined and futile dandies, having become the luxury of billions of people, may abruptly vanish. Will anything have been lost? On the day when some triumphant antitabagist crushes under his heel the last cigarette manufactured on the face of the earth, will the world have any reason to grieve, perhaps to mourn the loss of a cultural institution, a social instrument of beauty, a wand of dreams? Or what of those who have given their lives to cigarettes, who have died prematurely because they could not stop smoking? Do they deserve no respect, no admiration for their sacrifice? For them, as Sartre says, a life without smoking was not worth living. For them, as Zeno says, it was a way of life—their own way to death.

2 Cigarettes Are Sublime

Nearby is the grave of Carlos Gardel—who developed and popularized
the Argentine tango—where a cigarette is always kept burning in honor
of the chain-smoking, slouch-hatted musician.
—INTERNATIONAL HERALD TRIBUNE, October 3, 1989

Smoking a cigarette may be compared to making a poem: inhaling the hot
breath of inspiration, letting words on paper burn up in the visible air of
a muted elocution, exhaling swirling figures of desire, conducting with
gestures and modulating in smoke a lyric conversation overheard. This
chapter aims not only to consider cigarettes as poems but to evoke poems
that take cigarettes as their subject, for the most part hyperbolically, in lyrical effusions. The aim is to discover the nature of the imperious charm
that cigarettes exercise and the rhetorical facility they foster at the hands
of poets and, by extension, in those of all their innumerable admirers.

By no means the earliest example of the genre, "My Cigarette," authored
by a certain Charles F. Lummis, is not a very felicitous poem, but it is an
interesting compendium of the predicates poets frequently lend to cigarettes. It will also permit us to conjure the anachronistic effect that poems
about cigarettes inevitably produce, retrospectively, after the change in
value that smoking has undergone in the last thirty years. One is reminded
in reading this poetry of the letter that Sigmund Freud sent to his wife
celebrating the tonic virtues of cocaine, recommending it to her, to "make
her strong and give her cheeks of color" (Cocaine Papers 7). Freud's blithe
assumption that cocaine was harmless led to his famous fatal error of
prescribing it in enormous doses to a colleague as a cure for morphine
addiction. The best cigarette poems do not pretend to ignore the dangerous consequences of smoking. Another flaw in Lummis's poem is that it
claims that I can have a cigarette as my very own, have "My Cigarette"—
pretending to possess an object that, as we have seen, can hardly ever be

appropriated. This poem neatly illustrates the two sides of Sartre's insight: both the futility of the bourgeois desire to make a cigarette into personal property ("It tastes better when you roll it yourself") and the persistence of that futile desire. The passion to appropriate what is inherently inappropriable, under the illusion that it will give some secure ground to one's sense of self, motivates all the pathologies of consumerism. Shopping, like rolling your own, thinks Sartre, offers illusory protection against the anxiety of radical freedom (*L'être et le néant* 638). This poem does, however, have the virtue of confirming, as Sartre also demonstrates, that cigarettes, which cannot themselves be appropriated, are powerful instruments for appropriating the world symbolically:

My Cigarette

My cigarette! The amulet
   That charms afar unrest and sorrow,
The magic wand that, far beyond
   Today, can conjure up tomorrow.
Like love's desire, thy crown of fire
   So softly with the twilight blending;
And ah; meseems a poet's dreams
   Are in thy wreaths of smoke ascending.
(Knight 77)

The cigarette is endowed here with the magic of an amulet, producing effects on the world at a distance through the manipulation of a sign. A magic wand, like the star-tipped baton of fairies, it has the power to evoke the future "far beyond today," "to conjure up tomorrow." It allows the smoker to dream of possibilities unrealizable perhaps in actuality but not in the fiction of the magical space and time that the cigarette opens up for daydreaming. Cigarettes are fiery batons with which you can summon the future and conduct it, slim, white facilitators of anticipatory thinking and imaginative hypotheses, instruments of ecstatic projection away from the present to a future time in which the present for a moment no longer exists. Their magic derives perhaps from their capacity to moderate the anxiety occasioned by thinking about the future, all anticipation (anxiety is always directed to anticipating a future menace). They allow you calmly to project yourself forward to possible future worlds that may never be, but, for the time of a cigarette, are—more intimately than the present moment. Smokers playing chess and writing valentines smoke incessantly; so do journalists and actors in the wings. Waiting, hoping, fearing, the lover's condition (and the soldier's), require the assistance of the cigarette to ease and modulate, but sometimes to sustain, the not always delicious anxiety of anticipation.

Lummis's poem identifies the cinder at the end with love's desire, whose fire is mitigated down to the soft light and heat of twilight with which it blends—this flaming ash of desire at the edge of consummation, extinction. Sucking a cigarette nurses the smoker into a harmonious embrace of the twilight realm of sleep. In the poem, the smoke, mounting in wreaths or rings, initiates the spiraling movement of dreams; ascending thus transuming diurnal concerns, it opens the door to fiction, to poetic ambitions: "a poet's dreams / Are in thy wreaths of smoke ascending." Smoke rings are wreaths of laurel like that with which Petrarch, no Lummis, was crowned in apotheosis on the Campidoglio in Rome.

"My Cigarette" is embarrassing for the way it sounds unintentionally masturbatory (manipulating "my cigarette" while imagining someone absent prompts erotic satisfaction): the hot wand culminates, predictably, in the ascending writhing of spurting smoke. It might be that Lummis's desire to make it *his* cigarette is linked to his confusing it, unconsciously, with the phallus—an object of appropriation so notoriously inaccessible that many a man spends his life trying not only to have one but (in order to have one) to be one—a prick. The cigarette as phallus will be addressed in Chapter 5 when we take up "the Humphrey Bogart cigarette." Bogart— in the role of Rick, the great "prick" of *Casablanca*, incessantly smoking—is his cigarette.

The cigarette is often associated with communication at a distance, a vehicle for inaugurating transportation and travel: "I'd walk a mile for a Camel"; "Come to Marlboro country"; "You've come a long way, baby." The ecstatic transport of "coming" is also associated with the idea of a trip, a small orgasmic alteration of mental perspective. But the rush of a cigarette is a kind of negative orgasm; at the instant of inhalation, the poison kills a brain cell, perhaps, or discharges a synapse. Perhaps it induces a slight dementia, a scant forgetting (in Italian, *una dimenticanza*), that alters one's perspective just enough to give rise to another point of view so that the smoker feels as though a distance has been traversed. It is striking to see how frequently the cigarette is represented as a tele-instrument: -graph, -phone, -vision, but also a tele-aesthetics, touching at a distance and wafting its odor, a telaroma. The next poem, by Alfred Cochrane, illustrates the propensity of the cigarette to carry its magical messages across distances that are not only material but hierarchical:

From the Terrace

Go, little wreath of smoke, apace,
    Waft your illicit faint perfume
Across the interdicted space
    Of yonder lamplit room.

Tell her who lingers there and reads,
    Yet in my absence hides a yawn,
That the soft voice of summer pleads
    For her sweet presence on the lawn.

Say that above the deep-blue hills
    Hangs, fair to see, the sickle moon,
And that a mellow fragrance fills
    The orchard mown this afternoon.

Say that your soothing influence,
    With hopeful sentiment combined,
Inspires to rare benevolence
    A lover who hath newly dined.

And, if perchance, the garden seat,
    Where drowsy beetles wheel and hum,
Can tempt her not from her retreat,
    And if she still refuse to come,

Then whisper, cigarette of mine,
    Forebodings in her ear apart,
Of incense offered at a shrine
    That still hath something of my heart.
(Cochrane 29–30)

The "illicit" invitation of this "Cupid," its insidious pungent shaft, is all the more insinuating for being a "faint perfume." The fuming per-fume of cigarette smoke traverses the threshold and transgresses the "interdicted space" of "yonder lamplit room." The cigarette is a call to leave the yawn-ing lamps of culture for the titillating nature of a summer evening. A sexual landscape barely veiled is this spectacle of the sickle moon, which "hangs" down above deep-blue hills suffused with the fragrance of an orchard freshly mown, requiring that the lady come, look. This sickle is, as they say, hung, "fair to see," he says, sounding anatomical in a psychoanalytic third ear; the expression appears in the verse cut off by commas from the castrating-castrated figure of this hung "sickle," this pickle of a sickle, still hot from mowing. This is the sexy moonscape the cigarette invites the lady to come inspect. The cigarette as Cupid is charged with conveying the "rare benevolence" of the smoker, soothed and hopeful after having dined well; we clearly are intended to hear his postprandial "benevolence" as arousal.

The final, darkly cryptic stanza promises betrayal and revenge to the divine lady who may not be tempted by the sexy prospect of "drowsy beetles" and garden seats. The Cupid-cigarette is charged with whispering "forebodings in her ear apart," fearful promises that the poet will turn his incense to other shrines that have a piece of his heart. If she will not come for promises of beauty and pleasure, perhaps threats will extract her from the company of others. The cigarette smoke is both the sign of the poet's passionate desire to transgress the barriers that keep him from her and a threat—the bad smell of stale cigarette smoke that remains after someone has left. Cupid's arrow, at the end of the poem, is turned into a sharp reminder that she had better get her ass down to the lawn in a hurry or he will blow his smoke up other stacks. Not a very nice Cupid, this extortionist smoke. The power of cigarettes to convey messages at a distance, their link to the illicit and transgressive, their capacity to open somber as well as paradisiac perspectives are all represented in this poem. In a rhetoric that belongs to the nineteenth century, the poem anticipates twentieth-century attitudes toward romance. This Cupid carries a message from a tough guy, Bogart or Gatsby, standing around outside with a cigarette, impatiently shooting streams or tightly curled rings in her direction—a message that speaks more frankly and menacingly than the poem's Tennysonian diction would intimate. The cigarette in the poem is a very good avatar for the modern Cupid, one who deromanticizes romance, who gives it a keener edge of cruelty, irony, and raw seduction.

No doubt the greatest poem written about cigarettes was published in 1880 by the symbolist poet Jules Laforgue. It is a sonnet that Baudelaire, the father of symbolism, might have written if he had smoked cigarettes as compulsively as "la pipe" he celebrated in a famous poem written in 1837. Laforgue's sonnet may actually be a mocking echo of Baudelaire's, the jocular voice of a later, more with it generation that can kid the seriousness of Baudelaire's poetic diction, immensely self-important for all its heightened self-ironies. Baudelaire might have smoked cigarettes if they had been as popular as they were becoming when Laforgue wrote his poem fifty years later. By 1880, cigarettes were no longer the prerogative of the aristocratic elite or of loose women: they had become universal, under the influence of the Crimean war, from which French soldiers returned having acquired that compulsive pleasure from their enemies the Turks, and under the influence, as well, of such consummate smokers as Louis Napoleon and George Sand, both of whom smoked more than fifty cigarettes a day (along with smoking cigars and pipes and taking snuff in great quantities).

The sonnet form, since Petrarch, has been largely reserved by poets for addressing praise to women. But cigarettes, very early, were endowed with qualities of feminine seduction, as Théodore Burette wrote in 1840 in *La physiologie du fumeur:* "La cigarette est gentille, vive, animée; elle a quelque-chose de piquant dans ses allures. C'est la grisette des fumeurs" [The cigarette is congenial, lively, animated; she has something spicy in her charms. She is the *grisette* (the naughty, intoxicating lady) of smokers] (Burette 43). In chapter 1 I quoted Banville's metaphor comparing cigarettes to women: "the cigarette, which is the most imperious, the most engaging, the most demanding, the most loving, the most refined of mistresses, tolerates nothing which is not her, and compromises with nothing: it [*elle*] inspires a passion that is absolute, exclusive, ferocious like gambling or reading" (Banville 233).

A man in love with cigarettes is intoxicated with risk and imaginative adventure—intoxicated, says Banville, by the most "terrible, ferocious, demanding, but absolutely, passionately desirable [woman], who allows no compromise and no alternative to her jealously required devotion" (234). In chapter 4, "The Devil in Carmen," a name and a figure will be given to this terrible mistress, this infinitely desirable and dangerous woman, who is the emblem of the cigarette. In Laforgue's poem, the cigarette is a woman the way a woman is a drug: a source of hallucinatory experiences of the sort that Baudelaire conventionally solicits from his dark mistress or from opium.

La cigarette

Oui, ce monde est bien plat: quant à l'autre, sornettes.
Moi, je vais résigné, sans espoir à mon sort,
Et pour tuer le temps, en attendant la mort,
Je fume au nez des dieux de fines cigarettes.

Allez, vivants, luttez, pauvres futurs squelettes.
Moi, le méandre bleu qui vers le ciel se tord

Me plonge en une extase infinie et m'endort
Comme aux parfums mourants de mille cassolettes.

Et j'entre au paradis, fleuri de rêves clairs
Où l'on voit se mêler en valses fantastiques
Des éléphants en rut à des choeurs de moustiques.

Et puis, quand je m'éveille en songeant à mes vers,
Je contemple, le coeur plein d'une douce joie,
Mon cher pouce rôti comme une cuisse d'oie.
(Laforgue 333)

Yes, this world is flat and boring: as for the other, bullshit!
I myself go resigned to my fate, without hope,
And to kill time while awaiting death,
I smoke slender cigarettes thumbing my nose at the gods.

Onward, you living, keep up the fight, poor future skeletons,
I am plunged into infinite ecstasy by the blue meandering that
Twists itself toward the sky and puts me to sleep,
Like dying perfumes from a thousand smoldering pots.

And I enter paradise, flowered with brightly clear dreams,
Where elephants in heat are seen to mix
In fantastic waltzes with choirs of mosquitoes.

And then, when I awake, dreaming of my verse,
I, my heart full of the sweetest joy, contemplate
My dear thumb, roasted like a goose's drumstick.

It is worth noting that the poet says, "I smoke slender [fines] cigarettes."
The chic of the slender is indissociable from the idea of the mathematical
sublime—a disproportionately infinite wealth of pleasure confined within
the sleek slimness, the tailored lines of what is no more than is required to
be flawless—like a Chanel woman or a Fabergé egg. In French, the adjec-
tive fine predicates qualities of refinement that depend on moral or class, as
well as aesthetic, distinctions. It is striking how persistently brand names
are found that connote the most exalted aristocratic luxury, although—or
because—they lend their connotations to the most democratic and popular form of tobacco consumption: Duke of Burnham, Cameo, Duke's Best,
Elite, Les Élégantes, Jockeys, Petits Pages, Fashion, High Life, Old Gold,
Viceroy, Up Town. The beauty of the cigarette, compared, say, to that of

Coco Chanel
Photo © Henri Cartier-Bresson. By permission of Magnum Photos, Inc.

the cigar, has to do with the neatness with which it is rolled or "typed" by a hand-held or an industrial machine. The perfect symmetry of the cigarette's mechanically cylindrical form gives a tactile and visual pleasure distinct from that of holding a rough, naked cigar, of touching leaf instead of snow-white paper. Not only are cigarettes themselves "fines," but they have the power to produce refinement, metonymically, by the mere contiguity of their presence to fingers, mouth, and the air around.

Laforgue's poem begins by affirming the irredeemable flatness of our existence, in which no élan, no transcendence is possible, except to the credulous. As for the so-called otherworld, or afterlife, "sornettes!" [frivolous, hollow assertions based on nothing]—a word whose abrupt dismissiveness hardly authorizes its translation as "Bullshit!" except that in English that word vaguely rhymes with *cigarette*, the motive of Laforgue's choice in French. Laforgue is pushing Baudelairean ennui to a new, more modern despair in this poem that is a kind of parody of Baudelaire's defiant modernity; it consists not only in his contemptuous dismissal of the illusions of religion but in his fatalistic resignation to the futility of all ambition, of life itself, before the prospect of an eternity of death. Like Banville's hero, he abandons all productive activity, resigning himself to a fate without hope.

In the meantime, this mean in-between time between birth into a world of boredom and death with no promise of an afterlife, the poet finds a single activity worth pursuing—killing time. The instrument of his war is the cigarette, whose power derives from the capacity of its "blue meandering" smoke to plunge him into a state outside himself, outside the course of everyday time that seems to run its tedious ribbon to infinity. Alfred de Musset is quoted by Rival as having said: "Trois cigares le soir, quand le jeu vous ennuie, sont un moyen divin pour mettre à mort le temps" [Three cigars in the evening, when gambling bores you, is a divine way to kill time] (211). When even the diversion of gambling palls, smoking opens a cloudy parenthesis that interrupts the infinitely repetitive prose of a world ceaselessly beginning again at every turn of the wheel (no continuity with the future, no transcendence). As if invulnerable for the time of a cigarette, the poet thumbs his nose at the gods whose ascent to immortality mocks the flat finitude of mortal existence, from which he, the smoker, has, like a minor deity, momentarily escaped.

Putting thumb to nose, with a cigarette between his fingers, is the gesture repeated hundreds of times a day by the smoker defying the inescapable everydayness of his fate—an existence whose every pretension to transcendence collapses before the derisive fact of death. Smoking, he also thumbs his nose at those who keep on believing in the productivity of work, busily building their fortunes, here and now—those gravediggers, "future skeletons" all, to whom he offers sneering words of encouragement . . . and a drag on his cigarette, with its beautiful meandering blue smoke twisting into fabulous shapes in an airy dream above his head.

In Laforgue's poem, the poet smoking is plunged by his cigarette into an "extase infinie" and falls into something like sleep. The little weapon with which he fends off the banality of mortal existence, and the inevitability of death, induces a feeling of having died and gone to heaven in the time of a cigarette. The poison in every puff is killing him, like all smokers, but the pleasure comes from slowly dying. Against the infinity of everyday time, the poem, like the cigarette, invites the consumer to witness the visions it summons briefly into a paradise of daydreaming. But wait a minute.

To be sure, cigarettes here are endowed with the evocative power of perfume "dying" in *cassolettes* [little pots for burning perfume], the usual Baudelairean poetic props, evoking the melancholy beauty of whatever appears to be slowly vanishing. The "clear dreams" of cigarette-induced narcosis bear some resemblance to the visions that Baudelaire summons in his most influential poem, "Correspondances," which is often taken as the manifesto of the symbolist movement in poetry.[1] As in Baudelaire's poem, Laforgue's first line makes a dogmatic, doctrinal assertion about the nature of the world, followed in the second line by the evocation of a subject whose position is described as standing against nature in a nevertheless heightened relation of communication. In both poems, the second stanza describes the ecstatic identification of man and the universe in a movement of infinite expansion. The tercets of both sonnets exemplify with startling, vivid images the possibilities for supernatural, visionary experience that nature or the cigarette induces in a poetic observer. Laforgue's "infinite ecstasy" explicitly echoes Baudelaire's "expansion of infinite things."

In Baudelaire's poem, the word "*comme*" [as, or like], repeated six times, not only signals but enacts the analogical process that is the motor of what are called "correspondances," the synaesthetic communication between regions of experience and sensation that are normally held to be distinctly separate. In Laforgue, the word appears prominently in the fourth line of the second stanza, "*Like* dying perfumes from a thousand smoldering pots," where it establishes the identification between the smoke of cigarettes and the infinite expansion and vanishing of perfumed smoke. Laforgue's "mille

cassolettes" compares the cigarette to Oriental perfume pots that burn substances like those Baudelaire enumerates at the end of "Correspondances":
"Amber, musk, balsam, and incense . . . which sings the transport of mind
and senses." Just as in Baudelaire's poem, perfume is the medium through
which correspondences can occur. Of all substances it is the one that is
closest to the material consistency of thoughts or dreams, and its power to
evoke the most distant, deep, forgotten memories is a further sign of its
special link to the realm of imagination and poetry. When Baudelaire in
"La chevelure" wishes to celebrate the poetic adventures he experiences
through the woman he loves, he takes her hair as the synecdoche, the part
for her whole; and in her hair it is especially her perfume that is the ship
on which his remembering imagination sets sail for the most exotic and
the most poetic places. The smoke of Laforgue's cigarette has the same
function as the perfume in the hair of Jean Duval.

Not nature but Laforgue's cigarette is given synaesthetic powers to marry
realms of sensation that ordinarily are thought to have absolutely no relation to one another, just as Baudelaire, in his poem, conjoins the most
diverse sensations—the taste of an oboe, the sound of green, the odor
of infinity. The cigarette introduces the poet-narrator into what he calls a
paradise, one that unmistakably recalls the "paradis artificiels" that Baudelaire celebrated, as the realm to which certain drugs, including the mild
narcosis of poetry, could exalt the poetic sensibility. But look again: it is
clear that the line at the end of the quatrains of this sonnet is intended
to make us sick. A thousand pots of burning perfume in various stages of
going out would probably stink worse than the worst-smelling head shop
one could imagine. Cigarettes may be beautiful; they also stink—like many
modern things. And look again at the rhyme: *cigarettes* / *cassolettes*. *Cassolettes*
sounds pretty close to "casserole," to a pot of, say, *cassoulet*. Somebody's
goose is already being cooked.

The lines "Where elephants in heat are seen to mix / In fantastic waltzes
with choirs of mosquitoes" are a neat parody of the tercets in Baudelaire's "Correspondances." Compared to the elaborate, elevated syntheses
of Baudelaire's vision, those of Laforgue, dragging on his fag, look quick
and dirty. The only thing that singing in choirs has to do with being in
heat, ordinarily, is their equally opposite connotations: one is sacred, the
other profane. The only thing that mosquitoes have in common with elephants is their symmetrically opposite relation to the extremes of size:
among animals, the one connotes the infinitely macro compared to the in-

finitely micro other. The mixture, or coitus, of these extremes of nature is a grotesquely promiscuous paradise, a hell of a heavenly fuck—the mixing, mating of randy pachyderms and pious skeeters.

When the poet in Laforgue's poem gets back to business and awakens from his cigarette dream, he realizes that killing time has had its price. The narrator falls out of his brief paradise to discover that his thumb has been roasted like a goose, cooked like the goose of every habituated smoker. Himself, as figured by his thumb, itself a little phallus, emerges from the dream of the cigarette more butchered, let us say, a little deader than before. For Laforgue is not deluded, does not lead his reader to imagine that the drug is harmless, that it exacts no price for killing time; he knows that in that war against time the most decisive weapons hasten your own demise. Smoking cigarettes is a kind of self-sacrifice in terms of the logic of loss and profit that it affords the poet. But in a material world without transcendence, what better way to sacrifice oneself than as a roast goose—evocative, in a French poem, of the most celebratory occasions, poetic and sacred, profane and incantatory, at life's banquet tables. Perhaps the critical point is the tone of this last line—so different from anything in Baudelaire, whose self-importance, however self-ironical, would never allow him to worry in a poem about stains on his thumb. And that may be a way of Laforgue's saying, while writing a Baudelairean sonnet, that no one smoking cigarettes can take Baudelaire seriously anymore, that, for a certain modernity, all that is left of Baudelaire's high romantic ecstasy is available in cigarettes—at the small price of a pack and eventual death.

The beauty that Laforgue finds in the clear dreams that cigarettes give rise to is not positive; it is a negative beauty, alternately overcoming and suffering death. In that respect it may be thought to resemble the form of negative beauty that Kant in *The Critique of Judgment* dissects under the heading "Analytic of the Sublime." Kant's thesis is the necessary precondition for understanding the nature of the contradictory beauty and paradoxical pleasure with which cigarettes have provided the world.[2] For Kant, the sublime, as distinct from the merely beautiful, affords a negative pleasure because it is accompanied, as its defining condition, by a moment of pain. By pain he strictly means the normal feelings of shock or fear aroused by the presence of whatever impresses us by virtue of its sheer magnitude, giving rise to awe or respect.

Cigarettes are poison and they taste bad; they are not exactly beautiful, they are exactly sublime. The difference, to use the terms in which Kant makes the distinction, means that smoking cigarettes gives rise to forms of aesthetic pleasure painfully at odds with the affect arising from the contemplation in tranquillity, say, of a well-wrought urn. In Kant's terms, what we ordinarily consider beautiful, the object of what he calls a "pure [aesthetic] judgment of taste," is a finite entity; indeed, it is precisely its exquisite boundaries—the finitude of its means and ends, its margins and measure—that excite the feelings of calm enjoyment and reposeful exaltation that we normally associate with aesthetic satisfaction. By contrast, the aesthetic pleasure we take in the experience of boundlessness is not positive but negative, says Kant. The imagination suffers a shock in the presence of infinite perspectives that, in a first moment, is painful. But that negativity is the very condition of sublimity. Thus Baudelaire writes in his journals: "Il y a dans l'engendrement de toute pensée sublime une secousse nerveuse qui se fait sentir dans le cervelet" [At the conception of every sublime thought there is a nervous jolt that is felt at the base of the brain] (78).

The first moment of the encounter with what we call the sublimely beautiful, the feeling of awe or respect involving fear, is an experience of blockage: We discover in that fearful moment the limits of our capacity to imagine an infinite abyss—the harsh experience of recognizing the limitation of our faculty to represent in finite images the encounter with a magnitude that seems to be infinite. The imagination can invent things never seen in this world, but it staggers in the face of the task of representing infinity. Thankfully, the faculty of reason, says Kant, comes to the rescue of imagination by proposing the concept of infinity, the idea with which the mind can grasp, but not imagine, a boundlessness beyond all limitation, all finitude. Coming to the rescue of imagination, reason brings satisfaction after the moment of awe and fear, satisfaction derived from overcoming, if only in thought, the pain of recognizing the limits to our power to imagine. "The feeling of the sublime is a pleasure which arises only indirectly, produced by the feeling of a blocking of vital forces for a brief instant, followed immediately by an even stronger release of them; and thus as an emotion it does not seem like play but like a serious thing in the work of the imagination" (Kant 245).

Tobacco does not positively taste good the way, say, sugar does to children. The "pleasure" associated with cigarettes is negative, therefore not exactly a pleasure. One's first experience of smoking does not seem like play but like a serious act, accompanied by more dis-taste and dis-ease than the good tastes of innocent sweetness. In fact, tobacco makes one a little sick every time the poison is ingested. It announces its venomous character from the first, especially at the first puff, and subsequently as each successive puff distributes repeated jolts to the body. All the literature of cigarette smoking, no less than the testimony of universal experience, attests that it is not in spite of their harmfulness but because of it that people profusely and hungrily smoke. The noxious character of cigarettes —their great addictiveness, and their poisonous effects—not only underlies their various social benefits but constitutes the absolute precondition of their troubling, somber beauty.

The most magnificent poem about smoking is a sonnet by Stéphane Mallarmé whose subject, alas, for our purposes, is a cigar. The reason for his choice may have had more to do with considerations of rhyme than with Mallarmé's own predilections. At his regular literary gatherings, his *mardis*, he would speak to the symbolist ephebes, his disciples, from behind an oracular cloud of cigarette smoke. Mallarmé loved cigarettes, but, less bold or foolhardy than Laforgue, he must have blanched at launching a sonnet with rhymes in *-ette*. In most respects—in respect to breath, fire, cinder, and smoke—the cigar in this poem could be a cigarette; its explicitly cigarlike character is evident only in the rings it encourages the smoker to make and in the importance that its ash acquires as it grows firmly in place at the end of the fiery cinder. But it is not simply making a virtue out of necessity if we join this poem to others that have cigarettes as their nominal subject; for what Mallarmé in the end says about cigars, after the difficulty of his syntax has been unpacked, is that they are insufficiently like cigarettes, whose poetry consists in the all-but-perfect sacrifice of their matter to the sublimity of smoke, leaving but a scant remainder. The trouble with cigars, he says, is that they do not sufficiently vanish as cigarettes do as they smoke—all the way down to the insignificant butt.

Toute l'âme résumée
Quand lente nous l'expirons
Dans plusieurs ronds de fumée
Abolis en autres ronds

Atteste quelque cigare
Brûlant savamment pour peu
Que la cendre se sépare
De son clair baiser de feu

Ainsi le choeur des romances
À la lèvre vole-t-il

Exclus-en si tu commences
Le réel parce que vil

Le sens trop précis rature
Ta vague littérature.
(Mallarmé 73)

The whole soul summed up
When slowly we exhale it
In several rings of smoke
Abolished in other rings

Attests some cigar
Burning cannily if
The ash separates at all
From its bright kiss of fire

Thus if the chorus of romances
Flies to your lips
Exclude therefrom if you begin [to compose]
The real because [it's] vile

A too-precise meaning crosses out
Your vague literature.

Mallarmé's poem is smoking on many levels, not least of which is the graphic form it assumes on the page. The thin column of type, like a smoky plume rising, results from his choice of a brief, seven-syllable verse form that is rare in French prosody. The abundance of vowels in *o* and in *é* (with its acutely flying accent) encourages the reader to imagine the rising aspiration of encircling rings within rings that is the central image of the poem and the one whose implications it unfolds.

The whole soul, all souls, are resumed, summed up, in the exhalation. *Résumer* in French can be written to mean breathing back in again, gathered back into an essential interiority, a deep breath in which the whole self assumes itself all together—ré(s)-(h)umer. Here, the smoke emerging is not just a sign or representative of the soul; it sums it up, is its "vague," diaphanous but also wavy, correlative—the externalization and transformation of what before was the same thing within. Inspiration is expiration.

The abundant nasal sounds in the first stanza perform little exhalations at each line, and they serve to underline the importance of the word *lente* in the poem. The word repeats the full nasal sound in *Quand* to make an ex-

Pablo Picasso
Photo © Robert Capa. By permission of Magnum Photos, Inc.

tended exhalation at the beginning of the line; it has the effect of producing what the French call a hiatus—a pause or slowing down of articulation by the uncomfortable repetition, for the French, of vowels uninterrupted by consonants. The substance of smoke is matter as close to the demateriality of spirit as soul is to the corporeality of the body. When we say something has soul we mean that its energy is expressed palpably in its body—as far as possible from the abstracted cerebral spirit of "mind." These entities or beings—soul and smoke—lie on the borderline between the material and the spiritual, the sensible and the intelligible.

If the word *lente* were taken to read *l'ente* one might sketch a whole interpretation of the poem around this in-between being (*ent(r)e-ent(it)é*) that characterizes soul and smoke—substance less dense than matter, more corporeal than mind. The first two lines would then read something like: "The whole soul resumed / When slowly we exhale (the in-between being)." *Lente* of course may also be taken to sound like *l'hante*, which in French means "haunts it," and this smoke that resumes the soul has something ghostlike in its wreaths or wraiths, inhabiting a realm somewhere between life and death, between breath (*résumée*) and death ("expiring"). The soul at death is summoned to a summing up, as expressed by Mallarmé on the tomb of Edgar Allan Poe: "eternity changes him into himself." At death, the permanent human freedom to recast one's life vanishes, and that life assumes another form; it remains as a trace to be read by others. Only at the end can you make sense of a life, only death lets you read with certainty a life's destination, its destiny or meaning. You can only discover the plot backward from the end, resumed in its expiration. It is as if each time you exhale rings of tobacco smoke, you are writing the story of your life as seen from beyond the tomb—adding up and gathering in the evidence of the soul to which the smoke attests.

The smoke is exhaled in "several rings . . . / Abolished in other rings." The soul, like the smoke, is not unitary but heterogeneous and multiple; the several rings are at the same time all the same ring, indistinguishable from the next one that both abolishes and reiterates it. Both unified and unitary, multiple and heterogeneous, the soul exhaled, expiring in the smoke, is a temporal movement, is the movement of Aristotelian time itself. In the *Physics*, Aristotle elucidates the paradox of the "now": like the rings of smoke, each successive instant or "now" annuls a previous one to substitute itself in its place; like the smoke rings, the condition of the appearing of each new "now" is its vanishing into another: its appearance is simultaneous with its disappearance. And yet each now, says Aristotle, is the identical one present in this present instant, so that time in its succession may be thought of as circular, each ring vanishing into the following ring which it is. The whole soul resumed, Mallarmé seems to be saying, is nothing but the experience of what cannot be resumed: the soul's temporal succession—the multiplicity and unity of time's "movement" (if we can think of anything moving which is not already determined by time). The words *Quand lente* [When slow(ly)] are poised to point to the fundamental identity between the act of smoking and the temporality of being there.

The word *abolis* is one of those on which theses at the Sorbonne may be written. It is frequently taken to be the most characteristic Mallarméan word, whose importance is enshrined in the title and principal clause of his greatest poem, "Un coup de dés n'abolira jamais le hasard" [A throw of dice will never abolish chance]. The importance of the verb *abolir* lies in the way it operates in the poem as a negating word, an act of negation, and an idea of negativity, driving Mallarmé's whole poetic argument about smoking. His language ceaselessly tries to render positive and, as it were, palpable the minimal being of nothing—like smoke rings. Most nothing is not nothing at all: it is usually a *determined* nothing, as Hegel says—nothing in relation to something that it is not but that delimits it, fixes its terms, gives it a margin. The act of negating, or abolishing, for example, may have the most decisively determined existence. It is the absence of bouquets that Mallarmé aims to represent in the most heart-stopping evocations.

The word itself, *abolis*, had many attractions for Mallarmé whose meticulous interest in the graphic and phonic character of words led him to calculate poetic choices down to the smallest details of individual letters. In the center of the word is the letter *o*, as if to mark the nullity it accomplishes. Like a snake biting its tale, the letter *o* unifies a beginning and an end, like the totality of all possible signs from A to Z—in Greek, an alpha-bet-omega, the first three letters of *abo-lis*: O is the null that rolls a whole Hegelian universe, moved by the motor of ceaseless negations. That universe is like a hollowed sphere, in French a *bol*, or bowl; *bol-* is also an etymon from the Greek meaning *thrown*. *A-bol* means something *thrown down*, like the throw of dice marking a fatality—the fatal end of something. The letter *l* sounds in French like *elle*, of course—woman, who is traditionally identified with absence and negativity, compared to the so-called positive presence of the male; but the letter *l* also sounds like *aile*, which means wing. What is thrown down is also thrown, takes a hyperbolic flight to the ground in a moment of soaring departure—like the trajectory described by the head of John the Baptist in Mallarmé's poem "Le cantique de Saint Jean" (in that poem the letter i is used abundantly because its form embodies the decapitation of the prophet, with its little dot flying off at the top like a head about to roll, in the moment of being abolished). The letter s in *abolis*, the participial form of the verb, works in the cigarette poem to finish the word with a little vertical wave, like the smoke curling up from its fiery end.

The smoke attests a cigar that cunningly [*savamment*] burns with a kind of oracular wisdom; this cigar speaks veiled truths and conveys knowledge of some arcana. It burns as long as the ash is separated from its bright kiss of fire ("pour peu / Que la cendre se sépare / De son clair baiser de feu"). The ash of the cigar constantly threatens to extinguish its smoking; it grows firmly in place at the end, replacing the substance of the cigar by a ghostly but palpable negative form of itself, which progressively smothers the cinder and eventually puts it out. Cigars need constantly to be relit, unless scrupulously flicked. This fact governs the dominant comparison in the poem, accomplished by the conjunction *ainsi* [just as], which compares smoking the cigar to speaking romance or making poetry. If you want the kiss of fiery inspiration to touch your poetry, he seems to say, exclude vile reality from it, just as the cigar, in order to burn, must separate itself from its vulgar, dirty ash. The stuff of the real may have been indispensable for creating the conditions of there being smoke or romance, but once the fire is lit, one needs to exclude the real to keep the cinder burning. The ash is all too much a mimetic trace of the real, whereas the idea of poetry is to consume itself in a brilliant puff of ephemera; just as too much precise meaning erases the smoky vagueness of literature, says Mallarmé, too much ash extinguishes the resuming/expiration of the cigar.

The ash, in fact, is too precisely real, more essential than the thing whose trace or memory it preserves. Although only the remainder of the thing consumed, it may offer incomparable clues to the essence of the thing; the ash of something may reveal its truth. Thus Sherlock Holmes, for example, can reconstruct someone's personality by observing the ashes left from his smokes. Holmes was an especially systematic connoisseur of cigar ashes:

Yes [said Sherlock Holmes], I have been guilty of several monographs. They are all upon technical subjects. Here, for example, is one "Upon the Distinction Between the Ashes of the Various Tobaccos." In it I enumerate a hundred and forty forms of cigar, cigarette, and pipe tobacco, with coloured plates illustrating the difference in the ash. It is a point which is continually turning up in criminal trials, and which is sometimes of supreme importance as a clue. If you can say definitely, for example, that some murder had been done by a man who was smoking an Indian lumkah, it obviously narrows your field of search. To the trained eye there is as much difference between the black ash of a Trichinopoly and the white fluff of bird's-eye as there is between a cabbage and a potato. (Doyle 15)

The ash may be a mummy of the thing, perfectly preserving the shape of the absent thing, the outline of its essential form—guarding its memory. After the thing itself is consumed, the ash may be the only relic of its sacrifice, but no less precious for that. Indeed, a relic may be even more precious than the thing it survives, better able to perdure; the thing itself may vanish, but ashes preserve its memory, represent the idea the thing has become by vanishing. For Mallarmé, cigar ash, like a bad poem, resembles too mimetically the reality it replaces and thus snuffs out the fiery flare of burning imagination, which in this poem is the essence of smoking and literature. The ash must fall for the hot breath of poetic inspiration to continue to expire, flying or stealing from lips. Cigarettes, which are more perfectly consumed, leaving less ash, are what cigars ought to be if cigars were supposed to be poems.

In a short story titled "Une volupté nouvelle" [A new pleasure], Pierre Louÿs advances his extravagant claims on behalf of cigarettes through the mouth of Callistô, the palpable apparition of a beautiful Alexandrian woman, dead for eighteen hundred years. Her "shade," accompanying her tomb, "the stone which contained [her] refined ashes," has been brought to the Louvre from the ruins of Hellenistic Antioch. She appears unannounced at the narrator's door very late one night at the moment he has settled in, to meditate, to write, and to smoke—above all, to smoke:

One night, as I found myself at home, in silent conversation with two cats made of blue faience crouched on a white table, I hesitated in choosing between two pastimes of my solitude: writing a regular sonnet while smoking cigarettes, or smoking cigarettes while observing the oriental rug on the ceiling. The important thing is always to have a cigarette in hand; one must envelop the surrounding objects with a fine celestial cloud which bathes the light and shadows, erases hard edges, and, by means of a perfumed spell, imposes on the agitations of the mind a variable equilibrium from which it can fall into daydreaming. (Louÿs 65–66)

This overstuffed interior is drawn around the narrator like a womb. It recalls the rooms in Poe or Baudelaire where analysts and poets contemplate, ratiocinate, and dream. The two porcelain cats "crouched on a white table" are the sphinxlike emblems of this mysterious locale, poised between fiction and reality—between dreaming and writing. In this poetic space, the cigarette may be, as Sartre would say, an instrument for symbolically appropriating the world. Its smoke bathes the light and shadows, mitigates the press of hard reality, with an atmosphere that the smoker has taken into his mouth, past lips into lungs, and dreamily exhaled through his nose. Filling a room with my smoke is a way of taking possession of its volumes, its surfaces and edges, surrounding and transforming them with my own incorporations. But the magic of this perfumed spell also influences the conditions of poetic inspiration; it exercises a "variable equilibrium" on the mind agitated by daily preoccupations and inaugurates, as in the Laforgue poem, a space of dream. The balance it imposes is not boringly the same but a "variable" one that shifts equilibrium, that balances differently at different moments. The physiological effects of smoking, as we will see in chapter 5, "The Soldier's Friend," may explain the variability that Louÿs describes, the sudden passage from tension to relaxation, from speed to narcosis, that cigarettes procure.

Callistô appears unexpectedly at the door in the middle of the night, like Mimi with her spent candle or Poe's raven at the window. Knock, knock. He opens, and brushing past him is the sexy ghost of the most beautiful woman in antiquity, come to life, like a spirit loosed from Hades, brilliantly there in person. The narrator, who ends by making passionate love to her, insists in his account on her carnal presence in flesh and blood—particularly in the flesh. She is beautifully, erotically dressed:

> Her dress was of green watered silk, ornamented with gigantic irises stitched into the robe itself and whose stems mounted in ribs along her body up to a squared *décolleté* which displayed the naked tips of her breasts. On each arm she wore a little golden snake with emerald eyes. A double necklace of pearls gleamed against her dark skin, marking the birth of her neck, which was mobile and curved. (Louÿs 67)

A sort of Nefertiti, she is a royal priestess of *ars erotica*, a sort of encyclopedia of all the accumulated wisdom of antiquity, instructed not only in seduction and pleasure but in the knowledge, which may have been their indispensable concomitant, of all arts and sciences—including geometry

Beauty at the Beach
Photo © Robert Capa. By permission of Magnum Photos, Inc.

and pre-Socratic philosophy, as well as geology, architecture, and ancient techniques of metallurgy. Callistô's beauty is allied with a vast intelligence and a debater's ferocious argumentativeness; in that respect, she may be an emblem of what Louÿs, a (postromantic pornographic) modern, thinks is the difference between modern eroticism and that of antiquity: he imagines that in Alexandria and Antioch, in the first century, there was no separation between the most abstract forms of thinking and the most sensual forms of erotic pleasure. Even the narrator, a connoisseur, is taken aback in awe and nervousness at the daring prospect of Callistô's unnamed proposals of sexual pleasure. A courtesan of "rare intellectuality," she lectures the narrator in bed on the philosophical doctrine of Parmenides concerning the identity of thoughts and objects, and it turns him on beyond his wildest imaginings.

Having arrived unannounced to intrude upon the narrator's reverie, this ghost from eighteen hundred years past pours out her disappointment and dismay at what she has observed while wandering the streets of Paris. Not only does she find that things are worse: life is more stupid and people less happy than in the world she knew. But to her immense stupefaction, she discovers that so little has changed. She compares her own clothes, her shoes, her jewels to those of modern women and pronounces their superiority. When the narrator insists that the problem is a false one, that women in all times are equally beautiful in the flesh, she undresses in a flash to reveal such splendors as oblige him to acknowledge that she resembles nothing he has ever seen: "I could not explain how it is that her beauty could never be realized neither in our climate, nor in our time, for the evidence of it came to light in no single detail but in a general harmony and, perhaps, clarity" (Louÿs 73). The beauty of this classical beauty is harmonious and clear, like the Greece of Goethe. She is the gorgeous embodiment in this little allegory of the totality of what was different and superior about classical culture.

Callistô continues her "lecture," proving with irrefutable argument that nothing invented or discovered up until the end of the nineteenth century was not already known and fully understood in classical times. "I need to tell someone what disappointment I felt after my walk around and I am resentful toward your century for all the surprises it did not have in store" (Louÿs 79). What is called modernity is only the partial reinvention of the wisdom and techniques that have been for the most part irredeemably lost. There is nothing new or better, nothing known or practiced that was not already grasped before, and much has been lost to modernity, which is

poorer and sadder. Nothing is new under the sun, there are no new pleasures, not a single "nouvelle volupté," she argues, crushing the narrator's
last attempts to resist her point. But at the end of the story, just at the moment when the narrator admits to having lost every argument, he offers
Callistô a cigarette:

"Would you like a cigarette?" I asked her.
"What?"
"I say: Would you like a cigarette? No doubt that also comes from
Greece, since Aristotle who . . ."
"I would not go that far. I admit we were ignorant of that clumsy
habit, which consists in filling your mouth with the smoke of leaves.
But I do not suppose you are offering me this as a pleasure?"
"Who knows? Have you tried it?"
"Never! What, are you one of those who exercise this ridiculous
practice?"
"Sixty times a day. Indeed it is the only regular activity whose burden
I have agreed to assume."
"And you like it?"
"I truly think that I would sooner resign myself to never touching
the hand of a woman for a whole week than to seeing myself separated
from my cigarettes for the same lapse of time."
"You exaggerate."
"Not entirely."
She seemed to dream.
"Well. Give me a cigarette."
I offered it to her.
"Light it. How do you do it? Inhale?"
"Girls blow in it; but that is not the best way. It is in fact better to
breathe in. Take a puff. Close your eyes. Take another. . . ."
In a few minutes, Callistô had turned her little tube of oriental leaves
into ashes. She threw away the unsmoked half, where the rouge on
her lips had left lipstick traces. There was a silence. She even avoided
looking at me. She had taken the square pack in her hand, which to
me seemed agitated, as if by a slight emotion, and after she had examined it on all sides, I noticed that she was not giving it back. Slowly,
with the solicitude one has for the most precious objects, she placed
it near an ashtray, at the edge of the light sofa, on which she stretched
out her long, dark body. (Louÿs 84–86)

In the end, the smoking cigarette has the last word, the only word that modernity can answer to antiquity. But Callistô, stretched out across the page, is also a prophetic creature. Not the dandy, but the lady in command of her pleasure is the future of cigarettes in the twentieth century.

3 Zeno's Paradox

La cigarette est une étrange paradoxe: elle veut
dire tout en se taisant, rendre manifeste en
dissimulant, faire vivre tout en tuant; en
consumant. —Annie LeClerc

Any serious discussion of cigarettes that aims to determine their philosophical significance, judge their aesthetic pleasure, and weigh their cultural value must take account of Italo Svevo's masterpiece, published in 1923, *La coscienza di Zeno*. In English the title has been translated as *The Confessions of Zeno*, which is wrong: the word *coscienza* in Italian may mean consciousness or conscience, or conscientiousness, but not confessions—in the plural. The book, to be sure, is a kind of confessional recounting of Zeno's life by himself, and it is even sexy, like confessions in the popular sense, which exhibit or betray the idiosyncratic perversions and erotic transgressions of the narrator.[1] But if this novel is a fictional confession, it is principally a philosophical one: it traces a certain logic of consciousness, which it rigorously describes and conscientiously analyzes, at the same time that it discloses dramatic moments of the narrator's experience, exposing and probing his moral conscience. Zeno is much closer to the narrator of Augustine's and Rousseau's *Confessions* than to De Quincey, in his *Confessions of an English Opium Eater*, or, in *Confessions of a Confidence Man*, to Felix Krull.

Svevo's novel is the fictional memoir of Zeno Cosino, a figure whose life much resembles that of the author, Ettore Schmitz, whose nom de plume was Italo Svevo. Schmitz led a comfortable upper-class life in Trieste, much like the one he attributes to Zeno, the fictional author of these confessions. Both of them made principal distractions out of playing the violin and quitting smoking; but neither author nor narrator, Svevo or Zeno, had much success at either.

Svevo himself, in his correspondence with the great Italian critic Eugenio Montale, acknowledges the resemblance between himself and his narrator protagonist, even while he very strongly insists on their difference: "But just consider that this is an autobiography, and that it is not mine" (Svevo, *Écrits intimes* 235). Svevo tells Montale that he worked at putting himself in the mind of Zeno Corsini by miming his movements and mannerisms—the way he walks and smokes—before beginning to write this fictional autobiography. A friend of James Joyce, whom he knew in Trieste, Schmitz had to be playing a game of resemblance and difference with the mirror-glass disposition of this nom de plume, Italo Svevo, and the name, Zeno Corsini, of his fictional autobiographer: Zeno/Svevo cannot be an accident.[2] One is the fictional name of the person who is more or less Schmitz, and the other is that of his closely resembling fictional surrogate who narrates the novel. The play on names aims to confuse the genres of this narrative, making it impossible to decide whether and when to read these "Confessions" as an autobiography or a novel, even if, at the same time, the differences make it impossible to suppose that it is unimportant to distinguish between them, between fiction and truth.

Schmitz's journal, which he kept for the first few months of his engagement to Livia Veniziani in 1896, is replete with promises to stop smoking. Some examples, among scores of entries:

February 11, 1896: "While waiting, I will tell you that after so many, many promises, I have now, at this moment, smoked my last cigarette."

Later that afternoon: "7 minutes before 4 afternoon, still smoking, still and always for the last time."

February 13, 1896: "Last night I promised Livia not to smoke any more."

Later that afternoon: "Thanks to this outburst, with your permission, I smoked for the last time, and let's not speak about it any more."

February 19, 1896: "The cigarette that I am in the process of smoking is the last cigarette!" (Svevo, *Écrits intimes* 73, 74, 75, 76, 78)

The first chapter of *The Confessions of Zeno* presents itself as a self-analysis, in a way a psychoanalysis, written by the protagonist, Zeno, of his propensity to smoke, and a history of the stages in his long, unsuccessful effort to quit. He fails despite (perhaps because of) his having smoked "the last cigarette," just like Svevo, an innumerable number of times—"still and always" the last one. The fundamental paradox in the life of both the author and the character is that making resolutions to stop smoking is the indispensable condition, the sine qua non of continuing to smoke. This new paradox of Zeno, in turn, gives rise to the therapeutic question: How can a habit ever be cured if resolving to be rid of it permits, in fact ensures, its persistence?

In Italian, the first chapter of Zeno's confessions is entitled "Il fumo," which simply means "smoke" or "smoking"; it makes no allusion to the novel's preponderant theme of making and breaking resolutions. The English translation, "The Last Cigarette," although abusive, might seem to improve upon the original title, if it were not that clouds and smoke, all nebulous forms, occupy a preeminent place in the first chapter and throughout the novel, culminating, in its last line, in a postapocalyptic vision of earth "returned to its nebulous form wandering in the heavens."

Surely the most uncanny thing about this unobtrusively strange novel, which is intended to be the fiction of something more than just a book, is its last, prophetic paragraph, first published in 1923—a prenuclear post-ecological scenario. Here are the last four sentences of the novel:

> Perhaps some incredible disaster produced by machines will lead us back to health. When all the poison gases are exhausted, a man, made like other men of flesh and blood, will in the quiet of his room invent an explosive of such potency that all the explosives in existence will seem like harmless toys beside it. And another man, made in his image and in the image of all the rest, but a little weaker than they, will steal that explosive and crawl to the center of the earth with it, and place it just where he calculates it would have the maximum effect. There will be a tremendous explosion, but no one will hear it and the earth will return to its nebulous state and go wandering through the heavens, free at last of parasites and disease. (Svevo, La coscienza di Zeno 383)

If the invention of nuclear weapons seems to have confirmed the first half of Zeno's prophecy, that confirmation enhances the plausibility and hence the terror surrounding the second. But what does it mean to speak of Zeno's "prophecy"? Can fictional characters predict the future? Who, if anyone, is speaking here? With what authority or legitimacy? An analysis of Zeno's discussion of smoking must aim to trace the itinerary that takes him from the aesthetic and cultural implications of cigarettes at the beginning of the novel and leads him to this concluding anticipation of what sounds like total nuclear war or general plutonium contamination. Is there some logical necessity such that reflecting on cigarettes leads one inevitably to prophetic anticipations of apocalypse?

One of the threads that may help us trace that itinerary is the novel's explicit treatment of "Psychoanalysis," the title of the last chapter. The novel's initial premise is the fictional narrator's ongoing psychoanalysis—in 1923, one of the first to be represented in literature. The memoir is "prefaced" by Dr. S., who identifies himself as Zeno's analyst ("I am the doctor frequently depicted in this novel in not very flattering terms"). He coolly justifies his outrageous decision to publish this manuscript, without his patient's permission, as a form of revenge "to annoy him." He reveals that Zeno had interrupted the analysis "just at the most interesting point" and was refusing to recommence.[3] This extortionist shrink offers to share the proceeds from the publication of these memoirs with their author, his patient, from whom he received them in trust, on the sole condition that he agree to resume his analysis. Zeno, we learn in a postscript, defiantly refuses to go back to the talking on a couch; writing his memoirs has succeeded where psychoanalytic therapy failed to relieve him of his inveterate cigarette habit. Zeno mocks the therapeutic claims and the arcane methods of a psychoanalytic cure and proposes in their place the theory and practice of what he calls this "fumo-analysis."

However much the fictional narrator may believe he has departed from Freudian orthodoxy, the last lines of the novel, predicting catastrophe, an end to civilization and its discontents, uncannily anticipate another famous anticipation of total nuclear war. They antedate by sixteen years those passages at the end of *Civilization and Its Discontents* in which Freud offers an equally bleak prognosis for the fate of mankind—this species-being caught in the ever-more-fatal grip of increasingly destructive forces created by the progressive success and expansion of its technology. That this nuclear prophecy should come from Zeno's pen in memoirs written for his psychoanalyst that anticipate writings of Freud presents a surprising intricateness of fact and fiction, a strange temporal figure. It is as if a fiction written under the influence of Freudian psychoanalysis was able to arrive at some of the most significant Freudian conclusions sixteen years before Freud himself did; as if Freud's ideas were preceded by his own ideas, discovered by fictional minds he influenced.

Zeno's therapeutic alternative to psychoanalysis is not a talking but a writing cure, and it takes as the object of its analysis not the repression of infantile sexuality but the history of the patient's smoking—a history whose recall is facilitated by the patient's continuously smoking as he writes. Zeno indicates his reasons for rejecting psychoanalysis by narrating the circumstances surrounding his decision to abandon it. And the principal form that abandonment assumes is the resumption of the journal he had first taken up during the extended time his analyst was absent from Trieste. Zeno had dutifully put his pencil down when his analyst returned and for six months had submitted himself to an orthodox Freudian treatment. But convinced in the end of the failure of that treatment, and certain of the benefits of his own solution, he resolves at the end of the novel to abandon the shrink and the manuscript as well in the hands of the doctor who exploits him: "May 3, 1915. I have finished with psychoanalysis. After having practiced it assiduously for six whole months I find I am worse than before. I have not yet fired the doctor, but my resolution is irrevocable. Yesterday I sent to say that I was prevented from coming, and I shall let him expect me for a few days. If I could be sure of laughing at him without flying into a rage, I should not mind seeing him again. But I am afraid I should end by assaulting him" (380).

At the beginning of the first chapter, we hear the doctor, before leaving Trieste, prescribing to Zeno the unorthodox technique of writing down his life; he has no time to lose in getting cured, the doctor thinks: "After all he is old." He cautions Zeno not to insist on trying to remember his earliest childhood memories, which now seem remote and unreliable to him, but to begin with material closer in time, the history of his "propensione al fumo": "Scriva! Scriva! Vedrà come arriverà a vedersi intero" [Write! Write! You will see how soon you will get to see yourself clearly as a whole] (6). Zeno begins by evoking the material conditions of his fumo-analysis. He decides, for example, that he can write very well about smoking while sitting "here at my table," without "dreaming" on "that couch." The difference between psycho- and fumo-analysis is translated into a few decisive coordinates: his will be a vertical therapy rather than a horizontal one; it will consist in writing, not talking. It will appropriate the immediate certainty and hard-edged resistance of a pencil pressing against the surface of "my table" rather than yield to the cushy vagueness of talking on "that" couch.

Not knowing how to begin, Zeno inaugurates the epic narrative of his case history with the protocol of addressing a muse (actually, hundreds of thousands of them): he invokes "the assistance of cigarettes all so similar to the one I have in hand" (6). If he had made the calculation, he would have enumerated a staggering series of cigarettes consumed in a lifetime: 50 a day for twenty years amounts to 365,000 cigarettes, not including the additional 250 that get smoked in leap years. Some authorities think that smoking 300,000 cigarettes will pretty much guarantee the getting of cancer. Each one of those cigarettes implies the repetition of several small ritual actions, like those that Cocteau enumerates: the taking of a pack of cigarettes, the ceremony of extracting and lighting one, the strange cloud that penetrates you and that your nostrils breathe out. It may seem paradoxical that one could write a history of the succession of things and gestures "all so similar to one another." But the inevitable, ceaseless return of something indistinguishable from what precedes it and follows it is like the circle or cycle of time's passage, each "now," as we have seen, exactly identical to the now it replaces and anticipates. A history of smoking is, therefore, like a brief history of time—of the condition of history itself; this Zeno, smoking cigarettes, like the ancient one, is the philosopher of the paradoxes of movement in time.

When he invokes the muse of all those cigarettes similar "to the one I have in hand," Zeno's hand appears in the text to signal, in the fiction of this first-person narrative, that not a paragraph was written that cannot be assumed to have been accompanied, or interrupted, by a cigarette. Whatever the author Svevo/Schmitz may have been doing (probably smoking) while he was writing the fiction of Zeno's writing his memoirs, the fictional narrator, Zeno, is presumed always to have a cigarette in one hand (a pencil in the other). The reader is expected to discover that this novelistic fiction consists not only in what the narrator recounts but in what he is supposed to be doing (with his hands, lips, mouth, lungs, nose) while he is writing this autobiographical memoir.

Anyone allergic to cigarette smoking probably should not read this novel, for the same reason that entering into its fiction would be banned on all domestic flights. The performance of the fiction implies that it makes a difference whether you read the book smoking a cigarette: this novel was written for smokers only. If you are not holding a cigarette in your hand, you are probably missing the point, misjudging the relation of this self-history to the possibility of the cure it represents, and therefore misunderstanding the aim of the narrative, probably finding it foolish or naive. Smokers, conversely, will be powerfully motivated to read this fiction of a therapeutic process, which culminates in the final pages with the aged, principal character finally quitting smoking after a lifetime devoted to trying to do so. This memoir directs a pointed critique at psychoanalysis and claims to remedy its failings by proposing the itinerary of an authentic cure. The reader, reading the history of the cure all the while smoking cigarettes, may vicariously undergo the same purge as the narrator and may, at the end, abandon the habit. One can think of few works of fiction that

Lech Walesa in Gdansk
Photo by Corvin. By permision of Magnum Photos, Inc.

seek to have such an immediate and decisive influence on the lives of their readers.

James Joyce, who much admired Schmitz from the time he taught him English in Trieste, understood very well the aim of the book, or at least the transformative effect its fiction might have on its readers. Asked by the Putnam editors to write a preface for the English translation of La coscienza he declined but sent instead the following advice for its publicity:

> With regard to the other book by the author of Senilità, the only thing I can suggest as likely to attract the British reading public are a preface by Sir James Barrie, author of My Lady Nicotine [and of Peter Pan], opinions of the book from two deservedly popular personalities of the present day, such as, the Rector of Stiffkey and the Princess of Wales and (on the front of the jacket) a coloured picture by a Royal Academician representing two young ladies, one fair and the other dark but both distinctly nice looking, seated in graceful though of course not unbecoming posture at a table on which the book stands upright with the title visible, and underneath the picture three lines of simple dialogue, for example:
> Ethel: Does Cyril still spend too much on cigarettes?
> Doris: Far too much.
> Ethel: So does Percy (points)—till I gave him ZENO.[4]

The languorous chic of two charming ladies, one brune and the other blonde, like French cigarettes, is intended to seduce the philistine reading public into laying out its money, not for the art of this book but its utility—for the salutary effect it has, not on health, but on pocketbooks. Buy ZENO, Joyce advertises, because the more you read, the more you save.

For Zeno, the fumo-analysis begins to work immediately; no sooner does he evoke the muse of cigarettes smoked than he remembers something, not a thing that he had forgotten, he says, but one that he had never remembered before. He recalls that the first cigarettes he tried, so many years ago, no longer exist in commerce: in Austria around 1870 there was a cigarette that came in a little box marked with the two-headed imperial eagle. A negative memory, remembering the knowledge that something has disappeared, the first figure in this history of smoking is linked to the smoking of history. Never very far from the principal issues that dominate Western history since the sixteenth century (i.e., war and taxes), tobacco—the commodity that Napoleon considered the most eminently taxable—is the traditional locus of the most direct intervention by the state into the intimate pleasure of the individual, where politics is experienced with unmediated acuity, particularly during wartime, depressions, and revolutions. The rise and fall of the bicephalic eagle on the pack traces the figure of historical memory in the consciousness of Zeno, impresses the movement of history on the life of the singular smoker.

Zeno next hallucinates the image of several people gathered around the box of those Austrian cigarettes; he distinguishes their features only enough to remember their names. He is struck that he is in no way moved by them. Hoping to obtain more from their recall, he leaves off writing and goes to the couch to lie down, adopting a more orthodox psychoanalytic position. Immediately, the faces disappear and are replaced by grotesque masks that laugh at him. He gets up, despondent, and goes back to the table. Not only do the postures of psychoanalysis betray, mock, and depress him, but the role that Freud assigns to the affective power and determining influence of early memories is systematically discredited and disproved.

Zeno sits again at the table and lights up a cigarette. Once having renounced the humiliation of being supine, defying the grotesque inventions it puts in the place of memory, he now gains access to authentic scenes from his past that are linked in consciousness to the tangible chain of innumerable cigarettes he has smoked. Coming faster and more sharply, they begin to form a coherent narrative of absences, of disappearances, of forgetting and nonoccurrence. Attached to the memory of the cigarette box, with its bicephalic eagle, was the "figure" of a boy he used to know, Giuseppe, "with a rather hoarse [roca] voice" (6). Giuseppe is the first person remembered in this memoir, but his initiating role in this therapeutic analysis is confined to being a hapax legomenon, a first and last time. With none of the importance assigned to the earliest memory in a psychoanalytic cure, Giuseppe's inaugural appearance has absolutely no repercussions in anything that follows—no deeply encrypted psychological significance, nor any role in the anecdotal laying bare of Zeno's consciousness. The only thing Zeno tells us is that this boy received a lot of money from his father and used it to buy those Austrian cigarettes. Zeno is sure about one thing: Giuseppe never gave any to him.

Giuseppe's greed, which forces Zeno to steal the money he needs to buy cigarettes, runs counter to the popular ethic of democratic generosity associated with tobacco in general, and with cigarettes in particular. In this connection, it is worth recalling the opening scene of Molière's version of Don Giovanni, which begins with a long monologue praising tobacco for the generosity with which it inspires felicitous human exchange. Don Juan's valet designates tobacco as the panacea, curing all ills and, above all, instituting a more perfect universe of economic justice by encouraging the voluntary exchange of gifts: tobacco gives the gift of giving. Giuseppe, like the don himself, defies the utopian economy that tobacco installs.

Except in times of great scarcity, when they become a form of money —a universal token of exchange—cigarettes are normally exceptions to the regime of private property and are subject to the more expansive transactions of the gift. Even now, in many countries, just as formerly in America, anyone of whatever class can ask anyone for a light, and a request for a cigarette is never refused. Rival speaks of "the fraternity of smokers"— these days increasingly becoming a sorority. He quotes a letter of Mme de Girardin, writing in 1844 to the Viconte de Launay, in which she recounts that just recently a worker asked the Prince de J. for a light and he gave him his cigar. She notes that in Spain refusing to give someone a light may cause a serious quarrel. The least beggar, she says, has the right to ask the king himself for a light; he could not refuse. She concludes by opining: "If Prometheus had stolen fire from heaven in order to light his cigarette, they would have let him do it" (Rival 166).

Because of Giuseppe's avarice, Zeno began his career as a smoker by having to steal the money he needed to buy them. Since his only source of petty cash was the pockets of his father's waistcoat, frequently abandoned in summer on a chair in the hall, Zeno began buying cigarettes with the small change he filched. From the paternal pocket he stole "the ten soldi he needed to acquire the precious little box [scatoletta] and smoked one after the other the ten cigarettes it contained, so as not to conserve for very long the compromising fruit of the theft" (7). Beginning to smoke for Zeno was thus simultaneous with becoming a thief. It is not uncommon, it is perhaps the rule, that cigarette smoking begins under the sign of the illicit. Since moralists no less than doctors have disapproved of tobacco from its introduction, its use constitutes a form of defiance of authority, of the laws of man and God.[5] Laforgue, smoking, thumbs his nose at the immortals. Revolutionaries repeatedly arise to defy tyrants and dictators who have sought to repress smoking and constrain its easy commerce. Zeno understands very well that beginning to smoke is frequently, may always be, an Oedipal transgression; but unlike Freud, he considers that fact to be totally irrelevant to effecting a cure.

The case history that Zeno tells, unlike a psychoanalytic cure, does not proceed by the progressive revelation of some ever more deeply hidden secret of early sexual life. Rather, his rough chronology runs, consciously and analytically, from one paradox of smoking to the next. At each step in the narrative he enacts a further paradox that smoking cigarettes presents to his consciousness—to a mind that has a feel for the logical dilemmas of a philosopher or mathematician. Zeno after all, like Svevo, professionally studied law and chemistry.

Zeno began smoking by stealing, until one day his father caught him red-handed. "Then I remember that one day my father surprised me holding his waistcoat. With an effrontery that I would not have now and that even now disgusts me (perhaps that disgust will have great importance for my cure), I told him I was curious to count the buttons. My father laughed at my disposition toward things mathematical or sartorial and did not see that I had my hand in his pocket. To my honor I can say that his laughter directed at my innocence when it no longer existed was enough to prevent me from ever stealing again" (7). The consequence of his (not) being caught at the moment he was seen (unseen) stealing is paradoxical; his father's laughter at his innocence, just at the moment when, stealing and boldly lying, he had lost it, was enough, he says, forever to prevent him from stealing again. Why? What is the logical condition of this remarkably effective lesson that his father gives him inadvertently—effective precisely, it seems, because it was not the lesson he "deserved"? Being absolved of blame by his father who deems him incapable of imagining a crime, he applies the punishment to himself all the more thoroughly to prove how heinous he has been. If his father had seen him stealing and punished him, he might have determined to be more crafty the next time. To his credit [a mio onore], he applied the punishment to himself in the form of a mild self-loathing that effectively gave him the lesson the father had failed to administer. The law of the father is internalized and obedience becomes a matter of honor; now he is obliged to apply the punishment himself and to model his behavior on his own understanding of the principle. Not-punishing achieves the effect of punishment, whereas actual punishing would probably have inspired his continued defiance.

But suppose for a moment that the father's laughter is only feigned and that he sees very well where Zeno's hand has intruded. He also sees that the child thinks he is blind to the theft. The father does not disabuse his son; he allows him to continue to believe that he is unseen, in order to permit him, unaided, to draw his own moral conclusion that he should no longer steal for cigarettes. Perhaps the father knew that if he had intervened at that moment, in the paternal role, to arrest and punish his son, he would have ensured that Zeno would go on stealing. Instead, the son, obliged to punish himself, to prove he is capable of the crime, is a better father to himself than his father, punishing, could be. Feigning blindness to theft may be a model for pedagogy one does not wish to generalize; yet if the father had applied the same psychology and had allowed Zeno to smoke, instead of interdicting it, he might no more have become an inveterate smoker than he did an incorrigible thief. There are certain interdictions, paradoxically, that are better enforced by not enforcing them, and the taboo against smoking may be one of them.

The first paradox of Zeno is immediately followed by a second. Having decided never to steal again because he was not punished for what he had done intentionally, boldly, he now began to do unintentionally what he had forever forsworn: he stole again, but without considering it theft. His father left half-smoked "Virginia" cigars lying about on the edge of a table or chest of drawers. Zeno, thinking they were abandoned for the maid to throw away, began smoking them in secret, figuring they would never be missed. "Just the act of appropriating [impadronirmene] the cigars sent a shiver of loathing running through me, knowing how sick they would make me. Then I smoked them until my forehead was covered in cold sweat and my stomach twisted up. It cannot be said that I lacked energy as a child" (7). In Italian, the act of appropriating the cigars, of taking possession or gaining mastery, is said to be "enfathering oneself of them": "im-padron-irmene." The son becomes like the father by reappropriating in a paternal act of mastery the property of the father. But the only triumph he carries away from this act is a shiver of loathing in anticipation of how sick the cigars are going to make him. His expectations are perfectly fulfilled by the stomach-twisting cramps and cold sweat the cigars induce. It takes no little energy but an awesome expenditure to be able to procure for oneself such a complexly articulated pleasure-pain at the price of so much initiative. Not for a moment is the beginning of smoking identified with positive tastes, good feelings, or narcotic distraction; it is vicious from the start, loathsome in anticipation, sickening in the process, and revolting and shameful afterward.

He smoked the unused cigar butts he thought the maid would throw away until his father's paradoxical intervention once again cured him of his inadvertent theft. One day, as he lay curled up on a couch next to his mother, appearing to sleep, his father entered the room loudly wondering what had happened to the cigar butt he had left lying on the corner of a table: "I think I am going crazy. I'm sure I left half of a cigar on that buffet a half-hour ago and now I don't find it. I am worse than usual. Things are beginning to escape me." Zeno's mother responded, "with a hilarity restrained only by the fear of waking" her son: "And yet no one has been in this room after lunch." "It's because I know that too," says the father, "that I think I'm going crazy" (8).

Zeno stops stealing his father's cigar butts out of fear of driving him crazy by continuing to do what his father thinks it is impossible for him to do. He could not have taken the father's cigar butts because "no one [nessuno]" had been in the room—except him, Zeno, zero, "no one" adultly capable of wishing to steal cigars from his father. The laughter of the mother betrays her knowledge that the child is already lost to innocence, but the father has not yet conceived the possibility. Even if it leads him to question his own sanity, he refuses to attribute to his son the capacity or the will to transgress the parental interdiction. Once again Zeno internalizes the law that the father has failed to enforce. The father's seemingly inadvertent strategy (again the possibility of feint cannot be excluded) was brilliantly successful: it "cured" Zeno of stealing cigars by seeming not to see so as not to punish.

Conversely, where cigarettes are concerned, the parental failure is total, because prohibition achieves a result directly contrary to its aim. Zeno next writes this brief, fateful paragraph: "After this there was never any lack of money that made it difficult for me to satisfy my vice, but prohibitions sufficed to excite it" (8). If failing to punish cures a vice, prohibiting excites it. The power of interdiction to excite transgression is a psychological fact whose consequences are probably more widely known than those who are charged with combating drugs would officially acknowledge, for fear of seeming irrelevant. The paradox of prohibition as incitement may serve to explain, for example, the seemingly contradictory policies of the United States government, which places warnings on cigarette packs and subsidizes tobacco growers, which denounces the consequences of smoking even as it promotes America's tobacco exports. If the unwitting aim were, in fact, to increase the use of tobacco at home and abroad, then, according to Zeno's paradox, the most effective way of inciting its use would be to expand the scope of its prohibition. The statistically attested decline of smoking in America, following the surgeon general's report, may mask what is undoubtedly, and progressively, a vast increase in the amount of secret smoking. A Doonesbury cartoon intimated that when drug czar

William Bennett was forced to acknowledge using a nicotine dispenser, that meant there was probably a lot of sneaking cigarettes going on—quick little dirty ones, out of all public purview.

Under the menace of prohibitions, Zeno remembers smoking abundantly, "hidden in every possible place." He particularly recalls hiding in a cellar with two other boys, where they had a contest to see who could smoke the most in the shortest possible time. Zeno competes and wins. But what has he won? Staggering out into the sun and air, he has to close his eyes to keep from falling down: "Heroically he hides the sickness resulting from this strange exercise." It is strange to see the heroic excess to which the neophyte smoker will go to do abundantly something that makes him feel horribly sick and weak. When Zeno pulls himself together, he boasts of his victory. One of the boys says, "It doesn't matter to me if I lost since I only smoke as long as I enjoy it." Zeno says he "remembers the healthy words but not the healthy face that certainly must have been turned toward him at that moment" (9). His forgetfulness here is a kind of ironic revenge against his playmate. For Zeno, from the first, smoking has nothing to do with health or simple enjoyment. The idea that one could smoke just enough to enjoy smoking cigarettes contradicts the actual nature of the experience and the habit. Pope John Paul II is reputed, perhaps apocryphally, to smoke only three cigarettes a day, one after every meal—but only a saint can exercise such control over a practice that seems to have to be compulsively excessive or not at all.

From the beginning, Zeno could not tell whether he hated or loved smoking cigarettes. When he finally knew that he hated "their taste, their odor, and the state into which nicotine put him . . . it was all much worse" (9). Hating cigarettes is in no way incompatible with continuing to smoke; it only serves to provide the pretext for continuously smoking "the last cigarette." Hating cigarettes is the hatred one loves to hate.

At around the age of twenty he became a serious smoker as a consequence of the effort to stop. Suffering during several weeks from a violent sore throat and fever, he was ordered to bed by the doctor, who prescribed "absolute abstention from smoking." "The word, *absolute*, wounded me and the fever made it more vivid: a great void and nothing to resist the enormous pressure that is suddenly produced around the void" (9). After the doctor leaves, his father, with a cigar in hand, reminds him not to smoke anymore. The order produces an enormous uneasiness. It leads him to the next paradoxical stage in the history of his cigarette smoking. "Since cigarettes do me harm, I won't smoke any more, but first I want to do it for the last time [ma prima volio farlo per l'ultima volta]" (9). Even though it makes his tonsils feel on fire, he resolves to smoke a last one. "I finished the last cigarette with the meticulousness with which one fulfills a vow. And always suffering horribly, I smoked many others during my sickness" (9). The pain of smoking is nothing compared to the enormous disquiet of having vowed to stop, a promise which smoking "the last cigarette" nicely absolves. To stop, one first has to smoke the *last* cigarette, but the last one is yet another one. Stopping therefore means continuing to smoke. The whole paradox is here: Cigarettes are bad for me, therefore I will stop. Promising to stop creates enormous unease. I smoke the last cigarette as if I were fulfilling a vow. The vow is therefore fulfilled and the uneasiness it causes vanishes; hence the last cigarette allows me to smoke many others after that.

From time to time, his father would appear with a cigar in his mouth and would encourage him to stick to the resolution he had in secret, repeatedly violated. "Bravo!" said his father. "A few more days of abstaining from cigarettes and you will be cured." That sentence made him wish his father would leave immediately so he could run to his cigarette. Sometimes he pretended to be asleep to make him go away sooner; he didn't even need to hear the words to want to rush to smoke. His illness initiates him into the adult phase of his career as a smoker, one that continues up to the moment, after a long life, when he is writing this fumo-analysis: "This sickness procured me the second of my disorders: the effort of liberating myself from the first. My days ended up being filled with cigarettes and with resolutions not to smoke anymore, and to tell the truth, they still are. The dance of the last cigarette, which began when I was twenty, has not reached its last figure yet" (10).

In addition to his cigarette habit he had now acquired the habit of resolving to stop. And the determination to smoke the last cigarette increasingly became the dominant activity of his life. It still is, he tells us, in the moment he is retrospectively writing this memoir of his two habits. As he "grows older his resolutions are less drastic and he becomes more indulgent toward his weakness"—increasingly undeluded about his capacity to keep his resolutions. Nevertheless, he continues to make them even as he continues to smoke, apparently more than ever. "The resolution is less violent and my weakness finds in my old soul more indulgence. In old age one can afford to smile at life and all it contains. In fact I can say that for some time I have been smoking many cigarettes . . . which were not the last" (10). That is to say, the cigarettes he has been smoking lately are not only not

Kids Smoking
Photo © Ron Benvenisti. By permission of Magnum Photos, Inc.

the last cigarettes, they are not "last cigarettes"—those accompanied by resolutions, never kept, to stop.

Sartre, referring to letters of Dostoyevski that record his constant resolve to forswear his compulsive gambling, proposes an existentialist interpretation of the mechanism that permits the failure of even the most firmly made promise to abandon some habituating activity. That mechanism, or principle, he says, is nothing other than our possibility for freedom: the nonbearing of every past determination on our absolute freedom of choice in the present. Nothing in our past, even our most steely resolutions, can determine our action.

The feeling that comes over a smoker tempted by a cigarette is often represented as an interior debate between a tendency to smoke and a resolution that conflicts with it but that in the end is overcome despite good intentions. Sartre rejects that model, which depends too much on the hypostatized opposition of different "faculties":

> There is nothing in us that resembles an interior *debate*, as if we had to weigh motives and reasons before deciding. The anterior resolution ["not to smoke"] is always *there* and, in most cases, the [smoker] presented with [a cigarette] turns back to the resolution to ask its help: for he does not want to [smoke] or rather, having made the resolution the day before, he still thinks of himself as not wanting to [smoke], he believes in the efficacy of the resolution. But what he grasps then in anguish is precisely the total inefficiency of the past resolution. It is still there, no doubt, but frozen, inefficacious, *transcended* by the very fact that I am conscious of it. It is still *me*, to the degree that I perpetually accomplish my identity with myself through the temporal flux, but it is no longer *me* in the fact that it is for my consciousness. I escape it, it fails in the mission I had given it. (Sartre, 68–69)

It is not that the smoker's desire to smoke overwhelms his resolution and destroys it; it is still and always there. Confronted with a cigarette, he turns back to the resolution and asks its help. The determination not to smoke is still with him, still him, but the moment he asks it to help him face the new temptation, he discovers, in anguish, Sartre says, its total inefficacy in the present situation. The resolution still is him to the extent that he is the sum and the continuity through time of all his past determinations, but it is no longer him, having transcended it, by virtue of the fact that in the present he is conscious of it as something belonging to the past: "but it is no longer *me* in the fact that it is for my consciousness." Because I am not actually making a (new) resolution—an illocutionary speech act—but remembering one as something past for my consciousness—merely observing or representing it—"I escape it [*Je lui échappe*], it fails in the mission I had given it." Mission not accomplished, the smoker confronts the distance, the nonbeing [*le néant*], that separates himself from himself. He would have loved not to smoke. Yesterday he would never have taken the cigarette; yesterday he saw things clearly, in a synthetic vision of the whole. The relation he perceived between his health, his smoking, and the disapproval he received from friends and family, the opprobrium of society, *prevented* him from taking a cigarette. He thought he had erected a barrier between the cigarette and himself with the strength of his resolution. But now it seems only a distant memory of an idea, the ghost of a feeling he had yesterday. For his resolution to help him, he would have to make it all over again, from the beginning. But then that would be a new resolution, one of the options he has now in the present, like taking or not taking the cigarette. He would have to re-create in the present all those feelings of anxiety about his health, relive the unhappiness occasioned by social disapproval that he felt yesterday; otherwise the resolution is only a hollow phantom. The smoker had believed that it would prevent him from smoking in the future, but standing now before the temptation to smoke he realizes that he is as naked and alone as he was before, with no barriers between him and the cigarette, which he can smoke if he wants to. And he does.

For Sartre, the failure of even the most strongly taken resolutions is a proof of the absence of determinism, evidence of the inherent freedom in which we stand toward even the most powerful determinations of the past. The Sartrean smoker does not enjoy that freedom; rather, he experiences it in a mode of anguish, realizing that nothing protects him from the necessity of assuming responsibility for the choice of his actions in the present. To the extent that I am not absolutely what I have been, by virtue of being conscious now of what I was then, I open between then and now a space of indeterminacy which I experience as anguish but which is the irreducible space or time of my liberty.

"To cease smoking is the easiest thing I ever did; I ought to know because I've done it a thousand times" (Bohle 412). Mark Twain confirms that, whereas there can be only one first time for anything (a first time that is the last time it is the first), with cigarettes there are an innumerable number of last times, each only the most recent last time in a *perpetuum mobile* of smoking, with no power to determine when the next cigarette will be.

The paradox of the last cigarette is that it is simultaneously the last and the latest, no more cigarettes and another cigarette.

Zeno continues his narration by noting the following entry on the front page of a dictionary, beautifully written and adorned with a good many flourishes: "2 February 1886. Today I finish my law studies and take up chemistry. Last cigarette!!" He adds, "*Era un'ultima sigaretta molto importante*" (10). Zeno entertains the idea of a whole hierarchy of last cigarettes, associated with important dates in his life. It is as if his resolution requires the support of some momentous occasion to strengthen it as a barrier against smoking again. Conversely, resolving to stop smoking also serves to underline the momentousness of the occasion. The "last cigarette," noted with flourishes in the dictionary, acquires the force of its resolve from the importance of the change in his career with which it is made to coincide; at the same time, it lends that decision the visible public exteriority of a sign. Marking the passage from law to chemistry, "this last cigarette signified precisely the desire for activity (even manual activity) and for serene thought that was sober and clear" (10). Later, Zeno discovers on the cover of a book the date of another last cigarette—"also an important one"—marking his return to law. He realizes that he had little genius for chemistry and adds: "How was it possible for me to have had any [manual skill] when I continued to smoke like a Turk" (10).[6] Smoking the last cigarette results in his continuing to smoke like such a Turk that he can never develop the dexterity required for laboratory work. Smoking the last cigarette guarantees that he will be unable to acquire the skill that smoking the last cigarette is supposed to emblematize. What philosophers call a pragmatic paradox is at work here, insofar as the enunciation of a certain activity makes it impossible for the activity to occur.[7]

Once when Zeno was a student he changed his room and had to have the walls repapered because they were covered with dates. The room had become "the cemetery of his good resolutions and he no longer thought it possible to make any others in that place" (11). The paradox of making resolutions that Sartre diagnoses afflicts him with a vengeance. On the one hand, he needs to fix his resolution with the marmoreal stability and resistance of a visible, exterior monument in order to erect an insuperable barrier, a solid dam against the temptation to smoke again; on the other hand, he discovers with anguish that the more fixed and determined he makes the resolution the more it belongs to a past that has no power to help him with the immediately present temptation. The old resolution will no longer do because it is for his consciousness. He needs to repeat the act of seizing the present possibility for resolving to stop. Hence he needs to write a new date on the walls of his room, even more emphatic than the previous one, which can now be forgotten but cannot be erased from his walls. But what is a resolution that has been superseded by a more recent resolution? "The dates on the walls of my room were printed with varied colors and even in oil. The resolution, repeated with the most ingenuous confidence, found adequate expression in the force of the color that was supposed to cause to pale the one dedicated to the previous resolution" (11). An abandoned resolution normally can be forgotten, but when it has been painted with flourishes and in color on the walls, it may be dead but is not yet buried. It remains there, a ghost or phantom in the cemetery of the monuments inscribed on the face of the walls all around—powerless to have any effect, but refusing to vanish. A new resolution implies that one is no longer determined by the old one, which must be as if it never took place, and yet the requirement that it be forgotten conflicts with the necessity that it occupy space, as on a wall; but when each resolution requires a tabula rasa it is impossible to live surrounded by a tabula macula, entombing all the resolutions past and gone.

Certain dates, says Zeno, were preferred for "la concordanza" of the numbers—for example, one from the previous century that seemed as if it had "to signal forever the coffin in which [he] wishes to bury his vice": it was "the ninth day of the ninth month of 1899," as if such a concordance of nines could not be merely coincidental but stood in some significant relation to Zeno's personal destiny. His ultimate illusion is the belief that certain dates are destined to be the ones on which he will stop smoking. The new century quickly offers him new occasions for significant coincidence: "The first day of the first month of 1901." He writes: "It still appears to me that if that date could again come round, I would be able to begin a new life"—a "vita nuova" perhaps, at least "una nuova vita," as Zeno writes with his characteristic but undeserved modesty. The trouble with the system, he says, is that the calendar does not lack for significant numbers if one is prepared to exercise "a little imagination." He remembers one date in particular because "it contained a supremely categorical imperative": it was the "third day of the sixth month of 1912 at 24 hours. It sounded as if every figure redoubled the previous one." But positive ratios are not needed for a date to concord with stopping smoking; any excuse, he says, will do. He remembers having been struck by "the third day of the second month of 1905 at six o'clock," precisely because of the lack of any conformity in its numbers. "When you think about it . . . it has a sort of ring to it," Zeno writes, "since every single number seems to negate the preceding one" (12). Some important dates, like the death of Pope Pius IX or the birth of his son, are considered important enough to stop smoking. The family admires Zeno's remarkable memory for birthdays and anniversaries, not knowing that every one of them has been an occasion for his resolutions; they think it is his good nature. Making everything that happens in your life a pretext for resolving to stop smoking is not bad if it serves to endear you to your family.

And time goes by. Instead of the resolution producing a new life of health and good feeling, life becomes the history of resolutions unkept: "In order to diminish the appearance of stupidity I sought to give a philosophical content to the sickness of the last cigarette. One says to oneself, with a most beautiful attitude, 'Never again.' But where is the attitude if the promise is kept? It is only possible to have the attitude if the resolution is renewed. And then time, for me, is not something unthinkable that never stops. For me, only for me, it returns" (12). The word *atteggiamento*, which is translated as "attitude," is repeated three times in this brief paragraph. It is a word that has a particular resonance in Italian insofar as it is inseparable from connotations that belong to the theater and to the taking of Roman poses of nobility. "No more!" is the expression that accompanies the act and attitude of the cultural hero, the man who puts the devil of his vices behind him forever in favor of some purer, higher life. If that attitude of sacrifice is the very summit of nobility, how, asks Zeno, can one avoid making repeated resolutions in order precisely to be able, again and again, to assume that "bellissimo atteggiamento"?

But the most obscure and orphic assertion that Zeno makes in this paragraph is the last one: "And then time, for me, is not something unthinkable that never stops. For me, only for me, it returns [*Da me, solo da me, ritorna*] (12). A life that consists in constantly making resolutions is one whose history is not that of time passing but of time ceaselessly returning. His life is the succession of repetitions of the same resolution to stop smoking. Perhaps in that sense it is true that it is only for him, Zeno, that time returns. Like the temporal paradox of his namesake, Zeno's only act is virtual, the act of resolving to act. Like Achilles who never passes the tortoise, like the arrow that never strikes its target (it can never arrive because it must be forever going half the distance there), Zeno never catches up with the promise to stop smoking. No matter how hard he tries or how fast he flies, he never achieves his goal; no matter how firmly he resolves to stop smoking, smoking the last cigarette ensures that he will continue.[8]

The "last cigarette," repeatedly smoked, not only allows the smoker to preserve a heroic attitude to life, it also procures the most intense taste. Zeno writes: "I think that the cigarette has a more intense taste when it is the last. The others, too, have a special taste, but less intense. The last one acquires its savor from the feeling of victory over oneself and the hope of a near future of strength and health. The others have their importance since lighting them up protests on behalf of the freedom to do what you want, and the future of strength and health does not go away, though it has moved a little further off" (11).

The intensity of the taste associated with the last cigarette should not be taken to mean that the cigarette tastes good. Rather, it offers an antidote to the deadening of one's taste for cigarettes that the uninterrupted habit effects. Smoking a last one gives a reason for wanting to go on smoking something that, when it is the last one, tastes intensely. It explains as well, after you have begun to stop, the special savor of the one you smoke to prove that you are free to smoke if you want to. The mechanism Zeno describes seems like a perfect pleasure device. Smoking the last cigarette over and over induces repeated feelings of victory over oneself and the prospect of a healthy future; at the same time, continuing to smoke offers the savor of freedom from the harsh necessity of having to stop, without eliminating—only postponing—the future of strength and health that one is resolved to conquer.

Resolving not to make resolutions produces the same effect as making them, only by a more circuitous dialectical route. "Now that I am old and no one expects anything from me, I continually pass back and forth between resolutions and cigarettes. But what do these resolutions signify today? Like that old hygienist [igienista], described by Goldoni, I would like to die healthy after having lived ill my whole life" (11). To die healthy after having lived a life of illness, that is the paradoxical aim of Carlo Goldoni's hero, one that parallels the life of Svevo's Zeno, whose pursuit of health seems fated to succeed only when he attains the freedom from disease that the grave secures. Inherent in this paradox is a further implication that tends to revalue the value of health and illness: since his life is passed in the ceaseless pursuit of health, life is the disease from which only death will cure him; health belongs only to the tomb. The exfoliation of this central paradox of illness or disease [malattia] leads to the most apocalyptic anticipations of nuclear catastrophe at the end of the novel.

When the last cigarette has been smoked, after they have been banned worldwide in a universal prohibition, will nothing have been lost? Will that day represent an unequivocal triumph of humanity over disease? Will it constitute a progressive step on behalf of public health and human happiness? Health in America is increasingly a product that is sold. It has become one of the most profitable businesses of all, on the way to becoming this country's principal economic activity—in the form of what is called "health services." Yet, in fact, the more we hear about health and spend for it, the more diseased our society becomes, increasingly liable to weakness, ailments, and disablement of every kind. Every day we discover that more of what we eat and breathe and touch is bad for us, is making us sick. But what does "sick" mean?

Zeno excuses his doctors "for seeing in [his] life itself a manifestation of disease [malattia]": "Life does resemble sickness in a way; they both have crises and periods of calm, good days and bad. But unlike other diseases, life is always mortal. It has no cure. It would be like wanting to stop up the orifices we have in our body, believing them to be wounds. We would die strangled rather than cured" (12). He does not blame doctors for wanting to cure his smoking; they cannot help but want to as long as they see its effects as the manifestation of disease. But smoking is part of Zeno's life—in Zeno's case, it is his life. To want to cure it is to suppose that life itself is a disease that needs the attention of doctors. Doctors themselves like to think this is so. Those who want to cure us, who want to restore us to a condition of health, are those for whom the pains of life are symptoms of illness. Their impulse to cure is really an aggressive desire to kill life in civilization in the name of purity and health. Zeno's wife, herself not a smoker, had never considered smoking an illness; she had always said "that smoking was one way of living and not such a bad one either" (16). Smoking admittedly has some unpleasant side effects, but so does life.

Once Zeno realizes, at the end of his life, that smoking cigarettes is just another way of living (that is, of being diseased), once he no longer considers it bad for his health, he stops making resolutions to stop smoking and then . . . stops—smoking. To stop he had to stop promising himself to stop and believe that he was already healthy. Once he believed himself to be healthy, he freed himself of the paradoxical logic of "the last cigarette," and smoking no longer had any interest for him.

Zeno ferociously refuses, however, to underestimate the bad effects of smoking, what he repeatedly calls its "venom." Cigarettes deliver a small, regular injection of a very powerful poison. Nothing angers him more than when his psychoanalyst tries to persuade him "that smoking did [him] no harm and that when [he] had convinced [himself] of that it would really be harmless" (390). The psychoanalyst, fixated by the narcissism of the cure, wants him to believe that his smoking is only the symptom of other, more fundamental compulsions and complexes: Zeno, he says, took up the vice only to compete with his father and now considers it poisonous only to punish himself for the competition. Zeno himself, conversely, has no illusions, attributing the constant little pains and ills he suffers to its toxin. He understands that to stop smoking he must stop smoking, not cure his neurosis.

Fumo-analysis achieves its success where psychoanalysis fails by reinterpreting cigarettes, but in an entirely different direction. It achieves health by recognizing that there is no health—that health, as he says, is "a conviction." In the very last pages of his memoir, Zeno exults:

> It is not by comparison that I feel myself to be healthy. I am absolutely healthy. For a long time, I knew that my health could be nothing else but my conviction of it and that it was a stupidity worthy of a hypnagogic dreamer to suppose that one could cure it otherwise than with persuasion. Of course, I suffer from certain pains, but they have no importance in my overall health. I can put a bandage here or there, but for the rest it is a matter of keeping moving and knocking about and never yielding to the temptation of immobility. Pains and loves, in short, the whole of life, cannot be considered illness because they hurt. (410)

If health is a conviction, then persuasion—the power of rhetorical argument—directed to the self is more essential for achieving it than medicine. Zeno, this sophist, adopts a perspective that considers what we call disease or illness to be the name we give to the pains and infirmities that unavoidably arise as the consequence and the price of civilization. If only animals are truly healthy, it follows that old Zeno may be in excellent "health," once it is now understood in a different conceptual relation to disease, no longer its contrary or its ruin. If you accept Zeno's premise that you are "healthy" if you are still moving, then disease ought not to be considered to be bad for your health, merely something that occasionally needs to be patched. It is one of those things that gets managed as part of one's absolutely good health, which ought no more to be judged by one's diseases or illnesses than by the bruises and scratches we are regularly

Dwarf
Photo © Bruce Davidson. By permission of Magnum Photos, Inc.

obliged to bandage. Just because it hurts does not mean it is an illness: love hurts too; so, in short, does life. *Mallatie* they are not.

A smoker lives through his cigarettes, his cigarettes are his life, and to take them away would be to deprive him of a defining moment of his existence in the name of health. But he is already healthy; that is why he smokes. He knows that the poison in the cigarettes ingested all day long causes the many ailments and dysfunctions he more acutely observes the more he smokes. But he continues because he is making systematic use of cigarettes to perform tasks and procure pleasures, in a wide variety of situations, accompanying all his moods and movements. Would he have a healthier life without them? He would not have a life, his life; life itself would be impoverished. Moralists, of course, would disagree; but any smoker will tell you that what Sartre says is true: "Life without cigarettes is a little less worth living." If smoking is the way of life you are living (and there are worse ways), you will have good days and bad, says Zeno. If you give them up, that will not change.

Disease, says Zeno, is an ineluctable consequence of the pleasures and uses we derive from the technology of civilization. Every civilized pleasure we take and every successful enhancement of our physical and intellectual power produces ailments and disablement, illness and parasites. There is no pleasure we learn to love, no tool or machine we acquire that does not ultimately weaken the organism rather than strengthen it. In addition, we are progressively ruining our environment, Zeno notes, by overpopulation and by industrialization, giving rise to general strangulation. The result is that humankind is de-evolving in its body, as its evolving cunning makes it more and more able to compensate its enfeeblement with the prosthetic extensions of machines. Whereas animal species by natural selection develop new capacities to confront altered situations, growing stronger to meet the new challenge, humans grow weaker as their machines become more and more numerous and powerful. We are the "spectacled animal," says Zeno, supplementing our organic weaknesses with instruments—tools and machines—that are applied to the exterior of our organism, permitting it to accomplish what it no longer needs even to try to do on its own. Increasing disease and parasites, says Zeno, are the inescapable concomitant of progress, development, and growth; civilization is bad for your health—if you believe in health.

Doctors want us to believe that we can be free of illness—but that freedom belongs only to nature, which is not free. "Every effort to procure health is in vain. Health can only belong to the beasts, whose sole idea of progress lies in their own bodies," says Zeno (412). Life in civilization creates diseases faster than we can cure them. It is only a matter of dosing them, of choosing one or the other. The notion that by giving up smoking we will attain health is the illusion that feeds the impulse to stop smoking that smoking itself creates. Humankind succeeds at the price of growing weaker and weaker, more and more dependent on machines; more and more passive and dependent, it suck-seeds.

Ultimately, health is the realization that there is no health, only disease and parasites. But that's life. Fumo-analysis leads to the realization that the only cure for the disease and parasites of life is annihilation.

The connection between the first chapter of the confessions, "Il fumo," and the proleptic vision of total nuclear destruction begins to emerge. Svevo has understood that the impulse to blow up the world lies at the heart of the desire to put an end to smoking. Civilization, in creating machines, gave rise to sickness and parasites, which led humankind to wish to return to some precivilized condition of health by using machines to destroy it. Antismoking groups have an equivalent nostalgia for some state of nature from which civilization has fallen. But the problem is civilization itself, "the law of the greatest number of machines": "Under the law of the greatest number of machines, disease will prosper and the diseased will grow ever more numerous"; with the corollary: "Perhaps some incredible disaster produced by machines will lead us back to health" (412). Zeno diagnoses in the hysteria of antitabagism signs of a revenge of civilization on itself, in which it turns over its ultimate technological power to those who wish to use it to destroy civilization, to restore the world to some pre-civilized, purer, natural condition. "There will be a tremendous explosion, but no one will hear it and the earth will return to its nebulous state and go wandering through the sky, free at last of parasites and disease" (383).

4 The Devil in Carmen

De la vaporisation et de la centralisation
du Moi. Tout est là.
—Baudelaire, Mon coeur mis à nu

Take a long, deep puff on a cigarette; fill yourself up with its venomous smoke; let it touch the innermost convolutions of your lungs; then exhale it, slowly, past nose and lips in a swirling, expanding stream about your head. Tout est là. The smoke penetrates sharply, then exudes, softly envelops you in the experience of extending your body's limits, no longer fixed by the margin of your skin. The tobacco's vapor is atomized into atmosphere that halos your exterior form, after having been condensed within the cavities that harbor your most intimate interior. Joining inside and out, each puff is like total immersion: it baptizes the celebrant with the little flash of a renewed sensation, an instantaneous, fleeting body image of the unified Moi. An inhaling moment of concentration, centralizing the self to make it more dense, more opaquely present to itself, is trailed by a movement of evaporation, as the self exhales itself, ecstatically, in a smoky jag— as it grows increasingly tenuous, progressively less differentiated from the exterior world it becomes.

The double postulation of centralization and evaporation (which marks the rhythm of smoking, tapped out in every puff on a cigarette) has decisive psychological and aesthetic implications for poets, writes Baudelaire; it mimes the movement of the romantic lyric self, whose oscillation swings between the poles of fascinated immersion in the world and intense self-regard. In Baudelaire's mythology, the worldly figure of poetic experience who best embodies those two impulses, simultaneously, is the dandy: he exercises the most cruel, centralizing aesthetic constraints over the most vaporous, immoral imagination. A continuous self-invention, the dandy is both ruthlessly rigorous and infinitely ephemeral, the subjective correlative of a sonnet's mathematical effusions, or of the meticulously repeated satisfaction of a cigarette. The aesthetic religion of lyric dandyism, the morality of making a work of art out of a way of life, finds its most precious relic in the cigarette, whose invention roughly coincided with the invention, in 1830, of the Parnassian dandy, who called himself Art and whose doctrine was "Art for Art's sake."

Recall that Rival says that "the whole chic of the cigarette resides in its paper" (quoted in Rival 171). The paper in which the tobacco is rolled has qualities, beloved by the smoker, of whiteness, combustibility, absence of bad taste, resistance, and transparency. Differing from the uneven, naked leaf of the cigar, which Byron fancied, and the hard, lifeless forms of the pipe, paper lends both flexibility and rigor to the cigarette, whose chic, in its way, perfectly mirrors the dandy's stringent aesthetic discipline. Like the cigarette, the dandy is a subtle confluence, not an alternation but the marriage, of two distinct sets of qualities: the cruelty of discipline, of martial loyalty, and the generosity of unbounded love. Their coincidence is discovered in the unholy marriage of the Soldier and the Gypsy, two figures whose conjunction fatally summons strains of Carmen to the French mind. It is not only France's greatest opera, according to Nietzsche, the prophet of the superman, but one that will last in the repertoires, even as long as his own work will, even beyond the survival of what is now called man, beyond man, Übermensch: "I'm not far from believing that Carmen is the best opera there is; and as long as we will live, it will figure in all the repertoires of Europe" Lettres à Peter Gast, 80). Nietzsche wrote these lines from Genoa to his friend in music Peter Gast in December 1881, a week after he had heard the opera on the occasion of its first Italian performance, at the Gran Teatro, in front of a packed hall, before an elegant public (le duc de Montpensier, etc.); it was, he writes, "a veritable event." In those four hours, he says, he lived and understood more things than he usually did in four weeks. What, for example, did he understand?

In Le cas Wagner, Nietzsche contrasts the genius of the cold and foggy north with Bizet's tragic Latin spirit. He locates the disruptive energy of its paradoxical essence—a quintessence of sun and blood, laughter and fatality—in the tragi-passionate duo of Bizet's Gypsy heroine, the cigarette girl Carmen, and Don José, her ill-starred dragoon lover. In the plot of the story, the Soldier and the Gypsy are so fiercely bound together in unconsecrated matrimony that the death of one ineluctably condemns the other. It cannot be an accident that Carmen, in the story by Mérimée from

which the libretto was taken, is the first woman in fiction to smoke a cigarette, or that, since 1910, the two most popular brands of French cigarettes
have been Gauloises and Gitanes. No accident, because the paradoxical
qualities that Nietzsche attributes to *Carmen* are characteristic of cigarettes
themselves, beginning with those that are smoked by Carmen and concluding with those that were eventually to become the predilection of the
French. Cigarettes are everywhere present in Bizet's opera; *Carmen* may be
said to define the principal motifs surrounding cigarettes for modernity.

Gauloises were introduced in commerce on the eve of the Great War,
dressed in patriotic blue—the *bleu des Vosges*, the *bleu poilu* of the foot soldiers'
uniform—and stamped with an ancestral Gallic helmet encircled by unbroken chain links, symbolizing the strength of national unity.[1] Throughout the twentieth century, Gauloises have had a significant history of intensely patriotic associations that could be the subject of another book.
For our purposes here, we are interested in the other cigarette introduced
the same year, Gitanes, which were considered the first "modern" cigarette
because they came in a box accompanied by emblems of a hot woman.
On the dark blue box, the cartoon depicted a motif of fan, tambourine,
and Seville oranges, all elements in Mérimée's original story, each a feature
of Carmen's Gypsy wedding feast. When Carmen decides to spend a night
of love with Don José, to take him for her *rom*, to become his *romi*, she
gathers all their money and buys sweet things, "*yemas, turon* [sugared egg
yolks, honey nougat], candied fruit, as long as the money lasts"; she gobbles
down the candy "like a six-year-old child," spreads it around, and even
throws it against the walls to keep the flies busy (Mérimée 378)—as if there
were no limit to her avidity for sweetness and no bounds to the generosity
she displays toward herself and the accursed lucky ones she loves. She
improvises castanets from fragments of plates crashed against the floor;
swirling to the rhythm of their incomparable staccato, she cracks them as
if they were ebony or ivory, furiously, killing boredom. Nothing stops her
dancing, her wild Gypsy dancing, whose tight circles of passionate desire
are resumed in the rings rising from her cigarette.

The familiar Spanish Gypsy, drawn on the box, was first done by Giot
on posters for Gitanes, and in 1927 she became the official emblem. Her
image has acquired mythic dimensions, a cipher designating the absolute
power of seduction; it was recently the pretext for a show of graphic artists in Paris at the Espace Cardin. All her incarnations there were inspired
by the figure of the Gypsy dancer on the box, striking the pose of ¡Olé!—
the long, curved body with an arm upraised like a wisp of white smoke

silhouetted against the night blue. Like the cigarettes inside, her image on the box is the promise of a Gypsy wedding.

Gautier, in *Tras los montes*, is enchanted by the fake "exoticism" of "papel español para cigarittas," tinted with licorice, brilliantly colored, minutely imprinted with little romantic stories. Encircled with paper, endowed with its power to summon words, the cigarette from the first is a little scroll or volume that unfurls its romances in the air above the smoker's head. The cigarette, like Carmen, is an object of graphic legend and a source of fabulation, whose wispy undulations in space write worlds of imaginative reveries before the smoker's vapid gaze.

Spain in 1830 was probably the only place at that time on the European continent where cigarettes were widely known and universally enjoyed, particularly by women. The use of "papelitos," tobacco rolled in paper, in the Spanish colonies, is confirmed by the Jesuit Father Nurenberg in his *Historia naturae* in 1635. Casanova describes in his memoirs the "cigarito," made of Brazilian tobacco, rolled in paper, that his innkeeper smoked in Madrid, and Goya twice represents cigarette smokers. According to Rival, the cigarette arrived in France around the years 1825–30, having come "from Spain, where the Brazilians [had] made them known" (170). One finds the following definition of the "cigarrito" in the *Codes des fumeurs et des priseurs ou l'art de fumer et de priser sans déplaire aux Belles*, published in 1830 by "MM. E...D et C...P, anciens marchands de tabac": "Cigarrito, petit carré de papier à lettre dans lequel on fait entrer du tabac" [*Cigarrito*, a little square of letter paper into which one inserts tobacco] (quoted in Rival 171).

Spain is considered the country of drugs, especially tobacco, and of fabulations, often criminal—by Mérimée, for whom it is also the land of Gypsies. In the scholarly "dissertation" he appends to the story of Carmen, he writes:

> Spain is one of the countries where today are found in greatest numbers those nomads dispersed throughout Europe, and known by the names of Bohemians, Gitanos, Gypsies, Zigeuner, etc. Most live, or rather lead, an errant life in the provinces of the South and East, in Andalusia, in Estramadura, in the kingdom of Murcia; there are many in Catalonia. These last pass frequently into France. They are encountered at all our fairs in the Midi. Ordinarily the men exercise the professions of horse trader, veterinarian, and mule shearer; they join to those the ability to repair frying pans and copper instruments, not to mention smug-

Gypsies, Saintes-Maries de la Mer
Photo © Gilles Peress. By permission of Magnum Photos, Inc.

gling and other illicit practices. The women tell fortunes [disent la bonne aventure], beg and sell all sorts of drugs, innocent or not so innocent. (Mérimée 165)

Gypsy women in Spain, Mérimée continues, are rarely beautiful, but in the great cities of Andalusia certain of the girls, a little more agreeable looking and more painstaking with their appearance, dance in public for money. They do dances, he says, "that have been banned in our street balls at carnival" (167). But their apparent lasciviousness is belied by the loyalty they show to their own race and by the "extraordinary devotion [that they display] to their husbands. There is no danger or misery they will not brave to help them in their dire necessities" (168). Mérimée, a scrupulous student of their language (rommani or chipe calli), adduces an etymological argument in order to locate the identity of the Bohemian "race" in the "fidelity"— or "patriotism," as he calls it—that Gypsies, without a country, observe toward one another: "One of the names that Bohemians apply to themselves, Romé, or spouses, seems to me to attest the respect the race shows for the state of marriage" (167). Carmen, who "is infinitely prettier than all the women of her nation" (111), in the experience of the narrator, is also in the fiction the most bold, free, and, tragically, the most loyal Gitana in Spain. If one were to attribute her qualities to the cigarettes she smokes, one might lend them something of her illicit charm, her transgressive beauty, and the same fatal compulsion with which she marries those who dare to light her up.

The first time the narrator in Mérimée's story offers Carmen a cigarette (the first time in literature a cigarette is proffered), he is smoking one of the excellent cigars he carries with him in an elegant silver etui. A Frenchman, he is traveling on a personal archaeological expedition in Andalusia (just as the author, Mérimée, did) for the purpose of confirming his conjectures concerning the precise location of the decisive battle that Caesar fought with the sons of Pompey, the last defenders of the Republic. The story of Don José and Carmen is presented within the frame of Mérimée's novella as an accidental by-product of the narrator's scientific undertaking—a mere anecdote, mostly overheard, belonging to what the scientific aim of the expedition properly overlooks, and whose supposed triviality "prejudges nothing concerning the interesting question of the location of [the battle of] Munda" (92). But the narrator's dismissal is feigned, of course; the hierarchy of interests that pretends to take the story of Carmen less seriously than Caesar's victory is itself the object of his

irony: "En attendant que ma dissertation résolve enfin le problème géogra-
phique qui tient toute l'Europe savante en suspens, je veux vous raconter
une petite histoire" [While waiting for my dissertation finally to resolve the
geographical problem that is keeping all of scholarly Europe in suspense, I
want to tell you a little story] (92). The narrator's self-irony is doubly ironic:
not only is his discovery (the same as that of the author) archaeologically
irreproachable (it has been generally accepted by historians), but the narrator's gesture of detachment with respect to Carmen and Don José is a
patent mystification that serves, within the fiction, to mask his own passionate involvement in this "little" story. Despite the sobriety of his tone,
the narrator apprises the reader in several places that his point of view is
more engaged than that of an inquisitive but neutral observer of the tragedy
of Carmen. Even though the novella requires that we consider the narrator to be a fictional creation of the author Mérimée, we have to wonder
whether the author, any more than the narrator, the scientific historian, or
Don José, can fail to fall under the spell of Carmen, the most powerfully
seductive woman in the world. Can the reader escape her seduction? The
text itself, *Carmen*, is a Carmen: not only a fictional account of the heroine's
love and death, it literally bewitches the reader, exercises an incantatory
power, as she herself does within the story, that performatively transforms
not only the narrator and his characters but the author and his audience.

We learn the true story of Carmen's love and death from Don José, whom
the narrator meets in Seville on the eve of his execution for murder. The
story of Carmen is told in the voice of a man who is condemned and
with whom our very French narrator has virtually nothing, he assures us,
in common. Nothing except that, all the while he is ventriloquizing Don
José, narrating his narration, he cannot help reminding the reader, in his
own voice, of his lurid, rather sexy enthusiasm for outlaws in general and
for this bandit in particular.

At one moment, the narrator even imagines that he has become Don
José's rival for the attention of Carmen; he greets his outlaw "friend" with
annoyance when the murderer intrudes on his intimate séance with Carmen. The narrator's annoyance gives way to gratitude only later, when he
learns that she was intending to cut his throat and would have if Don José
had not intervened. (Of course, if the author of this fiction had wanted
to give his narrator an hour alone with Carmen, he could have contrived
to postpone Don José's irruption into their intimacy.) The jealousy he ex-
hibits toward Don José is the most perverse indication that the narrator has
been bewitched by Carmen's spells—it signals his submission, like that of

the murderer, like the reader's, to the irresistible violence of her charms. Who, exactly, is this veiled Gitana?

The first encounter with Carmen comes as the narrator is sitting at the top of the steps that lead down to the Guadalquivir, the myth-shrouded river that runs through Córdoba, where, we are told, the women of the city, old and young, have the habit of going at dusk to bathe. When the hour of the angelus is struck, officially marking the arrival of night, the women undress and enter the water:

> Alors ce sont des cris, des rires, un tapage infernal. Du haut du quai, les hommes contemplent les baigneuses, écarquillent les yeux, et ne voient pas grand-chose. Cependant, ces formes blanches et incertaines, qui se dessinent sur le sombre azur du fleuve, font travailler les esprits poétiques, et, avec un peu d'imagination, il n'est pas difficile de se représenter Diane et ses nymphes au bain, sans avoir à craindre le sort d'Actéon. (107–8)

> Then there are cries, laughter, and an infernal racket. From the top of the quay, men contemplate the bathers, look hard and do not see much. However, these white, uncertain forms, which emerge against the dark blue of the river, put poetic minds to work, and, with a little imagination, it is not difficult to represent to oneself Diana and her nymphs bathing, without having to fear the fate of Acteon.

The narrator thinks that he and the other men have nothing to fear from these bathers; because they see nothing in the dark, they must be immune to the punishment Diana inflicted on the hunter whose look transgressed the secret of her bath. In the Ovidian myth the intruder is splashed by the goddess, transformed into a stag, and chased by his own dogs. It is one of the further ironies of *Carmen* that the scientific narrator may, in fact, have fallen prey to what Sartre, a half-century later, called the "Acteon complex"—the psychosexual perversion whose sublimation drives the motivation of all research and investigation. He writes in *L'être et le néant:* "every kind of research [*toute recherche*] includes the idea of a nudity that one exposes by removing the obstacles that cover it over, as Acteon pushes aside the branches to better see Diana at her bath. And besides, knowledge is a hunt. Bacon names it the hunt of Pan. The scholar/scientist [*le savant*] is the hunter who surprises a white nudity and violates it with his look. Thus the ensemble of these images reveals to us something we will call the *Acteon complex*" (639).

The narrator of Carmen, hunter after historical truth, imagines he is safe from the fate of Acteon. Sitting on the top of the quay and seeing only the vaguest outlines in the darkness below, he supposes he risks nothing from Diana and her nymphs. But just at the moment when, lighting a cigar, he turns to poetic reflection, "a woman, climbing back up the stairs that lead from the river, came and sat down next to me" (358). The "bather," as he calls her [la baigneuse], is nothing other than the most dangerous woman in the world, endowed with Diana's power of metamorphosis, the magic to make men blind and mad, a "witch" of extraordinary powers, in league with daemons, herself an avatar of the devil. Having come to learn the truth of Rome, the archaeologist discovers in Carmen the diabolical power of Romé. "Arriving beside me, my bather let slide from her shoulders the man-tilla that was covering her head, and, *by the obscure brightness which falls from the stars [à l'obscure clarté qui tombe des étoiles]*, I saw that she was small, young, well built, and that she had very large eyes" (358). Like a curtain rising, her man-tilla falls. Mérimée italicizes the famous phrase he takes from Corneille's Le Cid (act 4, scene 3) as if he meant the reader to note the oxymoronic nature of the light in which this bather first appears, a luminosity that plunges into darkness what it illuminates, blinds what it enlightens with its stellar fire. Carmen, herself a creature of darkness, has very large eyes, we are told, the better to see everything, into the future as well as the past. Like a cigarette, she opens up perspectives on eternity, time seen from a standpoint out-side of the present, and entrances her admirers with the intensity of her penetrating regard.

Acteon's complex afflicts the man who hunts and dreams scientific dreams of unveiling some hitherto undiscovered nudity, some truth un-veiled of history or nature. His destiny reflects the immutable-seeming decree that discovering truth is a kind of crime, one the gods must punish by wounding the seeker or making him mad. To violate her nudity is the researcher's whole chance, he thinks—and his fatality, he learns, when he is devoured by his own dogs. His hunting leads him to the huntress Diana, or Carmen, who, heart-robbing, metamorphoses him into the hunted and sics on him his own most fond ideas, destroying him with the obsessive, fascinated curiosity she beguilingly provokes. The narrator-archaeologist of Carmen, chasing after the site where Caesar chased Pompey, finds what he does not expect to find, the emblematic figure of the whole aim of his search, and she is sitting on the steps in the surrounding darkness, still damp from her bath.

The narrator, lighting up, instantly makes a sacrifice to the goddess; she

of course, like all goddesses, loves the smell and smoke of it: "I immediately threw away my cigar. She understood this attention for a very French
form of politeness, and hastened to tell me that she very much loved the
odor of tobacco, and that she even smoked, when she found a very mild
papelitos. By good fortune, I had some like that in my etui, and I hastened
to offer her one. She deigned to take one and lit it on the end of a flaming
cord that a child brought us for a penny. Mixing our smoke, we chatted for
so long a time, the beautiful bather and I, that we found ourselves almost
alone on the bank" (358). The narrator's French "politeness," throwing
away the cigar when a woman sits down, displays the force of the taboo
against smoking in the presence of women. Carmen's transgressive character is instantly betrayed by her appetite for what women are supposed,
by the narrator, to hate. She wants a pleasure that a woman is not expected
to wish—to be the master/mistress of her own pleasure. The first time in
literature a woman accepts a cigarette, the gesture unmistakably identifies
her as an outlaw sorceress, a demonic whore, who transcends all limits
of feminine propriety. But it is her inhuman, unfeminine femininity that
makes her ominously beautiful, demonic because divinely beautiful—just
as the goddess Diana assumes the hideous form of Hecate, the witch. Her
pursuit and unveiling, like that of the truth, are dangerously compelling,
with similarly evil consequences. Carmen is the cigarette she takes, like a
jewel, from the silver etui of the narrator; or rather, she is the fiery heart of
the burning ember, carmen red at the end of the cigarette, in which every
brilliant dream is perpetually turned to delicious smoke and bitter ash.

Carmen's face is suddenly illuminated by the exotic flame burning at
the end of a cord bought from a child for a penny. Who is this child? A
witch's familiar? A sort of fiery Cupid who lights the demonic fire of passion between the narrator and Carmen? Or an imp of enlightenment? In
another text, "Spanish Witches," Mérimée writes: "In Spanish there is no
word which translates that of ghost [*revenant*]. *Duende*, which you find in the
dictionary, corresponds rather to our word imp [*lutin*], and is applied, as in
French, to a mischievous child" (*Lettres adressées d'Espagne*, 418). In Spanish
there is no word for "ghost," but this child is a *duende* whose function in
the narrative, like that of Hamlet's father's ghost, mischievously spurs the
plot that leads the poor searcher after truth into a bitter delirium of self-
doubt and hesitation. The mischief of this impish child holding a flaming
cord resides no doubt in its having lit the cigarette of passion that rivets
the narrator to Carmen, illuminating for him the face of what he had never
dreamed, had always only dreamed, of discovering.

The moment when two people gather around a flame to light a cigarette crackles with electric intensity; here is a journalist regretting the passing of its modern representation in film: " 'The man and the woman look into one another's eyes intently. He offers her a cigarette. She makes a sign yes, and gently extends a hand. He lights the match and takes her wrist, bringing the flame close, his eyes immersed in hers. A moment charged with electricity.' That is how a writer in Rome recently began a piece describing the change that has come over Hollywood movies, which no longer find that particular cinematic cliché acceptable, where only the wicked can smoke" (Anna Guaita, "Com'è trasgressivo, fuma," *Il Messaggiero*, December 5, 1989, p. 20). In Mérimée one finds the origin of that stereotypical "wicked" encounter. The little bolt of lightning generated by lighting a woman's cigarette resembles what the French call a *coup de foudre*: the flash, igniting love, produces sin in the instant when glances touch across a cigarette. The smoker-narrator, the author's surrogate, commits a transgression, looking into her eyes by the light of the flame brought close to her "*papelito*": "Mixing our smoke, we chatted for so long a time, the beautiful bather and I, that we found ourselves almost alone on the bank." The intricate implication of narrator, author, and reader into the dramatic presence of the bather-goddess is like a mixing of their respective ghostly positions in the smoke arising from Carmen's cigarette and links them, in some outlawed relation, to the narrative of a tragic destiny that stalks the Gypsy woman.

The mischievous child gives her the gift of light, a light, for a penny. In Carmen's world, money is the principle that governs all but one form of human relation—marriage, which is beyond price, outside the venal economy in which the Gypsy, an inner exile, must struggle to survive. She is often seen in rags, a poor courtesan, until she goes with officers, dances for money, and is dressed by them in jewels. She is a smuggler, who makes brilliant deals and leads the men on immensely profitable expeditions through the mountains; a thief, who steals the narrator's large gold timepiece (the price he pays, losing his time, for hers) and nearly slits his throat. (One says "nearly," as if it were a real narrative possibility, but the storyteller knows we know that there would be no story if she did.) Carmen is mercenary, treacherous, and cruel; money buys anything she has, except her love. "Don't you see that I love you," she says to Don José, enraging him, "since I've never asked you for money to do it?" (384). She is "a whore, a madam, a witch," says Mérimée; easy to buy, but, "like all Spanish women," she is difficult in her choice of lovers: "One has to please her, to merit her" (404). Where her man is concerned, her *rom*, once the marriage is consummated, she would rather die at his hands than abandon this "husband."

In *Le peintre de la vie moderne*, in the section "Les femmes et les filles," Baudelaire paints a cruel portrait of the lower-class whores whom Parisians called *lorettes*, the women who worked the area around the church of Notre Dame de Lorettes, in the Ninth Arrondissement. It is in the hands of these women at the bottom of the social scale that cigarettes appear, for the first and only time, in his writing—at the farthest remove from their mouth, at the tip of their languorous extremities, between fingers limp with boredom, killing time:

> In following the scale, we descend to those slaves confined to hovels, often decorated like cafés; unfortunately placed under the meanest authority, and possessing nothing of their own, not even the eccentric adornment which serves as a condiment to their beauty.
>
> Some of them, examples of an innocent and monstrous fatuity, bear signs, in their faces and their audaciously up-turned looks, of evident happiness to be alive (in truth, why?). Sometimes they instinctively find poses of an audacity and nobility that would enchant the most delicate collector of statuary, if modern statuary had the courage and the wit to collect nobility everywhere, even in the slime; and sometimes they display themselves prostrate in desperate attitudes of boredom, in barroom indolence, with masculine cynicism, smoking cigarettes to kill time with the resignation of oriental fatalism. (721)

Lorettes, more generally called *grisettes*, were the first women who dared to be seen publicly smoking cigarettes. The intimacy of their association with cigarettes, motivated perhaps by the rhyme in their name, is attested in an ironically disparaging sentence of Rival, who catches the rapid, loveless, bitchy pleasure of the cigarette by identifying it with impudent women: "C'est la grisette des fumeurs, tout juste bonne à distraire les lions et les lorettes" [It is the smoker's impudent lady, good only for distracting dandies and whores] (Rival 171). The cigarette gives the *gris* to *grisette*: the smoky grayness at the heart of every *gris-erie* (intoxication), which poisons as it elevates—half menace, half mourning. Killing time, smoking creates another time, a fumy atmosphere momentarily outside of ordinary duration, whose dreamy vanishing is postponed within the gray parenthesis of the time it takes to smoke a fag. The lowliest hovel is briefly transcended by rising cigarette smoke, elevating all who are humbled to the degree, to the distinction, of a ghostly, posthumous detachment.

The impudence of women smoking is what the soldiers sing as they stand outside the tobacco factory in Seville, watching the *cigarières* emerge onto the scene, with a cigarette "at the end of their teeth":

> Voyez-les! Regards impudents,
> mines coquettes!
> Fumant toutes, du bout des dents,
> la cigarette!
> (Bizet 11)

> Look at them! Their insolent stares,
> their flirtatious looks!
> Each one impudently smoking
> a cigarette!

It is notoriously more difficult for women than for men to quit smoking; perhaps because, even today, when a woman smokes she is seen as performing a brazen, transgressive act. For many women, at certain moments, lighting a cigarette is the socially countenanced mode of signaling hostile or aggressively sexual feelings aroused by the intrusion of another subjectivity. In circumstances when a man might display anger or come on to her, a woman will often light up, summoning fire and smoke, jabbing with the tip of her cigarette between nails or teeth. That explains why, among women, smoking began with those who got paid for staging their sexuality: the actress, the Gypsy, the whore. Such a woman violates traditional roles by defiantly, actively giving herself pleasure instead of passively receiving it. Lighting a cigarette is a demonstration of mastery that violates the assumptions of feminine *pudeur*, the delicate embarrassment women are expected to feel, or at least display, in the presence of what their innocence and dignity are supposed to prevent them from desiring. A woman smoking may be thought to be less "feminine" because more active, aggressive, masterful, but she is not therefore more "masculine"—in her own eyes or in those of many men; she may in fact be more desirable because she appears to be more free. No wonder it is so much harder for women to give it up.

"You've come a long way, baby" takes the measure of what is represented as a significant step in the liberation of women: in winning the right to smoke, women are deemed to have taken a walk away from infantile dependency in the direction of full adult responsibility. As a piece of advertising, the praise insults women's liberation, trivializing it by assuming that it is a long way, in terms of sexual equality, between whalebone and pantsuit—as if freedom meant only that you were free to cross your legs. Nevertheless, the appeal of the publicity may be calculated to touch an authentic chord in women, who recognize, historically and in their own experience, the discrimination to which women have been subjected, particularly in their use of tobacco, and the disapproval with which, smoking, they have been persistently viewed.

The synonymity of loose women and cigarettes appears in another little poem of the same era, which confirms the point of Baudelaire's description connecting the time of some transgressive eroticism with the time of smoking:

> Au quartier de Lorette
> L'on aime au jour le jour
> Et bien plus qu'un amour
> Dure une cigarette.
> (Quoted in Rival 171)

> In the quartier de Lorette
> Love is day to day
> And longer than love
> Lasts a cigarette.

Nothing is more fleeting than the time of a cigarette except the love aroused by *lorettes*; with them, love, like cigarettes, is for killing time, aborting the duration of whatever tediously endures.

The corporal Morales tells the moral of the story of cigarettes, in the opening measures of *Carmen*, in the first arioso of Bizet's opera:

> A la porte de garde,
> pour tuer le temps,
> on fume, on jase, l'on regarde
> passer les passants.
> (11)

> At the guardhouse door,
> to kill time,
> we smoke, we chat, we watch
> the people passing.

Smoking, not acting, talking for the simple pleasure of it, disinterestedly watching passersby, the smoker adopts an aesthetic standpoint, outside the realm of utility or ethics, that kills the time of work or responsibility in order to bear witness to the time, to the music, of pure passing. The drama of Carmen, Don José, and the Toreador may occupy the center of the opera stage, but it is framed by the smoke of countless cigarettes that are the circling, gauzy correlative of the music's temporal unfolding.

The bond of tobacco that links the narrator to Carmen in Mérimée's novella also ties him from the beginning to the fate of Don José. In Spain, the laws of hospitality, symbolized by the offer and the acceptance of a smoke, take absolute priority over civil codes. At the beginning of the story, the narrator recounts the moment when, exhausted and faint under the broiling Spanish sun, he comes across a little oasis among the rocks where a miraculously cool source bubbles forth, giving rise to an immaculate, prelapsarian garden of reeds and grass and jonquils. As he enters into this magic spot, the source of all his subsequent adventures and the starting point of his narrative, he discovers already present there a man surly in aspect, of the fiercest countenance, whom his guide instantly recognizes as a famous feral bandit. Spurred by his curiosity, the narrator brushes aside warnings and even ignores the pistol that the badman aims when he is surprised by the narrator and the guide:

> I stretched out on the grass and with a casual air asked the man with the pistol if he had a lighter. At the same time I took out my cigar case. The stranger, still without speaking, searched in his pocket, found a lighter and hastened to give me a light. Evidently, he was becoming more human; for he sat down facing me, without however putting down his weapon. Having lit my cigar, I chose the best of the ones that remained and I asked him if he smoked.
>
> "Yes, sir," he replied.
>
> They were the first words he had pronounced. I noticed that he did not pronounce his s in the Andalusian manner, from which I concluded that he was a traveler like me, only less of an archaeologist. (Mérimée 94–95)

The offer of tobacco humanizes the murderer and institutes civilized exchange. The bandit's words come in response to the offer of a cigar, and they permit the narrator to begin to situate the traveler in a social context, to begin to discover the origins of the extraordinary history of love that lies behind the savage mask of the outlaw's face. The gesture of offering and accepting the light establishes a *socius*, a bond or contract which on this occasion and others saves the narrator's life (and saves the tale for us).

"You will find this one rather good," I told him, presenting him with a veritable prize of a Havana.

He made a slight nod of his head to me, lit his cigar from mine, thanked me with another sign of his head, then began to smoke with the appearance of a very lively pleasure.

"Ah!" he exclaimed, letting escape his first puff through his mouth and nose, "how long it has been since I last smoked!"

In Spain, a cigar given and received establishes relations of hospitality, as in the Orient the sharing of bread and salt. (95)

It is rather astonishing to find exactly the same stereotype under the pen of Ernest Hemingway in For Whom the Bell Tolls (written over a hundred years later) at the moment when his hero, Robert Jordan, arrives in the cave of the loyalist partisans, where, before doing anything else, he offers round his Russian cigarettes. Simultaneously he has to acknowledge to himself that he cannot look at the dark-eyed girl without altering his voice. At that moment he "realized he was violating the second rule of the two rules for getting on well with people that speak Spanish: give the men tobacco and leave the women alone" (29). Mérimée's narrator understands Spanish laws of hospitality in exactly the same way: tobacco must be shared, but never women (they are reserved for exchange).

The power of tobacco to tame the beast, to institute a relation of civility between the archaeological Frenchman and the murderous felon, creates a moment of narrative felicity. Cut off from all help, with no arms or means of protection, entirely at the mercy of a man who shows no mercy, looking into an abyss (the narrator intuits from the fear of his guide the identity of his companion), he feels not the slightest inkling of fear: "I did not doubt that I was dealing with a smuggler, perhaps a robber; what difference did it make? I knew the Spanish character well enough to be very sure that I had nothing to fear from a man who had eaten and smoked with me. Besides, I was rather pleased to know that he was a brigand. One does not encounter them every day, and there is a certain charm at finding oneself in the presence of a dangerous being, especially when one feels that they are sweet and tame" (Mérimée 349–50).

Kant, in the "Analytic of the Sublime," writes:

Rocks standing out daringly and like a menace against the sky where storm clouds gather and advance with lightning flashes and thunderbolts, volcanos in their devastating power, hurricanes followed by desolation, the immense ocean in its fury, the cataracts of a powerful

Marguerite Duras
Photo © Bruno Barbey. By permission of Magnum Photos, Inc.

river, etc., those are the things that reduce our powers of resistance to something laughable by comparison with the force which belongs to them. But if we find ourselves in safety, the spectacle is all the more attractive insofar as it is more suitable to causing fear; and we willingly name those things sublime which raise the forces of the soul above its habitual means and make us discover in ourselves a power of resistance of a whole other kind, which gives us the courage to measure ourselves with the apparent all-powerfulness of nature. (261)

Mérimée's narrator, like Kant's traveler, is willing to confront the greatest danger, the violence most foreign to his ordinary experience, to look death in the face, because he knows he stands in a magic circle generated around him by the propitiating power of tobacco. Rather than fear, he experiences pleasure at the opportunity sublimely to encounter, unarmed but reassured, the menace looming before him. Whether Mérimée would display such temerity in life we may doubt; his prerogatives as the narrator of this story protect him, within its fiction, more surely than his offer of a smoke. But perhaps we are intended to identify his narrative invulnerability with the dreamy illusions of tobacco smoke; the circle of smoking, like the space of fiction, momentarily lifts the author out of the realm of ordinary mortality, "raises the soul above its habitual means," and transforms him into a narrator of the sublime.

Carmen, herself a thief and a murderer, is also beyond the pale. At their first meeting on the bank of the Guadalquivir, the narrator asks if she might not be "Moorish or . . . I stopped myself, not daring to say: a Jewess." But she is blacker than black, more exiled than the wanderer: "Come, Come. You see very well that I am Gypsy; do you want me to tell you la baji [your fortune in the cards]? Have you ever heard of la Carmencita? C'est moi!" (359). The narrator notes that he himself is such an impious infidel, has such passionate interest in those outside the laws of state and church, that not for a moment did he "recoil in horror at seeing [himself] alongside a witch" (359). Everything about Carmen, a Spanish sorceress, is doubled by its opposite: her beauty is inseparable from her ugliness; in the eyes of the narrator, she attracts as much as she repels:

In order not to tire you with a too-prolix description, I will tell you in short that to each fault she joined a quality which stood out perhaps all the more strongly by contrast. It was a strange and savage beauty, a face that first astonished, but that one could not forget. Her eyes above all had an expression both voluptuous and fierce that I have never since found in a human look. Gypsy eye, wolf eye is a Spanish saying which denotes a good observer. If you do not have time to go to the Jardin des Plantes to study the look of a wolf, consider your cat when it stalks a sparrow. (360–61)

Like her lover, Don José, she is both menacing and tame, a wolf and your domestic cat; in her black Gypsy eyes, voluptuous and fierce, the narrator glimpses the glint of the diabolical power she possesses by virtue of her grasp of the logic of love.

"Gypsy" signifies being black, says Mérimée, citing the word *Calés*, which means "black" in Romany and is the name "with which they most often designate themselves" (403). He suggests that the Gypsies came from India and brought their blackness from there. Nietzsche, however, when he praises Bizet's *Carmen*, attributes its power to another continent: "Its gaiety is African; fatality soars over it, its happiness is short, sudden, merciless. I envy Bizet because he had the courage of this sensibility, a sensibility which until now had not found expression in the music of civilized Europe— I mean that southern, coppered, ardent sensibility. What happiness those golden afternoons impart!" (Letter from Turin, May 1888). Nietzsche seems to be discovering the idea of a music which, in the twentieth century, will be invented as jazz, music whose pleasure is "short, sudden, merciless." The "southern, coppered, ardent sensibility" that Nietzsche hears in Bizet's music, with its soaring overtones of tragedy beneath an essential African gaiety, finds its emblem in music that evokes some gleaming metallic darkness—a brilliantly burnished place of secret cruelty, beyond good and evil. Carmen's seductive fierceness is linked to the innate mystery in the depths of her eyes that culminate for Don José in a single blackness. Arriving at the house of the officer, for whom Carmen has set a trap, he observes her observing: "The blind was half-open and I saw her large eye that was spying on me" (392). The same single eye appears to him obsessively fixed in his memory, at the end, after seeing it open beneath him under his knife: "I can still see her great black eye looking fixedly at me, then it became clouded and closed" (402). In her eye he sees a possibility of vision that sees into the heart of blackness.

Being black is the essence of Carmen's race. It is also synonymous, for her and for Mérimée, with the most absolute personal freedom: "I do not want to be tormented or especially ordered around. I want to be free and do what I please. *Calli elle est née, calli elle mourra.* Born a Gypsy, die a Gypsy" (401). At the end of the story, when Don José threatens to kill her unless she leaves Spain and follows him to America, she refuses to yield even though her prescience tells her that she will die at her lover's hands: "You want to kill me, I see it clearly; it is written, but you will not make me yield" (401). Her requirement for absolute independence coexists with the most obstinate loyalty until the oxymoron accomplishes its short, sudden, merciless dénouement. The cruelty of Carmen's death is joined to a defiant gaiety that comes, perhaps, from her prophetic power, which provides a posthumous perspective on her own demise, a freedom from the tyranny of the present, a vision of vengeance before the fatal insult occurs. Carmen, like the cigarette she smokes, is black as ash and red as ember; swirling arabesques in her eye evoke intimations of mortality, the gay wisdom of a cruel finitude, enlightened in every glance.

Don José was standing guard at the factory when he heard some bourgeois say, "There's the gitanella"; "It was a Friday and I will never forget it. I saw that Carmen that you know" (367). The *coup de foudre*, love at first sight, strikes Don José on Friday—the same day, of course, on which Petrarch first was struck by the look of Laura. As it was for Petrarch, the moment of the *innamorata* results in a kind of negative conversion; Don José in a flash sells his soul to the, watching, Devil:

> She had a very short red slip which revealed white silk stockings with more than one hole and darling red morocco shoes attached with ribbons the color of fire. She let fall her mantilla to show off her shoulders and a fat bouquet of red flowers [*cassie*] emerged from her blouse. She had another red flower in the corner of her mouth, and she advanced rolling her hips like a filly from the breeding stables of Córdoba. In my country, a woman dressed like that would have obliged people to cross themselves.
>
> And taking the flower that she had in her mouth, she threw it at me with a movement of her thumb, right between the eyes. Sir, that had the effect on me of a bullet which struck me. (367–68)

Her satanic redness—underlined by her name, which sounds like "red" in Latin—is complete down to her adorable toes. She is the Devil, she tells him, when she leaves him the day after the day of their honeymoon: "Bah! my boy, believe me, you got off cheap. You met the Devil, yes, the Devil; he is not always black, and he didn't twist your neck. I'm dressed in wool but I'm no sheep" (379). She is the wolf and he the lamb in this story; her power to captivate him is supernatural and ensures his destruction. The only defense against this werewolf is the cross. If she throws a flower like a bullet between your eyes, it cannot be forgotten, just as Carmen's flower, placed next to the heart, even "dried, smells good forever. If there are witches," says Don José to the narrator, "that girl there is one" (369). Mérimée devotes one of his four *Lettres adressées d'Espagne* to the subject of "Spanish Witches." He recounts his encounter with another Carmencita, the mistress of an inn where he and his reluctant servant stop, one "who has the Devil for a cook"; the servant, recognizing her, recounts fierce stories which he prefaces with a Spanish proverb: "Primo p..., luego alcahueta, pues bruja" [First a whore, then a madam, then a witch] (227).

Mérimée prefaces his story of Carmen with a well-known epigraph, taken from the Greek Anthology. It reads, in Greek:

Pasa gunei cholos estin. Echei d'agathas duo oras,
Tein mian en thalamo, tein mian en thanato.
(345)

All women are *cholos* [choleric]. Women have only two good days,
The day they get married, and the day they die.[2]

What may seem, in the epigram of Palladas (the cynical fifth-century Alexandrian aphorist), like vulgar misogyny, acquires a whole other resonance in the context of the Greek Anthology, which is obsessed, one might say, by the idea of the fatal bride. The repeated, moving inscriptions written on the tombs of girls who died on the day of their wedding find their dramatic enactment in Euripides' *Medea*, where Jason's young bride puts on the wedding garments sent to her by Medea, the wife scorned. The clothes are impregnated with a poison that burns the flesh from the body of the princess as she envelops herself in their folds: the metamorphosis of wedding clothes into shroud is the essential transformation that enacts what Nietzsche, referring to *Carmen*, calls "the tragic spirit that is the essence of love" (Letter from Turin, May 1888). The indiscernible difference between shroud and wedding dress is signified in the Greek of the epigraph to Carmen by the near homonym *thalamo/thanato*. The woman one marries is herself already dead and the bringer of death. In both Mérimée's and Bizet's Carmen, the identification of love and death is most strongly affirmed at the two most compelling moments: Carmen's marriage feast, and the scene of her murder. Two good days, Palladas might say.

Identifying the bride with death is the central motif of Freud's little essay "The Theme of the Three Caskets." It is an idiosyncratic piece, for it makes extended use of material taken from folktales and popular stories instead of from the usual sources provided by Freud's clinical practice. It allows him to define something like a myth of the collective male unconscious, whereby men identify their brides with death itself. He begins by examining two scenes from Shakespeare's *Merchant of Venice* and *King Lear*. In both, a man is confronted with the necessity of having to choose between three women, or their surrogates, and his choice in both cases settles on what seems at first to be the least excellent of the three but proves in the end to be most desirable. Bassanio in *The Merchant* chooses the lead—the least noble metal, instead of the silver or gold—casket and discovers there the portrait of Portia that allows him to win her hand. Freud notes that Bassanio's speech sounds strangely unconvincing at the moment he begins to have to celebrate the virtues of valueless lead. Similarly, at the end of *King Lear* the king is left with only the corpse of the least and last of his daughters, Cordelia, who proves to have been the most worthy of love.

The question at which Freud arrives is the following: Why does the man always face a choice among three women, and why does he choose the one who seems the least prepossessing? The third woman, he shows, is always predicated with attributes that link her to death: the muteness of Cordelia and the gray inertness of lead are, for Freud, eloquent emblems of mortality. Both of Shakespeare's plays, he concludes, illustrate the dream of a man choosing his own death, a dream all the more powerful and seductive because it is, in fact, always the other way around—death chooses man. It has been said that "bigamy means having one wife too many. So does matrimony." All marriage is bigamy, or polygamy, for in the life of every man, says Freud, there are three women, three mothers: the first one gives you life; the last one is Mother Earth, who receives you at death; and the second is the woman you marry, who is a figure for the first and the third. Every wife, he says, is actually three women—three mothers, as it were— and marriage is therefore a heroic act, insofar as in entering into it a man chooses his death, espouses it, and makes his life out of that choice. The woman he marries cannot fail to represent the past (his biological mother) and the future (the bosom of Mother Earth), while being in the present the simulacrum that mimes both the origin and the end: not merely gold and lead, but also the silver of the mirror in which he sees his destiny.

To be sure, there may be no such thing as a wife, as she is understood to be by men like Freud. Or if there is an idea, an ideal of a wife to which any woman (or man) might aspire, it might be the dream of being a Gypsy bride: "Tu es mon rom, je suis ta romi," cries Carmen as she marries herself to Don José. You are my Gypsy, my spouse, my man; I am your Gypsy, your spouse, your woman. Marriage to Carmen, like that of a smoker to his cigarette, is eventually fatal, but it embraces an impossible idea, a gauzy ideal of hymeneal union—a marriage that combines the most exhilarating perspectives on freedom with the most irrefractable bonds of habituated pleasure.

Thérèse Desqueyroux is another bad woman who is good. Her name links the name of Teresa, the martyred saint, to sonorities that evoke desperation (Dés-e-spérée) and the carmine color of the flames of hell (roux). François Mauriac, her creator, calls her odious, in his preface, and assimilates her to those whom Baudelaire calls monsters. In the same preface, he allows that he might have created a saint: "For a long time I desired that you be worthy of the name of Sainte Locuste," but canonizing her, he was afraid, would appear to the pious to be sacrilege (6). The second-century Roman chronicler Suetonius preserved the name of Locusta, the imperial poisoner, whose skill was employed successively by Agrippina and her son, Nero, to poison, respectively, the emperor, Claudius, and the rival, Britannicus. For Mauriac, a Catholic, the risk in canonizing Locusta would be that of committing the gravest blasphemy, arousing sympathy for the Devil, but it is precisely that risk which he decides to run in writing Thérèse Desqueyroux—the story of a woman who poisons her husband but whose spiritual example is more edifying than that of all the respectable, right-thinking, obedient Catholics in the novel. In the novel, her cigarettes are the emblem of both her sanctity and her evil.

For a long time, little of dramatic interest happens in the life of Thérèse: she marries a boring, complacent man, has a child she won't take care of, and smokes cigarettes, many cigarettes. She also dreams a great deal, mostly of destroying the acres of pine trees that are the principal source of her family's wealth in the arid region south of Bordeaux. She has grown up in the cruel landscape of the moors that stretch, a wasteland, from Bordeaux to the sea: barren lands (called landes in French), dotted with scraggy bushes, interrupted here and there by stands of pine whose cultivation since the end of the last century enhances the family's meager resources, they are, says Mauriac, lands "at the extremity of the earth" (29). Thérèse reflects the landscape in the burned-out grayness of her life—a product and the victim of the boring meanness, perverse cruelty, and desiccated rigidity of the Catholic haute bourgeoisie. She married Bernard Desqueyroux because he was the other large landowner in the region, and the union of their family interests had for a long time been envisaged; he is also less stupid than most of the men on the moor. She does not hate her husband; she has no motivating interest in his death. She is driven to add a few bitter drops of her own venom to his doctor's prescription out of the simple desire to see how he will react in the face of death, in order to trouble his immovable complacency. The act is one of gratuitous malice, a pure crime, whose absence of motive allows it to be seen as a gesture of revolt against the deadening, hypocritical, bigoted malignity of her bloated, reactionary class. Mauriac has won his bet: Thérèse/Locusta, by her attempt at murder, becomes the only saint in the novel, a martyr to the desire for transcendence.

The dose is ill administered and the husband lives. Thérèse is denounced by the doctor who discovers the crime. Only the intervention of her senator father and her husband's willingness to perjure himself on her behalf save her from prison. The price she pays is to become their virtual prisoner, hidden away to maintain appearances in the interest of preserving the father's political career and the family's respectability.

The power Thérèse exerts over the people around her is insidious and inexplicable, darkly magical. When she smiles, people find themselves agreeing: "You don't ask if she is pretty or homely, but you can't help submitting to her charm" (23). They also agree that she smokes too much: "Elle fume trop" (70). To be sure, everyone in the novel smokes; even her husband, Bernard, rolls a cigarette from time to time. But "she smokes so much that her fingers and nails are yellow, as if she had soaked them in arnica" (152). The stain of nicotine on her hands is the visible sign of the venomous impulse that leads her to administer "20 granules of aconitine"—a poison that rhymes with the one in her veins. Thérèse, in short, is a witch.

But smoking too much is also the sign, perfectly well understood by the moralizing class into which she is born, of her radical difference from them—a moral difference, of course, that they reprove and fear, but also a spiritual one, whose dark transcendence they cannot grasp but that the omniscient narrator never fails to underline. Her mother-in-law remarks: "She doesn't have our principles, unfortunately. For example, she smokes like a chimney [comme un sapeur]" (38). Smoking a lot, as always "too much," is the emblem in the novel of her refusal to submit to the deadening constraints of this provincial life, a refusal to follow the "ruts" [les ornières] in whose tracks all the rest of the family runs with a serene and untroubled good conscience.

The nicotine on her hands is an emblem of her cruelly paradoxical nature, a mind that refuses to accommodate the simple alternatives of good and evil with which this self-righteous society accumulates wealth, exploits its servants, preserves its privileges, hardens its heart against the intrusion of all adventure—avidity, curiosity, or change—and against others —like Jean Azévédo, thought to be a Jew, come from Paris, adept at books and the life of the mind. Thérèse promptly seduces Jean, then drops him after having fiercely contrived to detach him from her sister-in-law, who loved him purely and first. But cruelty like paradox flows in her veins, the double precipitates of blood spiked with nicotine; Thérèse exasperates her husband and the people around her by her "phrases," her "maniacal" joy at "splitting hairs" (178). The family cannot understand where she gets her ideas: "Thérèse says that there is nothing worse, to turn the head of young girls, than romantic novels, than the work of good books—but she is so paradoxical" (65). Bernard (the husband) "shrugged his shoulders: she killed him with her paradoxes. It does not require much cunning to be brilliant. One has only, with respect to everything, to affirm the contrary of what is reasonable" (77). The logic of smoking, as we saw in Chapter 3, generates paradoxes, often fatal, like those that slay Bernard and contaminate the intellectual and moral being of Thérèse with their irrefutable antinomies—their diabolical truth.

Her smoking represents a threat not only to the moral principles of this rigid Catholic society but to its economic well-being, even to its very survival:

> In the family there were endless discussions on the cause of the forest fires: a discarded cigarette? malevolence?
> Thérèse dreamed that one night she had gotten up, left the house, reached the part of the forest most dense with dried branches, thrown down her cigarette until an immense smoke tarnished the dawn sky. . . . But she dismissed that thought, having love for the pines in her blood; it wasn't toward trees that her hatred was directed. (111)

Thérèse is torn between her desire to wreak havoc and her attachment to her acres of pine trees: "She always had property in her blood"; "evaluations of property passionately interested her. No doubt that this domination over a vast stretch of property seduced her" (40). She knows that the least spark could start a conflagration in the pine forest: "She threw down her cigarette, and like the people on the Moor, crushed it out with care"

(172). But at other moments she dreams of the ruin that a cigarette care-
lessly tossed might accomplish—the apocalyptic destruction of the land
and all its inhabitants.

Cigarettes are a drug, both inebriating and poisonous: "But she was
wrong to smoke so much; *elle s'intoxicait*" (54). She in-toxic-ated herself; poisoning herself, she poisons those around her. Cigarettes are thus a weapon,
an instrument of her hatred, a tool of her revenge; conversely, for her to
refrain from smoking is understood by those around her as an unchar-
acteristic sign of love: "But Mme. de Trave gave assurances that [Thérèse]
loved her daughter in her way: 'Naturally one can't ask her to give her a
bath or change her diapers: that is not in her blood: but I've seen her stay
entire evenings, seated next to the cradle, keeping from smoking to watch
the little one sleep'" (108). "Bernard said, 'Watch out for your cigarette;
it can still start a fire; water has all gone from the moors.' She had asked:
'Is it true that ferns contain prussic acid?' Bernard did not know if they
contained enough to poison anyone" (41).

Against her husband, cigarettes are daggers. His ferocious defense of the
value of the family and of his family's values constitutes, in the eyes of
Thérèse, the most stultifying, censorious, and oppressive consequence of
his incurious complacency, his satisfaction "at seeing everything there was
to see in the shortest possible time. 'Look, Thérèse. Don't argue for the
sake of arguing; all Jews are the same. . . . And besides, it's a family of de-
generates—tubercular to the marrow, everyone knows.' She lit a cigarette
with a gesture that always shocked Bernard. 'Remind me what your grand-
father died of, and your great-grandfather?'" (57). The gesture of lighting a
cigarette prepares the coup; it administers a small initial shock to Bernard
that sets him up for the devastating attack on the whole system underlying
his defense of the immaculate integrity of the family genes. The indecency
of Thérèse's gesture, lighting the cigarette, presents him with the intolerable exhibition of feminine transgression. Very early in the novel we learn
that Bernard, on his honeymoon, "noisily quit a musical-hall whose spectacle had shocked him: 'Imagine foreigners seeing that! How shameful!
And that is what they judge us on'" (46). The seductiveness of her narcissis-
tic self-sufficiency and all the liberating possibilities it awakens could only
affront Bernard, with its refusal to entertain even the reassuring illusions
of feminine subordination.

A woman smoking in public offends those who think that women are
supposed to be veiled. In private, between a man and a woman, it becomes
the permanent signal of her determination to resist his male opinions, his

Wild Girl

Photo © Bruce Davidson. By permission of Magnum Photos, Inc.

will to inbreathe his adamic breath in her. Every puff she takes says to him that she is determined to take a breath, a puff, that is entirely her own. Before the First World War, when women's smoking was again tabooed, advertisements showed a woman sitting under starlight next to a smoking man, asking him to "blow some my way." In her fondest dream of escape to some unimaginable life of luxury and freedom in Paris, Thérèse imagines herself there on her own, blowing it her way: "In that resturant in the Bois [de Boulogne], where she had been, but without Bernard, with Jean Azévédo and some young women. She put down her tortoise-shell cigarette case [her etui] on the table, and lit an Abdullah. She spoke, opened up her heart, and the band played softly" (183). Mauriac has drawn the portrait of a woman who dreams of putting her horny box, up front, on the table. But her dream assumes a further dimension in the Abdullah she lights up. Who on the Bordelais moor had ever even dreamed of the possibility of smoking a gold-tipped, perfumed, Turkish cigarette, whose name contains the Arabic syllables of God? Thérèse, smoking there on the heath, imagines herself smoking in Paris, because for her, as for Mauriac, cigarettes are a means of seduction and a form of prayer—an expression of her deepest longing, a minor celebratory rite, a medium for opening oneself to one's own transcendent possibilities for freedom.

Before her cigarettes are taken away entirely, Thérèse has to battle against the oppressive odor of her husband's "pipe" that ties her to a hateful past, as distinct from the future for adventure that her blond cigarettes let her imagine: "Bernard did not go out that evening. Thérèse smoked, threw away her cigarette, went to the landing, and heard her husband wandering from room to room on the first floor; the odor of his pipe insinuated itself into her bedroom, dominated that of Thérèse's blond tobacco, and she recognized the odor of her old life. The first day of bad weather" (146).

At Thérèse's moment of greatest weakness, enervated by the isolation and despair that the family has imposed—hardly able to leave her bed— she eats and drinks only so she can smoke cigarettes. "She swallowed a few mouthfuls of confit and drank some coffee to be able to smoke (empty, her stomach no longer tolerated tobacco)" (151). Cigarettes have become more vital to her survival, more food than food. More important than her appearance, which she is inclined to neglect, her cigarette is the palpable manifestation of her interiority. Her identification with the cigarette she smokes is directly established very early in the novel, when her sister-in-law comes looking for Thérèse:

"Thérèse, where are you?"
"Here, on the bench."
"Ah! yes: I see your cigarette."
(71)

The ultimate punishment her captors malignly inflict—a form of psychic murder—is to take away her cigarettes; her worst fear is realized. Losing her cigarettes is all but equivalent to losing herself, her life. "Thérèse was afraid that they had taken away her cigarettes, she advanced her hand toward the table: the cigarettes were not there. How to live without smoking? Her fingers had to be able to touch that little dry, warm thing [cette petite chose sèche et chaude]; she had to be able to sniff them indefinitely [les flairer indéfiniment] and her room had to be bathed in a fog that her mouth had inhaled and rejected. She closed her eyes, and her yellow fingers were still making the accustomed movement around a cigarette" (172).

As she closes her eyes, her consciousness seeming about to be extinguished, she betrays only the faintest signs of life, halting peristaltic movements, like the last mechanical beat of her heart: fingers still closing around a nonexistent cigarette. The little warm, dry object is a kind of clitoral surrogate of herself, and to wrap her fingers around it is to enclose herself within an irreducible circle of masturbatory narcissism. Inhaling and exhaling smoke allows her to extend her body into the space her captors have imposed on her, to take possession of it and enclose it in a cloud of self-sufficiency.

When at last she begins to rouse herself from the torpor into which, imprisoned by the family, she had sunk, she begins to venture outdoors, to make plans, and to chain smoke. "Thérèse lit her cigarette with the one she had just finished smoking. Around four o'clock, she put on a raincoat, and plunged into the rain. She was afraid of the night, returned to her room" (172).

Smoking one cigarette after another is like the first tentative steps of a convalescent; each one marks a little victory, and each victory generates another, leading to her eventual recovery and final escape. She begins for the first time to dream the possibility of another life, in Paris, without constraints, available for adventure, luxuriously free, smoking exotic Turkish cigarettes, beautifully presented to her between translucent sheets of horn. On the last page of the novel, she realizes the dream and finds herself left alone, sitting in the Café de la Paix, as Bertrand, with relief, abandons her to her fate and returns to his well-trodden "path": "Like his carts, he needed his ruts." She savors her liberty and lights the fire of an attentive young man at a nearby table who holds out his lighter when she takes a cigarette: "A warm contentment came over her, thanks to this half-bottle of Pouilly. She asked for cigarettes. A young man at a nearby table held out his lit cigarette lighter, and she smiled" (191).

Mauriac in his preface tells us that he resisted the temptation, at the end of the novel, to turn his monster into a saint of negative transcendence, one who attains a spiritual elevation through her descent into the horrors of crime. But the possibility of such a conversion is adumbrated in the last lines, where she wins the right to smoke as much as she pleases: "Thérèse had drunk a little and smoked a lot. She laughed alone like a happy person. She powdered her nose, did her lips meticulously, then having reached the street, walked at random [au hasard]" (191). She puts on her face and plunges into the crowd, giving herself over to the unpredictable encounters and indeterminate itineraries of chance—the last word of freedom. Have you ever seen a cigarette walking?

5 The Soldier's Friend

You ask what we need to win this war. I will tell you,
we need tobacco, more tobacco—even more
than food.—General John J. Pershing
to the Minister of War

The image of the red Zouave on every packet of Job cigarette papers com-memorates what might have been the most decisive event of the Crimean War, were it not apocryphal. The story is that in 1852 a Turkish soldier, discovering that his pipe had been shattered by a bullet, fashioned the first cigarette by enveloping his tobacco in an empty paper cartridge shell and then smoking it. In fact, cigarettes arrived in France from Spain about twenty-five years earlier. Nevertheless, the story illuminates the possible origin of the expression "to smoke like a Turk," which designates compul-sive smoking and connotes, as well, the value assigned to tobacco in that culture, in which infinite ingenuity is applied to ensure that the Turk can smoke continuously, even in the midst of battle. The fable also intimates the symbolic identification between the bullet the soldier shoots and the sharp spike of courage he gets from repeated injections of tobacco smoke.

French soldiers returning from Sardonopolis brought the habit with them, and for a brief time cigarettes were in vogue in Paris. It is no acci-dent, as Marxists used to say, that cigarettes had an upsurge of popularity in 1848, when France and the rest of Europe were shaken by revolution-ary upheavals. All societies recognize the usefulness and value of ciga-rettes in periods of social disruption, war, or economic crisis, as judged by the jump in their consumption and the way public attitudes toward smoking abruptly change. The pattern is confirmed in the twentieth cen-tury: in periods of civil tension and social stress, cigarettes are widely tolerated and become objects of patriotic feeling and sentimental attach-ment. One striking example is the report written in 1925 by André Citroën, the automobile manufacturer, who was invited by the Régie, the French tobacco monopoly, to determine how it could better promote the virtues of French cigarettes. Citroën wrote an intensely chauvinistic elegy celebrating the qualities of *caporal*, the martial name that was given to "black" French tobacco: "Our ordinary *caporal*, crackling, bracing, male, healthy, a comrade, a good kid, a pal, what a personality it has! Unlike most exotic tobaccos, with their blond stringiness that supinely goes limp, soft, tasteless angel's hair soaked in perfume for sentimental neurotics" (quoted in Rival 227). To Louis Pauwels, French tobacco "smells like cut grass, turned earth, wool, wet leather, fire in the forest, the officer's club" (quoted in Rival 227). For Citroën and Pauwels, the tobacco of Gauloises was made for male bonding, whereas soft *blonds* were made for (by?) sentimental neurotics. Real men, who smell (of) the earth, prefer the bracing camaraderie, not to say butch homophilia, of the all-male officer's club.

Americans gripped in the current hysteria have naturally forgotten the affectionate identification of the doughboy's uniform with "Lucky Strike Green," and the European hopes and the American pride associated, in 1914, with the promise that "the Camels are coming." It might surprise Americans reading the letters of General Pershing, commander of the American troops, to hear the urgency with which he writes to R. J. Reynolds asking that he please send cigarettes. Or his even more insistent tone, in 1918, pleading with the Minister of War (quoted in the epigraph above).

What virtues or value, use or beauty, do cigarettes have in wartime? They feed no need and heal no wound, and yet in war they are the most precious of all commodities, as good as gold, more vital than food. A universal token of exchange, tobacco has been called "the Gold Token"; in America, Old Gold was a brand of cigarettes. According to Ned Rival, "In the invaded France of 1940 . . . tobacco became a gold-token [*valeur-or*] quoted daily higher on the black market" (219). Throughout the war cigarette rations were essentially equivalent to money, and a carton of American cigarettes bought GIs in Europe anything they wanted. More recently, for a brief time at the end of the Romanian revolution, Kents replaced lei, the local currency, as the principal medium of commodity exchange in Bucharest; in Tbilisi, in Russia, rioters took to the street, not to protest bread lines but to demand an end to the abrupt scarcity of cigarettes. At Drancy, the French concentration camp where prisoners were held before being deported to the East, the price of a pack fluctuated between two hundred and five hundred francs. "A cigarette," recounts Denise Aimé in *Relais des errants*, "sells for 150 francs on the eve of a departure for deportation, and for the right to take a single drag of one, ten francs, ten francs for a last puff of freedom and of dreams" (Rival 223).

The last cigarette performs the same function as gallows humor, which installs the perspective of the superego, says Freud: the locus of conscience, it also represents one's highest values, the most elevated sense of self, looking down at approaching death and laughing. Values being timeless, the superego does not believe in its own annihilation but feels indestructible in the face of its imminent execution. The benefit that cigarettes, like jokes, procure for those who are about to die, depends on their capacity to erect a posthumous (or divine) perspective—outside time, in another time and place where one is momentarily, gaily invulnerable. Recall the death of Walter Raleigh.

La Baïonnette, a newspaper edited in the trenches in 1917, confirms the saintly vocation of cigarettes to intercede on behalf of the soldier and bring solace to those in desperate need. The newspaper regularly published "Tobacco Litanies, "prayers written in gratitude and praise: "O Perlot [a variety of leaf], color of autumn leaves and of ripe oats [nèfle], ordinary caporal, be blessed, O tobacco, consolation of the soldier on campaign. You foster every kind of dreaming, mist over all pains, you even sometimes know how to smoke out [enfumer] the blues [le cafard], O divine consoler" (quoted in Rival 205).

The value of cigarettes, their use as a universal token of exchange, is linked to their insertion in a gift-giving economy. Cigarettes give the gift of giving—to the other, to oneself, to the beyond. They are the index and the tokens of the soldier's generosity; in a fraternal impulse he can offer them to comrades and receive them in return. In moments of great fear or anxiety, cigarettes help the soldier to gather himself together, repossess his self-composure. They are the little gift he gives himself to regain his self, his capacity for giving gifts or attacking. But they are also a deep well of consolation at which he may find occasion to drink forty times a day, a potion against loss, depression, and the boredom of waiting. They have something like the capacity of incense to connect the earth to the sky and hence to invite the smoker's spirit to turn away from the negativity of the here and now toward some higher realm—some more general perspective from which to view the horror all around.

At a time when tobacco has again been demonized, it is useful to recall that in pre-Columbian times it was considered to be a god, a minor divinity that found acolytes among Native American tribes stretching from the Iroquois of New York to the Mayans in the Yucatan. The glowing ember of the calumet unified the circle of the tribe with the spirits of their ancestors. With its power to give escape from time, to call up the past or evoke the future, tobacco linked Indians to their dead, in whom they saw themselves. It summoned their collective longing for future bravery rivaling the example of ancestors, so as to alleviate the burden of the spirits' haunting injunctions by imitating, then surpassing them.

Even in the private sphere, the simple act of inhaling and exhaling smoke in an attitude of unhurried concentration fulfills the conditions of prayer: it allows the one who smokes to "project onto one's suffering a quality of attention composed of acceptance and detachment . . . then to offer this suffering to God" (Limburg Stirum 98)—or to whatever one calls the transcendental. The connection is an old one; in 1856, *Paris fumeur*, a journal devoted to the pleasures of smoking, had as its motto "Qui fume prie" [Smoking is praying]. More recently Annie Leclerc in her book *Au feu du jour*, devoted to (stopping) smoking, writes that "the cigarette is prayer for our times" (49).

"Tobacco Litanies" evoke the capacity of cigarettes to "favor dreaming," to open up space and time so that daydreams may be prolonged. Each puff on a cigarette momentarily opens up a gray-blue balloon above the smoker's head, a beautifully defined space for dreaming, an escape from the harsh constraints of necessity and the cruel menace of death. Each puff is a last puff of freedom and dreams. The instant of inhaling and exhaling is free of anxiety; a little moment of meditation, it suspends reality and allows one to feel an infinite attachment to the universe, a brief taste of immortality. The cloud of smoke resembles a balloon in a cartoon or painting in which the imaginings of the smoker may be projected as onto a screen: in Italian the little cloud in which the speech or thought of a cartoon character is represented is called "il fumo." In the time it takes to smoke a cigarette the smoker can play out a personal little cinema fulfilling fondest wishes in imagination.

The condition of daydreaming appears to be forgetting, and tobacco smoke becomes a metaphor for the power of cigarettes to mask the cruel reality of war, to veil pain with mist, and to smoke over the mirror of negative experience, obliterating even the privation and misery of war. Smoking cigarettes promotes forgetting, and forgetfulness is the soldier's patron saint, what the prayer calls his "divine consoler." One historian of tobacco takes up the theme of forgetfulness: "The soldier smokes the way others drink, to forget. . . . One smokes to counter boredom, fear, cold or heat, against the discipline which produces the pitiable inertia of armies, against the injustice of living and dying; one smokes to replace love, liberty, the need to be clean and to walk bare-headed, alone, where the air is fresh and free" (Alyn 89).

It is hard to recall the value cigarettes once had at a moment when society is perversely passing laws against them, on the justification of protecting the general population from exposure to the smoke of other people's cigarettes. To deprive people in airplanes of the right to smoke, in their own section, where the air is powerfully conditioned, withholds from them, during a time of acute anxiety, the most powerful device that universal society has devised for finding prayerful consolation and resolute resignation in the face of danger. In time of war, it is with gratitude and love that one holds, between fingers and lips, the small, compact cylinder of paper and tobacco—cinder, fire, ash—like worry beads, rosary, or some other divine consoler: a little daemon, mediator of the gods, and a most intimate friend, a companion who never fails to speak to the loneliness of the self in moments of greatest heroism or of empty or splenetic boredom.

Cigarettes free the soldier by momentarily masking the cruelty of his condition; their effect is less that of producing a narcotic sensation than of permitting an intellectual stance detached from reality—one that, Janus-like, invites the return of nostalgia or speculates in dreamy anticipation. But cigarettes are more than therapy. It is not enough merely to assert that, though bad for health, they provide remedies for ills of the spirit. In fact, cigarettes serve soldiers in other ways, more puzzling and in peacetime less apparent. Consider the enigmatic assertion of General Lasalle (1775–1809), a Napoleonic hero who, before he fell, valiantly, at the battle of Wagram, is reputed to have said: "A hussard must smoke; a cavalryman who does not smoke is a bad soldier" (Alyn 87). What does this mean? The general's claim that there is a link between smoking and being a good soldier is not argued; it is merely asserted, apodictically, like one of those mute Marlboro or Camel advertisements that show only the vivid image of a man clearly accustomed to pitting his strength against the forces of nature.

At times in recent history refusing to smoke was considered anti-American, a rejection of a certain idea—some might call it a myth—of the heroic linked to the pathos of the frontier. By heroism is meant (in the strict, Hegelian sense) courage in the face of death, looking death in the face. When one smokes, one does not merely suck a tit of consolation; cigarette smoke is not always, not often, perhaps never mother's milk—it mostly tastes bad, produces a faint nausea, induces the feeling of dying a little every time one takes a puff. But it is the poison in cigarettes that rec-

Soldiers in West Germany
Photo © Cornell Capa. By permission of Magnum Photos, Inc.

ommends them to the heroic—a strong poison; it takes an infinitesimally smaller amount of nicotine to kill an adult than it does of, say, heroin or cocaine. In every puff there is a little taste of death, which makes cigarettes the authentic discipline of good soldiers.

Leclerc in *Au feu du jour* writes: "La cigarette est l'objet que je fournis à mon désir qu'il y transite, mais aussi pour qu'il y expire. Pour qu'il y ait lieu, séjour, et *mort*" [The cigarette is the object I furnish my desire so that it will persist, but also so that it will expire. So that it will occur, remain, and *die*] (16). The cigarette is not only an instrument that lets desire persist, it also kills it; it promotes the daydream in order to puncture it. It smokily entertains the moment of dreamy wish fulfillment and then interrupts it, punctually stubs it out. Cigarettes, in that respect, are unlike other drugs, like heroin, that have as the logical conclusion of their narcosis an infinite prolongation of the pleasure they procure, even to the point of death. One takes a cigarette with the knowledge, even the desire, that the wish will be momentarily entertained, forgetting reality, and then forgotten. Forgetting to forget is experienced as a sharp fall back into the world as the poison kicks in; the minute distance of that negative trip is all the more intensely felt because it is so brief. It is what gives cigarettes their bracing quality, heightening the sense of reality to which one abruptly returns from a momentary perspective outside it.

The last cigarette smoked before an execution is not equivalent to a shot of morphine; it stiffens the spine of the person condemned, kills escape, and promotes a resignation to necessity that gives one courage to endure the worst. It is because a moment out of time is born and then made to die that the cigarette serves as a simulacrum, a little enactment of death. It is as if the last cigarette plays out, in a controlled fiction, the death that is anticipated and feared. It creates the illusion that the death of all our dreams is willed, is chosen—that the execution is really a suicide that one will master till the end. The sublimity of smoking (like that of suicide, according to Schiller) lies in its capacity to promote the illusion that we are viewing our own death, determining it from outside ourselves, living posthumously, as it were, in the aftermath of the poison, in a moment of private heroism. At a time when war seems to have been banished from the West, cigarettes are one of the last adventures left. The notion that doctors' warnings will discourage people from smoking misses the seduction of cigarettes, which precisely depends on the risks and the displeasure they sublimely provide.

Moralists cannot understand why women are smoking more than ever at a time when society is imposing the most rigid constraints on smoking:

it is because women today are soldiers, increasingly at war with the mas-
culinist system that has for the moment slowed their struggle and seems
eager to reimpose old rigidities. One sees no signs for the Marlboro woman
because increasingly she is everywhere. Antismoking legislation, at this
moment in history, intersects the struggle for women's liberation—as it
always has. The degree to which women have the right to smoke in society
is an unmistakable indicator of the general equality they have achieved,
a test of their full membership in civil society. Antismoking legislation is
one of the subterranean forms in which that war for women's liberation is
still raging.

On the battlefield, "When cigars and cigarettes were distributed, it was
a sign that the hour of attack was near" (Remarque 75). Tobacco functions
not to numb soldiers but to steel their nerves and to permit them to master the ambient anxiety that is their permanent condition. Physiologically,
the cigarette is an extraordinary device for controlling anxiety; less clear
is its role in alleviating the symptoms of fear. The difference between fear
and anxiety, according to Heidegger—for whom the latter is a fundamental
disposition of being-in-the-world—is the indefiniteness that characterizes
the object of anxiety. Unlike fear, which flees from some determined, definable thing ready to hand, anxiety is anxious in relation to no definite
"here" or "there": "Anxiety does not 'know' what is that in the face of
which it is anxious" (Heidegger 186).

Whenever, feeling anxious, one takes a cigarette, the nicotine produces
two distinct physiological effects, which have a coordinated role. In the
first moment it enters the bloodstream, nicotine suddenly and often dramatically raises the pulse and arterial pressure, paradoxically acerbating
the feelings of tense displeasure that the cigarette was supposed to counter.
Taking a big drag of the cigarette, inhaling deeply, actually worsens the
physiological symptoms associated with anxiety. But the advantage of that
worsening is that it binds those physiological effects to a specific, determined cause—this cigarette I am smoking. Whereas, before, anxiety was
caused by a vague anticipation of indeterminate danger, now the feelings
of discomfort produced by the cigarette are punctual and pointed. Lending those feelings a single, determined origin is the first step in mastering
them, in taking them out of the realm of anxiety and locating them in
something ready to hand or present to hand—in the hand. The substitution
of a painfully precise origin for what was before a vaguely uncomfortable
source, is the first step toward eliminating anxiety and its dis-ease.

In Heideggerian terms, the cigarette serves to "transform this anxiety into fear in the face of an oncoming event" in a first moment; in a second moment, "the anxiety which has been made ambiguous as fear, is passed off as a weakness with which no self-assured *Dasein* may have any acquaintance. What is 'fitting' [*Was sich . . . 'gehört'*] according to the unuttered decree of the 'they,' is indifferent tranquillity as to the 'fact' that one dies. The cultivation of such a 'superior' indifference *alienates Dasein* from its ownmost non-relational potentiality-for-Being" (298). From the standpoint of the "existential projection of an authentic Being-towards-death" (298), the soldier's cigarette represents a fall out of an authentic condition of anxiety into an alienated condition of fear, which, for Heidegger, is more "ambiguous" precisely because it seems to make the source of the danger more clear, definable, ready-to-hand, turns the nonrelational character of anxiety into a relation to the "fact" of oncoming death, in the face of which one can harden oneself. Cigarettes effect "*a constant tranquilization about death*" (298) insofar as their mechanism assists in transforming it into a well-known event occurring within the world, a case that is happening all around, which I represent as something, of course, that will one day in the end happen to me but right now has nothing to do with me. For Heidegger's *Dasein*, the transformation from the "existential" certainty of anxiety's vague indeterminacy to the "ambiguity" of fear's determined relation to what is present to hand, a fact, or case of something happening in the world, represents a fall into alienated inauthenticity—for the soldier, it may be the condition of bringing himself to attack.

The capacity of a negative experience, a feeling of pain, a little death, to bind impulses is clearly articulated by Freud in his essay *Beyond the Pleasure Principle*. What he calls the "death instinct," which underlies the pleasure principle, organizes the otherwise intermittent and wildly modulating discharges of the organism into repetitive, predictable patterns. By smoking a cigarette, ingesting a certain quantity of nicotine, the organism is hastening its death, is producing in itself more noxious effects than if it endured the discomfort of anxiety. But the death it is hastening is its own death; it substitutes its own path toward death for the process over which it otherwise has no control. Using cigarettes to master anxiety may be understood as preferring a certain form of dying over an intolerable form of living. In that respect, it is a heroic activity, not nutritive or therapeutic at all. Under some circumstances, giving oneself more discomfort is preferable to passively enduring less; assuming a death of one's own choosing is more desirable than suffering a life over which one has no control. The only thing worse than war is to lose one's freedom.

But the physiological effect of nicotine has two stages. It not only raises blood pressure and pulse at the price of increasing discomfort—in the next moment it lowers them, producing a marked feeling of release and relief. After mastering anxiety by increasing it, by giving it a precise, punctual origin, at the cost of more intense displeasure the organism that has taken a puff of its cigarette gets a little reward for its heroism: the sudden burst of unease that accompanies the ingestion of the poison is followed by a moment of release as the organism relaxes the tension that the poison, now eliminated, had initially provoked. The distension of the vessels and the slowing of the heart create a feeling of relaxation after the body's exertion in eliminating the toxin and combating its symptoms. From a psychological point of view the contradictory effects, like those of the Kantian sublime, paradoxically reinforce each other: less ease is the condition of more ease. The mechanism is quite different from inoculation, for example, in which one takes a small amount of poison to combat a greater amount, or accepts a mild version of a disease as protection against a more virulent exposure. Cigarettes serve to defend against anxiety by elevating the disquiet as the condition of its transformation and mitigation. It is as if the pleasure that results from relaxation is strictly a function of the distance the body traverses between tension and distension, even if the final state is more tense than normal, and even if it was arrived at by passing through a condition of increasing discomfort.

The contradictory physiological effect of smoking permits a wide range of psychological uses of cigarettes. At different moments, under differing conditions, a cigarette may be smoked for its capacity to steel one's concentration, to focus on a fact in the world; at other times its power to provide release and relaxation, to encourage daydreaming, may be its principal value. At still others, the cigarette may serve to initiate a transcendent perspective.

To illustrate some of the many different ways cigarettes are used in war, I have noted all the cigarettes that are lit or crushed out, thrown away or unlit at night, shared and hoarded, detested and loved—instruments of torture and of surgery, tokens of friendship and signs of love—in several distinguished war novels, beginning with Erich Maria Remarque's masterpiece of the First World War, Im Westen nichts Neues (All Quiet on the Western Front). The list includes For Whom the Bell Tolls, Hemingway's fiction of the Spanish civil war; Norman Mailer's The Naked and the Dead, considered by many to be the best novel to come out of World War II; William Styron's Korean saga, The Long March; Platoon by Dale A. Dye, a novel of Vietnam based on Oliver Stone's moving screenplay; and finally, to confirm the cigarette's continuing imaginative role, Tom Clancy's latest version of the former cold war, *The Cardinal of the Kremlin*.

Im Westen begins with a scene that became a cliché in twentieth-century novels of war, the moment when something like normal civilian existence is seen through the eyes of soldiers just returned from the fighting. On this day, the fat cook, serving soldiers nine kilometers from the front, is eager to empty his pots, miraculously giving everyone double portions of sausage and bread; some soldiers are able to fill their canteens as a reserve. The effect is uncanny: what to the reader seems perfectly familiar appears from the soldier-narrator's perspective to be the most exotic thing imaginable; an act that normally might be taken to be satisfying some ordinary necessity acquires the unreality of the most extravagant orgy.

William Styron, a careful reader of the genre, also begins *The Long March* with a scene of a chow line, but one that has been devastated. In the opening paragraphs, Styron depicts soldiers near the large pots, dead and wounded by the blast of an artillery shell fired by mistake, fallen short, and landed in the middle of their mess. That moment when the farthest rear becomes the most forward front returns with the frequency of a hallucination in war novels. Perhaps it condenses the fundamental narrative law of the genre, the movement between the battle scenes and life away from the firing, between terror and unease, fear and anxiety. At the high moments of battle, the soldier's fear is directed toward the enemy; rather, it is the enemy that directs the fear, gives the self an object on which to focus anxiety so as to master it in the interest of action. All the soldier's reactions and gestures at the front are prompted by the necessity of facing up, of turning his face to the threat directed at him by a hostile force. Back in the rear lines, where the ritual of the chow line occurs, fear is mitigated and anxiety returns. (Styron's rear is a North Carolina boot camp in the midst of the Korean war.) The heightened anxiety is represented as a kind of madness that overcomes the soldier at a moment of intense orality, when, eating and drinking, he first starts to adjust to more pacific conditions, when he allows himself to think he might just have to live—anxiously, like everyone else in war who is not on the battlefield. The madness is a manic denial of the mostly unconscious awareness of our permanent tending toward death. Away from the place where one expects to die, death, it seems, is impossible. Styron cruelly erupts a shell among the soldiers at mess, interrupting the manic moment with the very thing that is most unforeseen, death's accidental intrusion. At the very moment when a soldier stops fearing, in order to live, he is killed by an instrument of the mortality his fear had been protecting him against. The entry back into life is the ironic occasion for a last exit. In the opening scene of Clancy's *Patriot Games*, the perennial hero, Ryan, almost gets killed on holiday in London by happening on a terrorist attack.

For Paul, the narrator of *Im Westen*, the double ration of food that day is not, however, what is most important: "But the most important thing is that there was also a double ration of tobacco. Ten cigars, twenty cigarettes and two packs of chewing tobacco per person, that's not bad. I gave my chewing tobacco to Katzinski in exchange for his cigarettes, and so I have forty cigarettes for me. This is in advance, for one day" (7). Normally cigarettes were rationed, distributed day by day according to their availability and the whim of the officers, who recognized the influence of tobacco on morale. The possibility of the soldier's having cigarettes in reserve, in advance of the time when he will smoke them, represents a fantastic luxury, marks a measure of freedom from the totalitarian control that regiments his life; it briefly institutes an economy of abundance in place of the normal condition of rationed scarcity. But the most important thing about double rations is that cigarettes, unlike mere food, differentiate man from animals.

Man, we have argued, is distinguished from animals in that he smokes. No other living creature willingly inhales the smoke of tobacco or other burning substances. And smoking in war acquires a preeminent value unrelated to satisfying natural needs but belonging entirely to fulfilling culture-induced requirements. Smoking does nothing for survival; it is even understood to be dangerous to soldiers—presenting a trace or a target to enemy eyes: "He decided to have a last cigarette before the dark and the need to remain invisible to the enemy made smoking impossible" (Remarque 208). Cigarettes provide the soldier in the jungle not just physical satisfaction or sensual well-being but the taste of civilized nature, of aesthetic pleasure, to the extent that it is not beastly but civilized to taste and judge, appreciate and discriminate.

Paul reflects: "And around us the prairie flowered. The blades of grass bent in the soft, warm air of the late summer; we read letters and newspapers and smoked beatifically. . . . It would have been easy not to have been sitting on those boxes today; we barely escaped it. And that's why all sensations today are new and strong: the red poppies and the good food, the cigarettes and the summer breeze" (Remarque 13). For Remarque's

German Army in Bonn
Photo © Thomas Hoepker. By permission of Magnum Photos, Inc.

narrator, it is as if having barely escaped taking a hit was equivalent to having taken it; life after is like afterlife. Reborn, as if he had died and gone to heaven, lying there in the warm sun smoking "beat-ifically," the soldier is raised up and blessed among the saints, with what seems like an eternal life in which all sensations are new and strong; at that moment, he is also Kerouac "beat"—very high, very real, very free. Once again able to taste and feel and smell, the parataxis of his language, the adding up of elements, things, and pleasure, enacts the return of his capacity to respond to stimuli other than those connected with survival; born again, he begins to discriminate between this and that, to sense the quality of the moment, to rediscover ephemeral beauty, the beauty of ephemera—smoke vanishing in a summer breeze.

Conversely, the worst moments in war are frequently represented by a character hating the taste of a cigarette. Here is Styron's character at a moment of desperate exhaustion: "Blood was knocking angrily at his temples, behind his eyes, and he was thirsty enough to drink, with a greedy recklessness, nearly a third of his canteen. He lit a cigarette; it tasted foul and metallic and he flipped it away. His knees and thighs, unaccustomed to so much pounding, were stiff and fatigued" (61). The soldier is losing it; he is at that point to which Styron frequently returns when the soldier's self-discipline gives way under the weight of past excesses, now taking their revenge. Nothing tastes good; cigarettes have gone to metal.

Or here are Mailer's men in landing boats, on high alert, preparing to take the beach: "Red had started to light a cigarette, the fifth since their boat had been landed in the water, and it tasted flat and unpleasant" (27). Or again: "He lit a cigarette and exhaled cautiously, his lungs still raw from the exertion of the march. The cigarette tasted unpleasant, but he continued to smoke it" (389). Like Styron, Mailer understands the incompatibility between the exertions of war and the pleasure of cigarettes; they don't improve your performance on long marches. But both authors also grasp the distinction between the physiological effects of cigarettes and their cultural role. They are the most important thing to a soldier, says Remarque, all that remains of civility when war has blasted away the imprints of a liberal education.

In Im Westen, Paul and his comrades, most of them from the same town and school, recall with contempt their teacher, Kantorek, who taught them only useless things and lies. Paul says that he has forgotten most of what he learned in school: "I don't remember much of all that stuff. It's true it hasn't been worth much. But no one at school taught you how to light a cigarette in the rain and wind" (Remarque 83). For a soldier, this knowledge is the highest form of culture, the only education worth having in war: how to light a cigarette hunched against the elements. It stands for all education, the vestige of *Bildung* in the breast of the beast-machine that the soldier must become in battle. Conversely, not being able to light a cigarette is experienced as the most brutal deprivation. The moment of the soldier's utter abjection occurs when his soaked cigarette disintegrates, spilling tobacco that falls to earth and mixes with the mud at his boots: "Toglio was trying to light a cigarette, but it soaked through and came apart in his mouth before he could get his matches out of his waterproof pouch. He threw it to the ground and watched it dissolve in the mud. Despite the fact that he was completely wet, the rain still hurt; every drop that went down his back was like a cold slug, shocking and loathsome" (Mailer 88).

Cigarettes defend the soldier against what is shocking and loathsome; they kill slugs . . . and leeches. Perhaps this explains a frequently encountered motif in war fiction, the repeated scene of a soldier using the tip of his lit cigarette to burn some parasite that has stuck to the skin: "Rhah had spotted a bloated specimen on Taylor's lip and used the lit end of a soggy cigarette to force the leech to release its grip" (Dye 158). The cigarette goes to the lip, fire end first, in a Promethean gesture, releasing the soldier from the grip of what is most vile in war.

Here is Norman Mailer's version of that allegory, wherein a long-haired caterpillar, black and gold, wearing heraldic colors of valiant death, is seared by a cigarette representing the fire of civilization wielded like a weapon against indignity: "It was struggling desperately to right itself until Wyman held his burning cigarette near the insect's back. The insect writhed, and lay prostrate again, its back curled into an L and its legs thrashing helplessly in the air. It looked as if it were trying desperately to breathe" (187). The soldier turns the loathsome excretion of the tropical jungle into a letter of the alphabet, itself the insignia, perhaps, of a woman's Love— "legs thrashing helplessly in the air."

The power of cigarettes to humanize the inhumanity of war has its limits in fiction. But it frequently extends its sway to include the enemy in scenes that evoke the arbitrary nature of war's divisions, when two men recognize themselves in the hostile other across the line of the front. Consider a scene from *For Whom the Bell Tolls* in which Robert Jordan is looking down at the sentry on the bridge that it is his mission to destroy:

The sentry sat leaning against the wall. . . . He looked sleepy and as Robert Jordan watched him he yawned. Then he took out a tobacco pouch and a packet of papers and rolled himself a cigarette. He tried to make a lighter work and finally put it in his pocket and went over to the brazier, leaned over, reached inside, brought up a piece of charcoal, juggled it in one hand while he blew on it, then lit the cigarette and tossed the lump of charcoal back into the brazier.

Robert Jordan, looking through the Zeiss 8-power glasses, watched his face as he leaned against the box drawing on a cigarette. . . .

I won't look at him again, he told himself. (Hemingway 433)

The act of rolling and lighting and drawing at length on a cigarette establishes an intimacy that almost makes the enemy a guest of Robert Jordan, who is observing him very close up through good German glasses. The sentry's cigarette is a mirror. Determined to kill him, Robert Jordan will not look at him again, lest in this civil war he see not antagonistic difference but the friendly sameness of a compatriot's pleasure—the same gestures, lighting up and inhaling, that have lit the same innumerable cigarettes on Robert Jordan's side of the glasses.

Cigarettes are frequently represented as being democratic, international, cosmopolitan. They overcome the barriers that war erects. In Vietnam, when the platoon enters a Vietcong village, not all the Americans are prepared to massacre old men, women, and children; some subscribe to the universal moral principle that a light cannot be refused: "Finally, the old [Vietcong] villager held up a knobby hand gripping a handmade cigarette and popped it into his mouth to hang from lips stained ruby-red from betel nut juice. 'He wants a light. Give him one, Tony.' Hoyt struck a match but had no chance to light the man's mangled cigarette" (Dye 119).

The stranger is made familiar by entering into the magic circle of smoke. When Robert Jordan arrives at the cave of the partisans who view him and his mission with the deepest distrust, he determines the degree of their confidence and their allegiance by their willingness to accept his smokes.

Anselmo brought him a raw-hide covered stool and he sat down at the table. Pablo looked at him, as if he were going to speak again, then reached for the cigarettes.

Robert Jordan pushed them toward the others. He was not looking at them yet. But he noted one man took cigarettes and two did not. (Hemingway 49)

"What are you looking at?" one brother, the one with the scar, asked.

"Thee," Robert Jordan said.

"Do you see anything rare?"

"No," said Robert Jordan. "Have a cigarette?" (52)

The cigarettes Robert Jordan offers the partisans are Russian, themselves a sign of his political reliability because they came from the supplies of the Russian general, sent by Stalin to help combat the Fascists. Their acceptance is lent a ritual signification, equivalent to what in regular armies would be the meaning of a salute.

"There is food soon," he said. "Do you have tobacco?"

Robert Jordan went over to the packs and opening one, felt inside an inner pocket and brought out one of the flat boxes of Russian cigarettes he had gotten at Golz's headquarters. He ran his thumbnail around the edge of the box and, opening the lid, handed them to Pablo who took half a dozen. Pablo, holding them in one of his huge hands, picked one up and looked at it against the light. They were long narrow cigarettes with pasteboard cylinders for mouthpieces.

"Much air and little tobacco," he said. "I know these. The other with the rare name had them."

"Kashkin," Robert Jordan said and offered the cigarettes to the gypsy and Anselmo, who each took one.

"Take more," he said and they each took another. He gave them each four more, they making a double nod with the hand holding the cigarettes so that the cigarette dipped its end as a man salutes with a sword, to thank him. (20)

The cigarette, dipped in salute like a sword, or a flag, betokens loyalty and acknowledges hierarchy. It is often, as here, bowed in gratitude. Accepting a cigarette may be a kind of salute, showing respect and recognition to a military superior; it may also signify some more radical submission to the other:

The interrogator saw that he'd won. You could always tell from the eyes. The defiant ones, the hard ones, didn't shift their eyes. They might stare straight into yours, or more often at a fixed point of the wall behind you, but the hard ones would fix to a single place and draw their strength from it. Not this one. His eyes flickered around the room, searching for strength and finding none. Well, he's expecting this one to be easy. Perhaps one more gesture.

"Would you like a smoke?" The interrogator fished out a pack and shook one loose on the table.

The courier picked it up, and the white paper of the cigarette was his flag of surrender. (Clancy, *Cardinal of the Kremlin* 173)

The role that cigarettes play as a universal token of exchange has already been emphasized. In *Im Westen nichts Neues*, they frequently serve in wartime as the facilitator of bribes:

I quickly intervened and began by offering the little guy a cigarette." But aren't you authorized to give them morphine injections?" . . .

I put in his hand another couple of cigarettes: "Listen, do this to be nice. . . ." "Ok," he said. (Remarque 18)

When we finally left, Kat says to me: "What would you say to a roast goose?"

"Good," say I. And we hopped on a truck carrying ammunition. The trip cost two cigarettes. (70)

But more than a bribe, the cigarette is above all a bond, a token of the camaraderie that rivets soldiers to one another. It is a veil like the dusk at the end of a day of fighting that throws a beneficent shadow over fears and inspires generosity, allowing even the most miserly to communicate their solidarity with their comrades:

It was a warm evening, the dusk is like a veil, in whose shadow we feel secure. It brings one another closer together, that's why the usually miserly Tjaden treated me to a cigarette and helped me light it. (Remarque 42)

We felt like brothers and gave each other in turn the best pieces. The meal finished, I lit a cigarette and Kat a cigar. (73–74)

It is not merely that one cannot refuse to give a cigarette (or offer a light) but also that one cannot refuse to accept it, even if it is the last one. Even if a soldier tenders the last "dime" he has left to exchange in the barter of wartime economy, it is worse to refuse than to leave him with none. " 'Got a smoke I can borrow, man?' Chris stared into the soldier's haggard face and felt embarrassed about asking for anything from a guy in such pitiful condition. . . . The man stuck two fingers in an upper pocket of his shirt and fished out a C ration four-pack of Winstons. There was one crumpled cigarette left in the box. Chris nearly refused to accept the man's last smoke but he was afraid to do that" (Dye 208–9). To accept a last cigarette from a man in a pitiful condition, with nothing else to give, is to give him the gift of giving, which his self-respect needs most when he has nothing. To refuse it signals your own lack of generosity, your unfriendliness, or suspicion—a hint that you want to deny him the freedom of his liberality, to insult his gifts. It ends all possibility for trust or dialogue.

One of the most powerfully moving scenes in Remarque's great novel comes at the end, at the moment when Paul is given leave to return home. After the hell of war, he might be expected to exult; in fact, he is melancholy at the thought of abandoning his comrades. Many have already died; he wonders how many will still be alive when he returns:

> Of course, I have to pay for drinks, and we all lift a few. I am melancholy: I'll be gone for six weeks; naturally I have to be thankful, but how will it be when I return? Will they still all be here? Haje and Kemmerich have already gone.
>
> Whose turn is next?
>
> We drink and I look them in the face, one after the other. Albert sits next to me and smokes, and slowly we all gather together. . . . Over our heads a cloud of smoke spreads out. What would a soldier be without tobacco? (110–11)

The munificent cloud of smoke draws a ring around the battle-hardened comrades and circles them in its embrace, drawing them closer together. What would a soldier be without tobacco? He would be totally alone with his melancholy and mourning. The smoke of cigarettes holds the ghosts at bay—or rather, Indian-like, brings the departed spirits into the diminished circle of the living, joins the past to the present, and creates the beneficent illusion of an eternal present with no loss. A fleeting antidote to depression, cigarettes are the greatest treasure to the bereft.

But cigarettes also stimulate and sharpen the mind, promoting action. In war novels, they are frequently lit by officers at the moment they have to fix a plan or give an order. It is almost a requirement of command that decisions be taken only after a moment of self-concentration, the sign of reflective detachment and considered restraint before committing men's lives. "Lieutenant Wolfe . . . 'We're too damn vulnerable in here.' Barnes calmly lit a cigarette. 'How 'bout the flanks, lootenant? You got anybody on the flanks?' " (Dye 108). The lieutenant's alarm prompts the tough old sergeant to light up calmly before giving his superior orders in the guise of pointed questions. The pause to smoke is the sign of his having taken command in this situation, acting with deliberation in contrast to the officer's nervous indecision. In films, thinking is often represented by having a character light a cigarette, but war novels depict the reality behind that convention. "Cummings sighed, lit a cigarette. 'We've got to co-ordinate the staff work on this more thoroughly. Will you tell Hobart and Conn I'll want them with you this morning'" (Mailer 332). "The General lit a cigarette and extinguished the match with a slow wave of his hand. 'I assure you, Robert, there are a few other concerns in my mind'" (Hemingway 149).

Lighting the cigarette is a measure of the time of decision, the time it takes to conclude that one has done enough thinking. In fiction, the gesture often occurs at a critical moment, signaling that a fateful conclusion has been reached. "With luck some penetration might be made by them, but it was unlikely the frontal assault would be that successful. As it was, the timing might be very opportune. He lit a cigarette. The thing had its appeal" (Mailer 342).

As it often is for women, the cigarette for the soldier is sometimes a weapon to be wielded in the parallel war he wages with those who are entitled to command by virtue of the wisdom their position in the hierarchy presumably (but rarely) bestows. "Barnes [the tough sergeant] accepted a light for his cigarette from O'Neil's Zippo and blew a distracting stream of smoke into Wolfe's eyes [Wolfe, the cowardly lieutenant]. . . . Barnes's expression was caught somewhere between a grimace and a sneer. He silently took a long drag on his cigarette" (Dye 125). But it is sometimes also a token of the love that soldiers feel, a vehicle of romantic sacrifice. In Remarque's novel, our friends have met French girls whom they decide to try to visit. They have to wait until dark to swim across the canal; the bridge is forbidden and guarded. In the meantime, drinking beers in the canteen: "We are prey to an agitation without truce. We can't stay still. . . . Our hands are restless, we light innumerable cigarettes, until Kropp says: 'Really couldn't we also take them back a few cigarettes?' Then we put them back in our berets and saved some for them" (106).

A powerful source of consolation, an escape from anxiety, a form of pleasurable release, killing hunger and boredom—an instrument of civility, an aid to decision, a spur to alertness, Cupid's arrow, and a weapon against superiors, the cigarette a soldier smokes is everything he needs. What would a soldier be without cigarettes? He would not be himself. In novels, the cigarette is often a surrogate of the self, a visible sign of mind and heart. Smoke is the material substance that most closely resembles thought; the glowing tip represents the fierce fire of the soldier's will to live and to overcome. When it is extinguished, he dies. The most grimly surreal moment in *Platoon*, in the whole zoo-full of horrors it recounts, is described in a flash, a soldier's corpse glimpsed in the midst of retreat: "Another had the whole lower part of his torso torn away, with the legs. He lay dead in the trench, face down, his face yellow as a lemon; between the reddish hairs of his beard, a cigarette was still lit. It gleamed, until it went out between his lips" (Dye 92). The still-burning cigarette between lips has the surreality of a dream in which life and death are inverted; what is dead was only now living, and what is living, briefly, is only a dead thing—a tube of paper and tobacco. The alive soldier's cigarette was only a banal extension of his fingers, an insignificant adjunct to his activity, trying to survive. It becomes in death the last burning metonymy of his just-stilled breath, posthumously signaling death's imminence and the still-warm presence of his life. Only when his cigarette dies does the soldier's body become a corpse. In the ghostly in-between time before it goes out, the lit cigarette on a dead man's lips marks the time of the unthinkable passage from the fiery energy of life to the ash of extinction.

A signal change has occurred in the conventions that govern descriptions of cigarette smoking in war novels. Until roughly 1970 a cigarette was only a cigarette, the identity and uses of which were generally understood. With the Vietnam War, the unsuspecting soldier who took a cigarette from a comrade was liable to be surprised by a whole new possibility for mitigating the horrors of war.

> King disengaged and lit a C-ration match to what looked like a hand-rolled cigarette. . . .
>
> Crawford exhaled loudly and giggled. Chris had watched him inhale smoke but nothing came out of his mouth.
>
> "You volunteered for this shit, man?"
>
> Crawford just shook his head and sucked down another mouthful of smoke. King took the cigarette from his hand and turned to face Chris. . . .
>
> King profered [sic] the cigarette he'd been sharing with Crawford. It was sweaty, squashed and not very inviting. "Heah. Have some of this. You won't feel a thing after a few hits."
>
> The comments confirmed what Chris had suspected. The smoke was grass. (Dye 74–76)

If a smoke is grass, is a joint a cigarette? And if grass, is it the same thing to "profer" a joint as to proffer a cigarette?—assuming this is the author's misspelling, and a telling one. Perhaps the error was simply motivated by the fact that *profer*, accented on the first syllable, sounds more like "reefer." Subliminally, the sound of the misspelling prepares the surprise at the end of the paragraph, when the convention of the soldier's gesture is turned around, parodied: a smoke turns out to be grass; it acquires a new content, evoking other connotations, and assumes a different value. But conceptually, the neologism, *profer*, accented on the second syllable, as in the phrase "to profer a (marijuana) cigarette," makes the distinction between passing grass and offering a cigarette a question of prefer-ment. Smoking a cigarette is normally an individual act, except in times of penury. Smoking grass is usually a communal one; it draws the initiates into a circle of preference, including them and excluding others. To prefer is to give priority of rank, to erect a hierarchy. Some are high and some are low: the stoned and the straight. In *Platoon*, the protagonist goes from taking a little toke to shotgunning dope through the barrel of a rifle. The moment marks a rite of passage, a kind of promotion, the sign that he has arrived as a soldier:

> It was a matter of trust, Chris supposed. Either you were with 'em or you were against 'em. He cautiously pressed his lips against the cold muzzle of the weapon and blinked at the cheers from around the circle of heads. . . . Chris felt a warm flush from his armpits to the top of his skull. He closed his eyes and barely heard King's exclamation.
>
> "Can you dig it? In one night mah man Chris be goin' from a little toke to shotgunnin' dope. Ah bleeve the man has arrived." (Dye 96–97)

6 "l'air du temps"

Je ne veux pas travailler je veux fumer.
—Guillaume Apollinaire

Why do I laugh when I look at the photographs in this book? I find some of them beautiful, some moving, but all inevitably funny. I ask myself, Is there something inherently comic or witty about pictures of people smoking? Not much, you might think, these days; in the present climate of alarm, every one of them seems to be shadowed by its latent negative, like an X ray, showing the smoker's martyred lungs. A few of the pictures in the book were taken with an intention to make you laugh—the portrait of Cocteau (p. 5), for example—but you have to adopt a very peculiar perspective to find any humor in most of them, and even then you may not be amused. Roland Barthes hardly ever finds photos funny, and he doesn't like it at all when he does. In *La chambre claire*, he disparages a picture by the great Hungarian photographer André Kertész that features two statues standing behind a window facing the street: "I like Kertész, but I neither like humor in music nor in photography" (59).

Conversely, Barthes likes pictures that wound him—that prick. In the photographs he loves he can always discover a point—some punctual, telling detail—that touches him deeply, pierces him, and produces a little poignancy, a melancholic occasion for mourning the irrecoverable pastness of the moment the photograph records:

A word exists in Latin to designate this wound, this prick [*piqûre*], this mark made by a pointed instrument; this word suits me all the more in that it alludes to the idea of punctuation, and these photos of which I am speaking are in effect punctuated as it were, sometimes even spotted with these sensitive points; precisely, these marks, these wounds are points. So I will call this element . . . punctum, because a punctum is also that: a prick, a little hole, a small spot, a little cut [coupure]—and also a throw [coup] of dice. The punctum of a photo is that element of chance in it that poignantly pricks me [me point] (but also bruises and makes me suffer). (49)

Cigarettes in these photos touch me just as pointedly, but the bruise is more like a hot little poke in the ribs; I laugh. And unlike the chancy, unpredictable nature of Barthes's punctum, whose locus can never be known in advance, for me it is always the same point, the identical little white tube in the photograph that provokes hilarity. In my eye, the wittiest punctum is invariably located at the top of the cigarette, at the burning point of fire that is rarely recorded by the photograph.

Fire is not normally "seen" like other substantial things; its energy is rendered visible by the effects of movement that it makes in the air. Fire is its movement; freeze it, it's out. It does not lend itself to the immobility of what Barthes calls a "pose." Observing a photograph, he says, "I include fatally in my look the thought of that instant, however brief, when a real thing finds itself immobile before the eye" (122). But fire is not exactly a thing, it is its mobility, the work of energy, ergon, force in movement over time. Its representation defies the photograph's power to create the posed illusion of time frozen in a frame, the lure of the stopped moment, whose image can be seized and represented with fixed limits, within the coherent unity of two dimensions. Artists represent fire with icons of it (which are like valentine hearts standing for love); they don't draw it so much as they indicate it by drawing conventional signs for fire.

A still camera cannot capture the fiery heart at the end of a cigarette any more than it can shoot the sun (except under certain highly technical conditions). The emulsion cannot record the condition of its own chemical transformation—the darkening of its silver halide salts by the light that comes from burning sources. The light of fire is the god of photography whose face is forever forbidden to be seen but whose metonymical surrogate, like a little idol, is always popping up at the ends of fingers or touched to lips. Every cigarette in a photo is a fetish of the god at its tip, invisible in the photo that worships it.

The general impossibility of photographing smoking is the little joke, the witty point that all the cigarettes recorded in these photographs diversely illustrate. Every photograph of the act of smoking a cigarette records the cigarette but not the smoking—the conditions of its possibility, the means of its enactment, but not the act itself. The white tube in the picture is only a metonymy for the smoking of burning tobacco at the end. The eye is inevitably drawn to the tip of fire, the twinkling surrogate for the smoker's own spirit, and both are invisible in the frozen frame. Like the moment it records, the glowing cinder is extinguished in the photo. It is as if being observed photographically stubbed it out. The camera kills, as many cultures believe; Barthes explains the refusal of many Chinese to be photographed because they fear the camera's malevolent eye. The dead cigarette in the picture is the permanent index of the aggressive intrusion of the photographer's foreign, spying eye into the subject's private life. It marks the violence performed in fixing an external perspective, hence a kind of death, on the subjective standpoint of the spirit whose mask is frozen—captured in its frame. The dead cigarette in the photograph bears witness against the illusion to which photography succumbs, the claim that the camera lays bare the truth of the subject; it is the witty revenge of the subject on the camera's mythifying pretension to represent the life of the spirit in front of it. It signals the unrepresentable inner life of the subject, whose habits, thoughts, and intimate pleasures are evoked because it is a picture of someone smoking. The dead cigarette points up the limits of the camera's power to represent what it "sees," its ability to record only facticity, not transcendence, as Sartre would say. Photography records an *en-soi*, the image of a corporal self present to itself in its substantial being; but it cannot represent, except figurally, the *pour-soi* of the self's capacity to be radically other than how it appears, how it is, at this frozen moment.

I know I am not alone in finding pictures of people smoking funny. During a few months in 1927, Jacques-Henri Lartigue took ninety-five photographs of famous and unknown women smoking (or pretending to smoke, for his camera), and published them in a little album he called *Les femmes aux cigarettes*. The contemporary viewer would interpret it as a hymn to the beauty of feminine gestures and poses. But Lartigue's attitude toward his subjects, which he acknowledges in his brief introduction, is a hoot. He writes that he could not look at a woman smoking a cigarette without laughing: "To me, a woman smoking cigarettes was something extraordinarily funny. The absurdity of a woman putting in her mouth a rolled slip of tissue paper filled with tobacco really puzzled me. More than that it amused me. And I have never taken a photograph without one thought in my head: to amuse myself. My interest has always been to do something funny, and *les femmes aux cigarettes*—that was funny" (1). Lartigue admits to being puzzled by the "absurdity" of women smoking, but for all that he is no less amused. Whatever remains mysterious but provokes laughter must owe its origin to the return of some repressed possibility. Here, no doubt, it is the spectacle of women's freedom, which the male taboo against their smoking, violated at the camera's behest, has for centuries interdicted and masked with denials. Women ought not to, therefore they do not smoke. That is the contradictory, wishful assertion contained in Hitler's proclamation: "Deutsche Weiber rauchen nicht." Smoking cigarettes is both a source of visible sensual pleasure and an emblem of women's erotic life. At least that is how it appears to men, for whom the sight of women smoking is both threatening and intensely, voyeuristically exciting.

Frequently the smoker displays a resistance to being photographed by brandishing the lit cigarette between lips or fingers in a gesture that is provocative or hostile. Frequently in photographs, the cigarette is wielded with effrontery or coquettishness, as a weapon or a veil against the eye of the camera, refusing and therefore soliciting even more its curious intrusion. In general, the closer cigarettes appear to the mouth of the subject the more aggressive is the gesture they convey. Women holding cigarettes between their teeth or dangling from lips, like the bold women in this book, are wittily (perhaps wittingly) telling the photographer where he can stick his lens. Mary McCarthy (p. 161) is doing many things with the cigarette in her upraised left hand—conducting a score, extending the dance of her pen, taking digital pleasure, striking a pose, and giving the finger to the intruder on her meal. Lartigue's laughter at the spectacle exactly fulfills the double requirement that Freud specifies in *Wit and Its Relation to the Unconscious* as the general condition of its production. A compromise formation between fear of the law and desire for pleasure, laughter erupts whenever some dangerous psychic content (like aggressive feminine sexuality) is exposed but mitigated under the guise of some trivial, neutral form—such as a rolled slip of tissue paper filled with tobacco. The reader may find nothing funny in what makes Lartigue laugh, but if she is inclined to be charitable, she may decide that it makes him a dupe, someone whose laughter is foolish—itself an occasion for mirth.

Lartigue's nervously giddy reaction, of course, had some historical parallels. An excellent example is the movie *Casablanca*, where everybody smokes all the time—except for women. None is ever seen actually to take a drag. In one of the opening scenes of the film, an anonymous woman, sitting next to Sam's piano in the crowd of Rick's American Café, can be seen holding a lit, half-smoked cigarette at the end of her fingers. She starts

Mary McCarthy
Photo © Inge Morath. By permission of Magnum Photos, Inc.

to take a puff, but interrupts the movement of the cigarette to her lips and smiles as if she were suddenly inhibited by a distracting thought or momentarily enchanted by Sam's tone. In fact, she was probably checked by a sign from the film's director. The strength of the taboo in 1942 that prevented Hollywood films from showing women smoking allows us to appreciate the little scandal of Henri Lartigue's *Femmes aux cigarettes*.

But times have changed. What amused Lartigue is not what we find funny today. Conversely, now *Casablanca* is the scandal—not only because women are not allowed to be seen smoking, while men do nothing else, but because that convention belongs to a whole repertory of chauvinist assumptions that make it a paradigmatically phallic film. A woman looking at *Casablanca*, if she is not charmed, is angry, and if not angry then amused watching men manipulate their cigarettes, playing out their unconscious assumption of mastery with all its fears and hollow pretension, in the gestures with which they offer, accept, light up and throw down, inhale, exhale, choreograph, and punch their cigarettes. If Lartigue, like other men, finds it funny to look at women smoking, women looking at men smoking in *Casablanca* may equally be amused, but for reasons that are symmetrically inverse.

Through most of this book I have studiously avoided mentioning the phallic character of cigarettes. The metaphorical operation of identifying a phallic symbol any time a textual detail resembles the male organ debases the notion in Freud, where its function is considerably more complex.[1] Finding phallic symbols has become such a vulgar critical gesture that it is virtually the only one American adolescents learn to perform in school. (The most trivial phallic symbols are pistols, bull horns, telescopic lenses, and naked cigars favored by rough men; it is a joke when they are all pointing in the same direction, as in the photograph on page 163. The joke is on the seated tough guy, making a movie of the revolution, who does not know that multiple penises in Freud are the sign not of virile potency but of castration; see "The Medusa Head.")

However reductive the phallic equation, nevertheless it cannot be denied that there are times when a cigarette is more than a cigarette. Most critics, for example, agree that Humphrey Bogart in the role of Rick, the protagonist of *Casablanca*, plays him as a "Prick."[2] At the beginning of the film he refuses to protect a member of the Resistance from the clutches of the Vichy police, and treats women who love and need him with indifferent cruelty, even brutality. His phallic character is emblematized by his cigarette, which identifies him from the first. After the camera has passed

Sam Fuller Shooting a Film
Photo © Micha Bar-Am. By permission of Magnum Photos, Inc.

through the smoke-filled bar of Rick's Café and entered its inner sanctum, where the roulette tables are, Humphrey Bogart appears for the first time in *Casablanca*. Before we see Himself (i.e., the Face), a hand—his hand—crosses the screen on its way to a crystal ashtray; it is holding a cigarette, characteristically, at the end of thumb and index finger. Imperceptibly it flicks the ash before abandoning the cigarette in the ashtray, where, for a few frames, it smokes anonymously. The now-free hand receives a notepad from a waiter, puts it down, and takes up a pen; it signs "O.K. Rick" on the line dotted for an "*autorisation*," authorizing that a thousand Moroccan francs be paid by Rick's American Café. The hand hands back the pad. With one finger it then touches the mitered point of a white bishop that has been taken off the board; Bogart, in the film a "thinker" (in life a serious student of the game), is playing chess with himself. Are we also supposed to deduce that the player has some high episcopal dignity in this congregation of Casablancan society, or is he *fou*? Touching the tip of the bishop may be a subtly sexual sign, or it may be a way of establishing the prickly, punctilious nature of Bogart's character. The hand next reaches for the still-smoldering cigarette. We first see the Face of Bogart as he takes the cigarette to the corner of his lips, between his thumb and first finger, curling his fingers around the slender tube the way a soldier might shield it with his palm. He takes a big hit, unfiltered; inhaling deeply, he grimaces as he toughs out the sharp malaise accompanying a violent nicotine high. Then, exhaling the poison, luxuriating in the little victory over himself, he wickedly blows the smoke back up his nose and effusively streams it above his head, now haloed in gray.

"O.K., Rick" is what Bogart may be seen to sign on the bottom of the chit before we see Bogart playing Rick, the owner and author of his place—this play—into which the camera has just ushered us, at the political and sentimental center of *Casablanca*—this allegorical interior of the world at war. "Everybody Comes to Rick's" is the name of the never-produced play from which the screenplay was originally taken. But in case there were any doubt about the authority or the author of the performance we are about to see, Bogart signs a second time, endorsing his performance by introducing it with the little scene of smoking his signature cigarette, what Annie Leclerc in *Au feu du jour* calls "the 'Humphrey Bogart' cigarette." The indistinction between the actor behind the role and the role assumed by the star immensely complicates the task of biographical attribution even as it invites us to speculate on the relation between the man, the persona, and the characters he plays in film. Throughout *Casablanca*, a beacon plays across the set. One critic rightly reads it as a sign of "escape or confinement," evoking one of the dominant, explicit themes of the film, set in a city at the furthest extremity of war-torn continents, where everybody is "waiting, waiting, waiting." It is also a spotlight illuminating Bogart, frequently following his exits and entrances, touching him alone with a halo of light. The only time we see him silhouetted in the film, against a round shadow like the negative of the beacon's spot, he has gone to the large wall safe of his office to extract the money that appears to be his character's—perhaps his own—principal motive for action. Silhouetted against the wall in profile is a cigarette jutting from his lips. Bogart's genius orchestrates the way he constantly displays the material underside of the persona he is playing—the idiosyncracies of the star beneath the role he plays. The cigarette he smokes is not only Rick Blaine's, it is also Humphrey Bogart's. Bogart is known to have improvised most of his lines in *Casablanca*; the multiple signatures are intended to signal his proprietary role in casting the character of Rick in the hard-boiled mold he had invented and continuously refined. That persona has a life of its own, one that many, like Woody Allen in *Play It Again, Sam*, have taken for a model—including Bogart himself.

Assuming there is something she calls "la cigarette 'Humphrey Bogart,'" Annie Leclerc gives it what might too quickly be called a "feminist" reading, except that she introduces it anecdotally with reference to its being smoked by a woman—one who resembles herself:

Now I remember the taste of that cigarette, its vile, raw taste of lying. It's not a bland cigarette. How many films would lose their savor, how many characters their intensity if one took from them this cigarette. It's the "Humphrey Bogart" cigarette. The cigarette of the cop, the journalist, the bad guy, the cigarette of someone "in the know" [*avertie*], forewarned. It's the cigarette of the politician, the scientist, the militant, man or woman. It is always the military cigarette, colonial, imperial. It is the phantom of power desired, aspired to, smoked for so long that it ends by assuming form, becoming solid. . . .

Now, I don't say that all cigarettes are made of the same stuff [*tabac*], nor even that every smoker at sometime or other has smoked one of these. I simply say that the other day I saw a "Humphrey Bogart" cigarette in the hands of a woman, and that woman could have been me, I could have smoked that cigarette, and that horrified me.

Why was it necessary, why is it always necessary to convert humiliation into arrogance, to suppress infirmity with orthopedics? Why does being afraid of everything hide itself behind being afraid of nothing? (108)

The lie that Humphrey Bogart's cigarette tells is, at bottom, the lie of what Leclerc elsewhere calls "phallocracy," some of whose turgid masks she enumerates: cop, soldier, politician, militant. Phallocracy gives rise to phantoms of power, whose swaggering self-assurance masks the arbitrary character of their claim to possess authority and to know how to use it. The "Humphrey Bogart" cigarette is one of those masks, posing as fearless arrogance, concealing the lacks that lie beneath the lie of a role. Annie Leclerc diagnoses the castration beneath the insolence of the tough-guy pose, the male's self-doubt that Bogart enacts in the gestures of smoking the phallocratic cigarette in a film that may be taken to be its textbook. Smoking there on his curled lip, the cigarette is the erect visible embodiment of power aspired to, the phantom of power become solid and taking form.

In this respect, Leclerc's reading of the Humphrey Bogart cigarette seems to follow an orthodox Freudian reading of *Casablanca*, which similarly finds beneath brave appearances unmistakable signs of impotence, inversion, and rage. Harvey Greenberg, M.D., a practicing psychotherapist, has written a book called *The Movies on Your Mind*. He brings the blunt instrument of his vulgar Freudianism to bear on the carefully polished surfaces of Hollywood movies. In a trumpeting tone, he lays bare, beneath edifying appearances, barely repressed Oedipal family romances, which he sees as paradigms of castration violence and paranoid perversion. His triumphalism leads him to write sentences like this one: "Other sound interpretations of *Casablanca*, in my obviously biased opinion, still suffer from the failure to account for the Oedipal theme" (104). His success in revealing these subterranean sexual themes may owe as much to his bias as to their having been consciously written into Hollywood movies by writers and directors whose sense of intellectual modernity in 1940, when *Casablanca* was made, included the recently disseminated, American ego-psychology interpretation of Freud's discoveries; the movies he examines may well have been made with viewers like Dr. Greenberg in mind.[3]

It may be ungenerous to take as a sign of Greenberg's misreading how the film seems to confirm his reading at every point—triumphantly too true to be good. It is certainly no simple error that leads him to consider Rick, the principal character of *Casablanca*, as if he were the barely displaced surrogate of the doctor's real patient, Humphrey Bogart, whose conflicted sexuality is the analyst's real subject. He is too good a reader to have missed the way Humphrey Bogart seems to countersign in the film the character of Rick Blaine, and he does not fail to perceive that there are other hidden themes as well as the Oedipal one: Casablanca, he says, is "the silver screen's headiest blending of patriotic and sexual fantasy"(81). Dr. Greenberg's reading of the film need not be contested, but what he calls the blending of the political and the sexual is in fact a more forceful articulation of that relation than he sees. It is what makes this film one of the most remarkably successful pieces of political propaganda that America produced during World War II, at a time when enormous artistic resources were being invested on both sides of the struggle. Like most propaganda, its real aim was to influence domestic political opinion, and the principal sign and instrument for using the sexual to pass political messages is the innumerable cigarettes smoked in the film.

Dr. Greenberg, of course, never analyzes the cigarettes. That is part of the interpretive price he pays for failing to make explicit the premises of his assumption that he is authorized to address the unconscious of Hollywood characters. But he pays the rest of the price when he writes, for example, "Rick's murderous [unconscious] impulses towards Laszlo [the leader of the Resistance] find an acceptable displacement in the person of [the Nazi] Major Strasser" (120).Greenberg lends to the fictional Rick a dimension of unconscious moral choice, an Oedipal compulsion, and a notion of what is acceptable (shooting Nazis) that suspiciously resembles an autobiographical, identificatory projection; the doctor can invent the unconscious of Rick Blaine at the price of unwittingly revealing to the world the dreams of Harvey Greenberg. Greenberg's own identification makes him resemble Humphrey Bogart less than Woody Allen, whose Oedipal remake of the final airport scene of Casablanca in Play It Again, Sam anticipates the doctor's conclusions. He half acknowledges this in a "postscript" in which he cites "the amusing commentary" of Woody Allen, whose "nebbish hero bolsters a sagging ego by hallucinating Humphrey Bogart as sexual mentor." What the nebbish view of Casablanca advanced by Allen and Greenberg ignores are the heroic historical struggles the film not only evokes but seeks fiercely to decide.

What is a nebbish? Unlike conventional thematic critics, who discover the content of the text at the surface in its ostensible declarations, psychoanalysts like Greenberg dig a little deeper and bring up latent contents (homosexuality, castration, incestuous murder) that now manifest their once occulted meaning. Glossing over the political drama of loss, betrayal, and heroism, Greenberg reads *Casablanca* as enacting castration fears, Oedipal defeat, and the mourning resulting from abandonment by a beloved woman: a nebbish is a phallic ego that sags. The doctor presumes to demonstrate that beneath the image of the incomparably seductive tough guy is the latent homosexuality of the "strange" character played by Humphrey Bogart: "The idea that Rick has been a closet queen all along is lunatic (and to members of the Bogart cult, heretical). But his rejection of Ilsa [Ingrid Bergman] in favor of a friendship that will thrive in the sacrifice of combat is certainly informed by Rick's fear of women and his corollary misogyny" (103). The psychiatrist must join the company of lunatics (and heretics) if he is to affirm his slightly crazy notion that Blaine-Bogart is "a closet queen." Greenberg says that Rick's "rejection" of Ilsa-Ingrid is "certainly informed" by his Oedipal fears and hatreds, precisely because it is not at all certain in the film that her departure should be seen as a rejection, let alone one "informed" with sexual motives. Nor is it ever clearly explained how Rick's decision to abandon Ilsa "in favor of a friendship that will thrive in the sacrifice of combat" is compatible with his "fear of women and his corollary misogyny."[4] What value is the doctor assigning to friendship and to the sacrifice of combat? Is Blaine-Bogart forgoing Ilsa-Ingrid in the name of something exalted or frightened? Are we dealing here with sublimation or repression? Noble or nebbish?

At the end of the film, Rick renounces the woman in favor of a cause more important than himself, despite having repeatedly said throughout the film, "I stick my neck out for nobody." Like what Freud, in "The Moses of Michelangelo," calls "a cultural hero," he sacrifices love and assumes his castration to promote higher interests of humanity—the struggle of the Resistance against a cruel Occupation. The conjunction of love and sacrifice is represented in the film by the innumerable cigarettes that are smoked.

Cigarettes are everywhere in *Casablanca*; they are the dominant visual feature of Rick's Café, which is a micro-polis because it is the political nerve center of the wartime city, crowded with refugees, spies, criminals, and soldiers of fortune, rife with prostitution and corruption, picturesquely colored with the cynicism occasioned by the permanent spectacle of desperation. The camera's attention is not so much on the character of Humphrey Bogart as on the place he owns and runs, whose prominent sign on the roof, frequently seen in the film, spells out "Rick's American Café."

Before Bogart appears in the film, the camera cuts to the front of Rick's bar. At night, from outside, its sign seems to float above the place. The name in lights is surrounded by a curly neon bubble, as if the place could speak, as in a comic book, in balloons above its head—as if it were a character, the principal character in the film. The café at night is a kind of brothel, visited by the whole cosmopolitan society of Casablanca seeking pleasure and escape. As in a brothel or a movie house, at Rick's Café, says Ferrari, the head of the black market, "people are the principal commodity." At the center of this bordello is the tinkling piano of Sam, whose music, brilliantly performed, is the guardian of the memory of the place, of its place in the momentous history of the war going on all around and within.

A long, wordless sequence of camera shots takes us into the café, as if we were the paying customers (we are), past the usher at the door, past the long bar, into the inner sanctum of the roulette wheels, to the elevated solitary table where sits—in front of a chessboard, an ashtray, and a calendar—the boss, Bogart—thinking, smoking, as time goes by. At the beginning of the sequence, camera-right of the door, two well-dressed couples go in; cut to the sign, Rick's American Café; pan down: two American officers escorting a woman are followed inside by two Arab men unaccompanied (no women for the Arabs). Then, as the camera begins to move forward, we see the back of an elegant woman going through the door followed by a man in a white suit, which proleptically resembles the gorgeous white one that Laszlo, the hero of the Resistance, wears throughout the film—an adumbration of his and Ingrid Bergman's approaching (smashing) entrance together, and in contrast to the black uniforms of the Nazis in the film.

As the camera goes through the door it receives a slight nod from the fezzed doorman. It is blocked for a moment by the arm of a passing waiter, which moves off to permit us to catch a glimpse of a man, sitting in profile at a table, carrying a cigarette to his lips and quickly taking a puff. He exhales rapidly as the camera moves to follow the progress of the couple to their table. The camera momentarily loses them behind a screen just as it cuts to a different angle, inside the smoke-filled café behind the back of the band, at the right hand of the drummer, whose slightly elevated position affords him the best possible view of the whole foggy place. As the couple vanish, a waiter carrying two champagne coupes on a small round tray emerges on the right hand side of the screen in the middle ground. The camera picks him up and follows him across the room as he weaves in and out of view, with one hand brilliantly directing the tray in front of him, like Sartre's *garçon de café*. He is blocked from view just as he comes behind the beautiful couple for whom the champagne is intended, darkly profiled against the brilliant haze. Suddenly there is a flash as the handsome soldier elegantly lights his own cigarette, at the same time in one movement turning toward the turning profile of his stunning, dark-haired companion. At that instant the waiter appears between them and with a slight inclination holds up the tray of champagne glasses. The soldier exhales, and for an instant, before they take the glasses, the screen is filled with the brilliantly centered image of the glasses of champagne over which momentarily hovers a perfect little cloud of gray smoke. Framed by the darkly beautiful profiles and seen slightly from below, the smoking wine glasses catch all the light of the café—an epiphanic moment of unspeakable beauty in the film. "Everyone Comes to Rick's" for the experience of that epiphany—a moment frozen in a frame but moved by the projector to represent the ecstatic suspension of time, or the fiction of another time, outside the war, that the multiple diversions of Rick's American Café temporarily propose. For Umberto Eco the bar evokes multiple archetypal scenes: Foreign Legion, Grand Hotel, Mississippi River Boat, New Orleans Brothel, the Gambling Inferno in Macao or Singapore, the Smuggler's Paradise, the Last Outpost on the edge of the Desert (204).

But Rick's is also the place where refugees from the war are obliged to come to get a visa to leave Casablanca on the plane to Lisbon, the first step on the way to freedom in America. The bar is the real, effectively the only, embassy in town that provides the service. Its bustling success is attributable not only to Rick's meticulously calculated enterprise but also to his political neutrality and moral ambivalence. He practices an easy camaraderie with the representatives of the Vichy government, lending them his place to carry out their often brutal operations, gaily bribing them, all the while maintaining an amused indifference to the hypocrisy of their pretended independence of Nazi overseers, whose *droit de regard* and indirect commands are seen actually to determine the political essence of Vichy's *soi*. In most respects Rick's politics in *Casablanca* is indistinguishable from that of the American consul in North Africa in 1941; his neutrality toward the bitter political struggles that pit Vichy and its Nazi masters against the Free, the "Fighting French," exactly mirrors the stance of the Roosevelt government. The similarities even include the fact that Rick is hostile toward the leader of the Resistance movement, just as Franklin Roosevelt despised the arrogant obstinacy of Charles de Gaulle (who was leading the struggle from London) and suspected, wrongly, that it signaled his bonapartist ambition to make a coup d'état. We can appreciate some-

Humphrey Bogart
Photo © Dennis Stock. By permission of Magnum Photos, Inc.

thing of Roosevelt's impatience with the sanctimonious self-importance of de Gaulle and gauge its tone from the response Rick gets in the film from Laszlo, the leader of the Resistance. Rick asks: "Do you sometimes wonder if it's worth all this? I mean what you're fighting for." "If we stop breathing, we'll die; if we stop fighting our enemies, the whole world will die," answers Laszlo-de Gaulle, modestly staking the fate of the world on the continued breathing of what smacks as a royal "we" (Koch, *Casablanca* 160–61). Rick's irritation is forgivable when he protests to Ingrid-Ilsa, the wife of the great man: "Do I have to hear again what a great man your husband is? What an important cause he's fighting for?" (154). In the film, Laszlo, like de Gaulle in life, smokes cigarettes with great dignity and calm, continuously; nearly every breath he takes in the film is filled with cigarette smoke—the very air of political struggle.

The politics of Rick's "American" café, taken as a smoky displacement of the American consulate in Casablanca in 1942, reflects this country's continuing recognition of Vichy, despite the growing number of voices inciting the American government to withdraw its diplomats, as the British and Canadians had done, and throw its support to the forces struggling under the banner of the Cross of Lorraine. In the opening scenes of *Casablanca*, the Vichy police shoot and kill a man who is clutching papers emblazoned with the Free French emblem. In the café Laszlo and Ilsa are approached by a man who pretends to want to sell them a ring. He is Berger, a secret agent of the Resistance at the service of his leader, a man ready for any sacrifice:

> Berger.—You look like a couple who are on their way to America. You'll find a market there for this ring. I'm forced to sell it at a great sacrifice. The ring is quite unique. (He opens the ring to show the Cross of Lorraine concealed within.)
> Laszlo.—Yes, I am very interested.
> (Koch, *Casablanca* 86)

The plot of the film that leads Bogart from a compromising neutrality toward Vichy to solidarity in arms with de Gaulle may be seen to enact, allegorically, the desire of many, particularly Jewish, producers in Hollywood to see American recognition withdrawn, the way Rick at the end abandons his café in unoccupied French Casablanca. In the final scene of the film, Captain Renaud, until now the chief of the local police, becomes a "patriot," decides to join the Resistance, and trashes a bottle of Vichy water in disgust. He and Rick, former cynics, decide at the end to leave Casablanca together and join the Free French forces in Brazzaville, a West African colony that in 1940 had rallied to de Gaulle—the place from where he had broadcast the first calls to free France. "Louis," says Rick, at the end, as if he were apostrophizing an avatar of the Bourbon monarchy, "this looks like the beginning of a beautiful friendship."

In the foggy final scene, as in a dream of solidarity, the American and the now Fighting Frenchman go off together arm in arm into the mist of the airport to the swelling strains of the "Marseillaise," whose motifs are heard accompanying the opening frames of the film, the closing ones, and some of the most stirring moments in between. The film's emotional high point is the symbolic victory that the Resistance wins over the Nazis when the "Marseillaise" taken up by the people in the bar progressively drowns out the strains of Nazi soldiers singing "Die Wacht am Rhein." Dr. Greenberg entitles his chapter on *Casablanca*: "If It's So Schmaltzy, Why Am I Crying?" (which seems a little strange; schmaltzy movies and national anthems always make me cry). The strength of the movie's sentimental appeal is closely linked to the power of that great French hymn to awaken, even in Americans, dreams of collective triumph over tyrannical oppression, and to embody those dreams in the surging progressions of its melody and the exalted imperatives of its rhetoric. The film evokes the dream of America in its opening frame as a globe turns from the New World to the Old and a radio speaker narrates:

> With the coming of the Second World War many eyes in imprisoned Europe turned hopefully, or desperately, toward the freedom of the Americas. Lisbon became the great embarkation point. But not everybody could get to Lisbon directly. And so a tortuous roundabout refugee trail sprang up. Paris to Marseille. Across the Mediterranean to Oran. Then by train or auto or port across the rim of Africa to Casablanca in French Morocco. Here the fortunate ones through money or influence or luck might obtain exit visas and scurry to Lisbon and from Lisbon to the New World. But the others wait in Casablanca, and wait, and wait, and wait. (Koch, *Casablanca* 12).

The film's immaculate hostility toward American foreign policy is purified of any suggestion of anti-Americanism. In case the point were missed, Carl, the cuddly waiter at Rick's, brings an elderly, visibly Jewish couple some best cognac to celebrate their imminent, emigrant departure. They raise their glasses and each in turn toasts: "To America. To America. To America." The political allegory is never more explicit than when Bogart-Blaine, drinking heavily, slams his fist down on the table and turns to Sam:

> "If it's December 1941 in Casablanca, what time is it in New York?"
> "My watch stopped."
> "I'll bet they're asleep in New York; I'll bet they're asleep all over America." (28)

If America is asleep to the cynicism of U.S. policy toward Vichy's collaboration, the film is intended to awaken it to what are presumed to be its true interests. As a piece of propaganda, the sentimental enactment of a political message, it was remarkably and almost immediately successful in changing Roosevelt's diplomacy.

On the eve of the New Year 1943, Franklin Roosevelt screened the recently released *Casablanca* for his guests, at a time when his government's policy toward Vichy France was becoming daily more intolerable to a country at war with its masters. Vichy, which had sentenced de Gaulle to death in absentia, was not only recognized but courted by the United States: the American ambassador to Vichy was Roosevelt's close personal friend, Admiral William Leahy. In January 1943, ten days after seeing the film, Roosevelt flew to Casablanca (the first American president to travel by air while in office) for a historic meeting with Winston Churchill. The first priority of the conference was to coordinate Allied diplomacy toward the representatives of France in North Africa. General Jean François Darlan, who had been the commander of Vichy forces in North Africa until his assassination in December, had supported French collaboration with the Nazis until the Allies landed in North Africa in 1942; he had then ordered Vichy forces to join their side. Roosevelt condemned the assassination, calling it "murder in the first degree." Darlan was immediately replaced as high commissioner in French Africa by General Henri Honoré Guiraud, a close friend of Marshal Pétain. De Gaulle, living in London with the support of Churchill, accompanied Churchill to Casablanca and with much reluctance agreed to be photographed shaking hands with Guiraud. Within six months, he had succeeded in eliminating Guiraud's influence over Free French forces. In Casablanca, Roosevelt, at Churchill's urging, overcame his suspicions, agreed to abandon his recognition of Vichy and his support for Guiraud, and shifted American diplomacy in favor of de Gaulle's Free French—a move that culminated in August of that year with

America's lending its full support to the French National Committee. That decision made Roosevelt and de Gaulle objective allies in the struggle against Nazism.

The beginning of a beautiful friendship between (f)Ri(n)ck(lin) and "Louis," at the end of *Casablanca*, is interpreted by Dr. Greenberg as a "homosexual" choice. But the necessity that requires cementing a bond between French and American brothers is not internal to the plot's psychological logic; rather, it uses that logic to conceal its implication in the fierce struggle for loyalties that was about to begin. The film itself was a major player whose lobbying on behalf of the Free French actually may have made a difference in the course of Roosevelt's foreign policy and the history of American relations with France. Roosevelt's showing the just-released film at the White House on New Year's Eve, ten days before flying to Casablanca, corresponds to the moment in the film when Bogart-Blaine, abjuring his moral neutrality, gives the nod to the band in the club to strike up the "Marseillaise," drowning out the voices of soldiers singing a Nazi hymn. Roosevelt, weeping in the dark of the White House screening room, may have decided then and there on the shift in favor of the Free French that the conference in Casablanca made tangible. Humphrey Bogart, playing the patron of Rick's Café, must certainly have known he was playing Roosevelt. Did Roosevelt, at Casablanca, entertain the suspicion that he was enacting Humphrey Bogart?

Dr. Greenberg says nothing about the cigarettes in *Casablanca*. If he had he would have probably been content to consider them "phallic," but he omits them precisely, perhaps, because he feels the resistance they would pose to his reading of the Oedipal drama—because they would force him to modify his idea of the phallus. He allows himself to be duped by the film into believing he has discovered its unconscious message, while the movie uses his interpretative satisfaction to slip him another, starkly political message. He has failed to see that the cigarette as sexual fetish had by 1942 become such a commonplace cliché that it could be used, even by Hollywood, to conceal other more subtle themes. As Bogart says at the end, as if addressing Dr. Greenberg's family romance: "The problems of three little people don't amount to a hill of beans in this crazy world" (175).

Cigarettes in *Casablanca* may be masks behind which frightened men hide their doubts, their cowardices, their hesitations, and their impotence. The cigarette hides fear behind an aggressive pose, one that expresses contempt for the fear and weakness of others. The Humphrey Bogart cigarette, held between thumb and index, allows the tough guy to smoke and to show his knuckles. Whenever two men are engaged in a relation of competition or rivalry, whether sexual or political, they are scrupulous to show each other the back of their hands, usually balled into a fist. That gesture is in contrast to the way women, in Lartigue's book, frequently smoke cigarettes between two extended fingers, curling the others down to the palm. Half-seductive, the woman's hand holding the cigarette veils her, concealing, inviting, just as the smoke softens her outlines; half-defensive, the curled fingers sketch a fist in the direction of the other while holding toward herself a little secret hollow in the hand.

Peter Lorre is one of Casablanca's principal victims. He chain-smokes nervously, holding the cigarette close to his body, taking rapid, short puffs, twirling the cigarette between his fingers, as if to offer a visual emblem of the inverted phallus of his castration. If the act of pointing a lit cigarette at others and blowing smoke in their direction is often an aggressive gesture, a response to the unwelcome intrusion of other subjectivities, turning the cigarette inside one's palm is a sign of self-immolation. As a general rule, the farther one holds the cigarette from one's body, the more confident and peaceful is the pose.

Claude Raines, who plays Captain Renaud, also smokes continuously in the film. His intimate connection to Bogart is reflected in the way his smoking mirrors that of his rival, his companion and political compatriot—he is Bogart's homosexual object choice, if one were to believe Dr. Greenberg's "camp" interpretation. At other times, caught in the increasingly contradictory constraints of his impossible position, cynically trying to serve many masters, sentimentally and politically repulsed by the Nazis, Captain Renaud is shown by the camera taking long, deep puffs of a cigarette and blowing vast clouds of smoke slowly in the air, the visible manifestation of his complexly textured ruminations. Cigarette smoke is one of the material substances in the world that closely resemble the substance of thought. Both Laszlo, the leader of the Resistance, and Colonel Strasser, the Nazi commander, smoke continuously as well. Nothing is more revealing than the way cigarettes serve in the film to indicate what they have to hide. Laszlo smokes his innumerable cigarettes held between inordinately long, tapered fingers joined together, the flat palm deployed like a screen in front of his face. Forming the background of the underground, the hand holding a cigarette not only serves to mask his intentions and hide from the world the secrets on his lips, it also is waved with the solemnity of a censer by this political pope, the repository of higher values and uncompromising principle. The Nazi colonel is all fussy compulsiveness, smoking his cigarettes down to butts that he sucks, holding them precariously at their extremity.

Annie Leclerc, after having diagnosed the phallocracy implicit in the Humphrey Bogart cigarette, with seeming hesitation reconsiders the question and elliptically nuances her judgment at the beginning of a subsequent chapter. She writes:

> Which makes me think that perhaps I was cruel toward the "Humphrey Bogart" cigarette. This little guy with the devastated look in fact needs a cigarette at least to pretend. At bottom I think I can also understand the epaulets, the cop trench coats with the collar turned up, or all the minute or blunt instruments of phallocracy. It suffices to acknowledge that the menace is considerable. That the manipulator, male or female, of the mechanisms is in the first place someone who is afraid. That perhaps there is good reason to be.
>
> Pretending is not the evil. The evil is that one is fooled. If no one believed, one would not feel so obliged. . . . (115)

She breaks off, unwilling or unable to pursue her thought to the end. The implication seems to be that both men and women smoke phallocratic cigarettes to give themselves courage and to conceal the fear they may feel in the face of situations that may be truly menacing. The cigarette is a tool for maintaining the calm, unexpressive exterior necessary in the face of threats to one's integrity. It is the disguise of power and a mechanism for giving oneself the power to maintain one's composure. Leclerc's hesitation surrounds her apparent defense of the usefulness of the phallocratic mask, the one she earlier had unequivocally denounced. Revising her opinion, she allows that wearing it may not, in all circumstances, be bad; sometimes it is necessary for men and women, in the face of real danger, to appear arrogant, hard-boiled, afraid of nothing. The moral error occurs when one starts taking one's mask for oneself.

Toward the end of her book on cigarettes, Leclerc remembers what she may have always forgotten, the air of smoking. She writes this wonderful passage:

> I had forgotten, perhaps since forever, in the night of my time, that food was not the only thing that passes through the mouth. I had for-

gotten air. Air that passes through the mouth and by the tender throat. Air. The air of breath, the air of cries and laments, the air of song and words.

Air. . . . As if the word itself had been forgotten. Strange little word. A suspended word, withdrawn from other words. A fresh word, in-augural, unfinished, which opens itself between tongue and palate, a word so light, inconsequential, that as soon as it is said it is already in the air. A downy word. A bird word. Air. . . .

Didn't I use to smoke as well to repair this forgetting, to remind my-self of air, of throat and lungs? To smoke so that it passes through me, so that it circulates and is exchanged? It is not amusing to be always oneself. To be alone, singular, separated. I must have smoked to try to open the shell, to split open the all-so-heavy, onerous pouch of emo-tions, of food and thoughts. To smoke in order to try, to try again an exit from this receptacle-self, garbage-can and tabernacle.

To lift the lid of suffocating repetition. To smoke in order to pass beyond. And to breathe even beyond breathing. (123)

Annie Leclerc smokes to remember not to forget . . . air. Not even to forget the word, air—which is itself, she says, airy, winged, a downy bird word, no sooner said than in the air. She smokes so as not to forget her throat and lungs and air, to be traversed by something that circulates between inside and out. The puff of the cigarette is air that reminds her of air, a breath beyond breathing that recalls the fact that we live not only within ourselves but outside ourselves, in and of the air we breathe. Cigarette smoking allows us to effectuate an exit from our boring, repetitious, con-fining, sacred, worthless little selves, to experience ourselves as part of what we are not, outside our familiar interiority. The air of smoke reminds us that we are smoking air, that we are always outside the inside of our-selves, in the air like the word when it leaves our interior and flies in the air, like a downy word—like a bird, the word, air.

Air is not just the gases in the space around us and in us, it is the word for the space-time that accompanies every breath. We are in time the way we are in the air, hence "l'air du temps," like a whiff of perfume, names the ambient quality of the moment, the particular tone and tenor of a moment in space and time. Each breath we take, each puff we smoke, is an air of time, a mode or mood of time passing.

The cigarettes being smoked in *Casablanca* are the visual embodiment of the film's most memorable song, "As Time Goes By." The city is the place for waiting, waiting, waiting, in this mean in-between time, for the visa that will allow one to leave this place which is an exile but not yet the place where one is going. Time passing has a double significance, evoked in the first and last verses of the film's theme song:

> You must remember this,
> A kiss is just a kiss.
> A sigh is just a sigh.
> The fundamental things apply,
> > As time goes by.

> And when two lovers woo,
> They still say I love you.
> On this you can rely,
> No matter what the future brings,
> > As time goes by.
> . . . . .
> It's still the same old story,
> A fight for love and glory,
> A case of do or die.
> The world will always welcome lovers,
> > As time goes by.

The song may be heard as referring to the sentimental story of Rick and Ilsa: their bad timing, falling in love the day the Germans marched into Paris; the time lost since the time, five minutes to five on the clock in the Gare de Lyon, when Ingrid-Ilsa failed to leave Paris with Rick; and the time gone by since their reunion in Casablanca.

Sam—the "boy," as Ingrid Bergman calls him—plays the piano at Rick's and is his most faithful retainer, maternal and protective of his "boss." When we first see him in Rick's he sings:

> Cause my hair is curly, cause my teeth are pearly,
> Just because I always wear a smile,
> I'll see the weather in the latest style.
> (Koch, *Casablanca* 47)

He is the soul of the place, the sentimental and aesthetic center of the film, whose music gauges the moral climate of the action and serves as a running commentary on the progress of the plot. When Bogart hides the stolen letters of transit in his piano he plays "Who's Got Trouble?"; and when Ilsa enters Rick's for the first time, on the arm of another man, he plays "Love for Sale." He is the guardian of the past and holds the secret of time's reversal. When Ingrid-Ilsa sits down at the piano, Sam says: "I never expected to see you again, Miss Ilsa. A lot of water under the bridge." She asks him to play one of the "old songs." He tries to appease her first with "Avalon." That is not what she wants to hear. "Play 'As Time Goes By'" (86–88).

But Sam's watch has stopped; like every one else in Casablanca, he is waiting, waiting. As time goes by, time is being lost while America remains suspended in benevolent neutrality toward Vichy. Patriots are those who wait impatiently for a new alliance between the United States and the Free French forces.

A Polemical Conclusion

This book seeks to suggest that the present campaign against cigarettes in America, with its spreading international echoes, stages an upsurge of censorious moralizing under appeals to notions of health. Judging by the history of antitabagism, this upsurge is probably a moment in a cyclical process of repression and the return of the repressed, guaranteeing that the pendulum will ineluctably swing in the other direction—particularly under conditions of social tension brought on by political or economic crises. The swing may already have begun. The rising tide of hysterical overreaction, by its stridency, has succeeded in drowning voices raised to recall the social and cultural benefits of cigarettes—the mystery of their having conquered the world, as Cocteau said. It is after all a world in which, for almost a century, a third (at least) of all adults have smoked billions of cigarettes a day.

In 1631 the Parlement of Paris, alarmed by doctors' reports on the health of inmates, outlawed smoking in prisons; in 1659 the city fathers of Colmar prohibited bourgeois from smoking and incited the population, in the name of civic virtue, to denounce offenders (Vigié 58). We can only guess at the success of their efforts among the criminal class, but perhaps one measure of the persuasiveness of their arguments is that Molière, in the opening lines of *Don Juan*, played before the king in 1665, felt free to put into the mouth of Sganarelle an exaggerated paean to tobacco, which affirms sententiously: "A life without tobacco is not worthy of being lived." The repression of smoking often ensures that when the repressed returns, it does so violently, hyperbolically. Whenever what is unhealthy is demonized, it becomes irresistible, with all the seduction of vice and the fiery allure of what ought not to come to light. Censorship inevitably incites the very practice it wishes to inhibit and usually makes it more dangerously compulsive, because illicit, in the bargain. Think of masturbation.

In *The History of Sexuality*, Michel Foucault distinguishes between two historical sorts of laws that have been promulgated to control pleasure. On the one hand are the interdictions, like those in the Middle Ages, against adultery that effectively discouraged the practice. On the other hand are incitations, like the rules and regulations against masturbation that were promulgated in the nineteenth century by pedagogues, doctors, priests, and family moralists: making it a vice did not cause it to diminish; on the contrary, suddenly everything became masturbatory. What once might have been taken to be scratching an itch became subject to moralizing suspicions that had only to be pronounced to be true. Like masturbation, what are called drugs have spread into every segment of society; for years the government and the clergies have been waging war, and the problem may be worse now than ever. Cigarettes are bad enough; they do not need to be demonized. As was the case with masturbation, not only truth but the public health might be better served if at least some sympathy were shown for the Devil.

To speak of censorship with respect to smoking presupposes what this book has tried to demonstrate, that smoking cigarettes is not only a physical act but a discursive one—a wordless but eloquent form of expression. It is a fully coded, rhetorically complex, narratively articulated discourse with a vast repertoire of well-understood conventions that are implicated, intertextually, in the whole literary, philosophical, cultural history of smoking. In the present climate, the discursive performance of smoking has become a form of obscenity, just as obscenity has become an issue of public health. Of course, censors always claim that they work on behalf of the moral and physical well-being of the body politic, which they wish to protect from the harm that is supposed to follow from the proscribed symbolic behavior. Since smoking is wordless, it is a form of expression especially vulnerable to being suppressed by censors who hesitate before banning speech. The increase of attacks directed against smoking in the last decades could be seen as the harbinger of the wave of censorship that threatens to engulf America. Like the Gypsy dances that were banned at French carnivals, smoking cigarettes has become an act that arouses irrational fears and excessively repressive impulses, even if it deserves to be civically disapproved. Cigarettes are bad for your health,

Edward R. Murrow

Photo © Elliot Erwitt. By permission of Magnum Photos, Inc.

like many things that are consumed thirty times a day; perhaps they are worse than most. But historically, the laws that are devised to suppress them fail to do so, may in fact produce the opposite of what they intend, and this paradox gives rise to suspicions about the motives and attitudes that underlie their imposition.

The first chapters of this book aimed to show that the demonic predicates that cigarettes have acquired in the last twenty years are the negative obverse of deific attributes that at other times have attached to smoking. A daemon is an old god, whose cult has been repressed but whose still-haunting power to enthrall the celebrant reverses its sign: what once was blessed now appears frightful and hideously tempting. Combating the Devil, witch-hunters find evil everywhere because it is the face they give to their own repudiated impulses. Unholy measures are usually called for to suppress unholy practices, and, like wars of religion, the campaign against smoking lends itself to cruel fanaticism and self-righteous indignation. Smoking is forbidden in public buildings where some space for smoking could be assigned. Fanatical persecution usually reinforces the cult it aims to banish, giving rise to secret ceremonies and underground movements that have their own perverse theology. This book has the remystifying aim of revealing the god behind the unrelievedly evil mask that cigarettes have assumed, to expose their power to continue to possess us. If there is any chance that society will ever renounce tobacco, it will not be because of censorship, which will only foster its use. Not until society has glimpsed the aura of divinity behind the hideous mask will it grasp the nature of its old fascination and begin to invent new gods for these times.

In the preceding chapters we have examined many of the benefits and pleasures, the wisdom and beauty attached to smoking cigarettes. We have seen how it has been represented, in literature and philosophy, as exemplary of the high ambition to appropriate the world symbolically. It induces forms of aesthetic satisfaction and states of reflective consciousness that belong to the most compelling varieties of artistic and religious experience. Cigarettes have regularly been linked to strong currents of sexual and political freedom. They have served generations of men and women, in periods of acute distress, as an incomparable tool for managing and mitigating anxiety and as a variety of prayer. They constitute, in the hands of many, a subtle but efficient instrument for mediating social interaction— a weapon against the intrusions of other subjectivities and a sort of magic wand that seductively invites intrusion. And yet despite the multiple benefits and undeniable beauty of cigarettes, their value these days is exclusively determined with reference to their noxious effects; to banish them it is enough to say that they are very bad for your health. But we have been led to ask, What is the value assigned to health that makes it, in this case, the sole criterion of what is good and beautiful? Perhaps one cannot simply weigh the advantages of cigarettes against the risks, if it is their very harmfulness that makes them sublime—if no one ever would have smoked them were they harmless. Good health, according to Svevo, is fundamentally at odds with the progress of civilization, which by its nature increases infirmity. Life itself is a progressive disease from which we only recover posthumously; for if health is freedom from disease, then it is only available by dying. Living means choosing your poisons. The hero of Svevo's novel is able to abandon his lifelong habit of smoking only at the end of his life, at the moment when he abandons his persistent illusion that someday he will finally be healthy.

Healthism has become part of the dominant ideology of America for reasons that seem alternately naive and sinister, serving to mask the depredations of a cruel industrialization and to foster the immediate interests of a major sector of the economy. It has distorted and obscured more appropriate views of our biology and of the relation between life and survival. It has given rise to forms of hypocrisy whose transparency is more visible abroad than here, but with consequences for the quality of life in this country and for social freedom that are visible all around us.

In 1990, in a speech at a dedication at the University of Pennsylvania, Louis W. Sullivan, secretary of health and human services, declared war again on smoking, borrowing the rhetoric of Pope Paul VI, in 1965, at the United Nations, when he called for the end of war: "Let this just be the beginning of an all-out effort to resist the tobacco merchants' attempts to earn profits at the expense of the health and well-being of our poor and minority citizens. This trade-off between profits and good health must stop. Enough! No more" (New York Times, November 7, 1990).

On the very same day, the White House chief of staff was reported, in the New York Times, to be negotiating with the majority leader of the Senate in order to eliminate congressional proposals amending the president's clean air legislation. Trading off profits and good health, the White House strenuously resisted a plan, strongly supported by environmentalists, to restore a provision that had originally been included in the first Clean Air Bill, passed in 1970. The earlier bill had proposed a second, mandatory round of controls on auto emissions in 2003 after the first round in 1993, but the administration sought its elimination from the new bill. It also opposed provisions that would have put controls on the emission of toxic chemicals and improved fuel efficiency in automobiles to reduce the carbon dioxide in exhaust, the presumed cause of global warming. The administration stood fast against efforts to cut the emission of sulfur dioxide and nitrous oxide, the principal contaminants in acid rain. In these instances, it did not denounce the merchants who were earning profits "at the expense of the health and well-being of our poor and minority citizens"; rather, it was looking out for mercantile interests with what environmentalists consider to be precious little regard for the general welfare.

Perhaps it is too cynical to assume that the administration was being deliberately hypocritical, denouncing cigarettes while promoting the profits of polluters. We learn from the *Times* that Dr. Sullivan, the first African-American secretary of health, was moved to make this speech blaming cigarettes and reproving R. J. Reynolds, not in a policy-making session but on a plane, returning from a conference, "as he settled in for the long ride from Rome to Washington." Sinking into his first-class seat, the health secretary must have had a benevolent thought for "poor and minority citizens" less exalted than himself, perhaps noting with professional annoyance that smoking was still allowed on transatlantic flights. From the tone of his speech we can imagine his indignation when he turned to the newspaper and read the account of Reynolds's plan to promote the sale of Uptown cigarettes in a targeted black population: "At a time when our people desperately need the message of health promotion, Uptown's message is more disease, more suffering and more death for a group already bearing more than its share of smoke-related illnesses and mortality" (*New York Times*, January 19, 1990). In a flash he must have decided to make this the first major initiative of his cabinet post, a cost-effective crusade on behalf of those whose suffering he acutely understood.

Hawking the "message of health promotion," in an administration not noted for its solicitude toward the plight of poor minorities, Dr. Sullivan's message is a negative (or positive) echo of the one that Uptown advances. He doubtless does not suspect, what his rhetoric unwittingly betrays, that health itself has become an advertised commodity, whose promotion is perversely tied to the success of the competition. Nor does he hear any irony in his compassionate reflection on the victims of "smoke-related illnesses"—sickened by effluvia that pollute the clean air. At a time when urban misery has increased immensely, the illness and death resulting from the smoky emanations of unregulated industrialization are not high on the list of Dr. Sullivan's priorities. In an administration that has been faulted for not vigorously addressing problems of the inner city, its minister of health and well-being seeks to mobilize the indignation of the citizenry against the traditional luxury of the poor—the ultimate consolation of those who are bereft, who sacrifice much of the little they have for the solace and comfort that cigarette smoking provides. Like playing the lottery, smoking is a frivolous expense that recommends itself to the very poor who, buying a pack, get a share in the dream that sells Viceroy, Old Gold, Elites, and High Society on the most miserable streets in the world.

Dr. Sullivan must also have recognized, perhaps obscurely, the value of a harsh attack on the tobacco merchants in countering the administration's bad press resulting from the recent action of the U.S. trade representative. For some time the administration had been threatening Thailand with reprisals if that country implemented its ban on cigarette imports and cigarette advertising. Asked about this, the secretary of health and human services allowed that promoting cigarettes to Thais is problematic:

> "I know this is one of those areas that is problematic," Dr. Sullivan said. "It is my job as the nation's chief health officer, my responsibility is to. . . ." He paused. "But on exports, this gets into the area of respon-sibilities of other people," he said, alluding to the office of the United States Trade Representative.
>
> But not satisfied with the sound of that, Dr. Sullivan said, "Let me just say at this juncture, I want to focus on the serious problems we have here in the United States." (New York Times, March 19, 1990)

Dr. Sullivan's wish to distinguish his bureaucratic responsibilities from those of the trade representative allowed him to cast the policy contra-diction as a problem to be resolved by an appeal to patriotism. America may promote the sale of its cigarettes abroad, poisoning the Third World, but it must not countenance harming the health and welfare of "our" mi-nority poor. But the paradox of a government's promoting what it actively combats is only a seeming one; it conceals a deeper consistency.

An editorial in the New York Times illustrates what at first appears to be the absurdity of that logic—a dilemma that not even the editors can con-ceal from themselves. Entitled "Exporting Cigarettes," the piece begins by citing, approvingly, the outraged reaction of then Surgeon General Koop at U.S. efforts to break down barriers against the exportation of American tobacco products: "I don't think that we as citizens can continue export-ing disease, disability and death" (New York Times, quoted in the International Herald Tribune, August 8, 1989). In fact, America continues to export them

fiercely, the Times acknowledges; tobacco is one of the few American products that the rest of the world is eager to buy, just as they have been for
three hundred years. Last year America sold abroad $3.7 billion worth
of tobacco, a sum not inconsequential for the country's balance of trade.
Earlier the Times had written: "In a decade where American goods—from
sweet corn to stereo components to semi-conductors—are losing ground
in Asia, cigarettes represent a rare and fiercely defended success story.
Tobacco exports to the region rose by 76 percent last year alone" (New York
Times, July 10, 1988).

Asian countries, the largest new markets, are enthusiastic consumers of
our cigarettes, preferring them to inferior local products, and they would
doubtless continue to smoke them in increasing numbers if governments
allowed cigarettes to be imported and advertised freely. Not yet considered illegal, like opium, cigarettes are surely entitled, thinks the Times, to
the government's protection from trade discrimination. Yet the editors
wonder: "But doesn't the United States have a moral responsibility for haz-
ard resulting from its product?" Their solution to the dilemma displays a
peculiarly American optimism about the power of self-righteous nagging
to disculpate the pursuit of crass economic interests—especially in this
case, where they seem to glimpse the way the former promotes the latter.
The editors write: "A better way to resolve the contradiction would be
to open those markets also to American information. Wherever the U.S.
representative opens a market, let the surgeon general follow, issuing his
annual report on smoking, and nagging and scolding foreign governments
as well as his own" (New York Times, quoted in International Herald Tribune,
August 8, 1989).

The logic of this argument was earlier illustrated by Jimmy Carter, in
1978, speaking to farmers in North Carolina, promising tearily to support tobacco subsidies on the very day that Joseph Califano, his secretary
of health and welfare, was launching a $50 million scolding campaign
against smoking—the most expensive nagging in history. But the paradox
is only apparent: we have already observed that the sublimity of smoking
is linked to the awareness of its dangers. The more vigorously government
denounces the danger of cigarettes, the more it serves to incite people to
go on smoking or to struggle with taking it up. The New York Times seems
almost on the verge of understanding the (perhaps) unconscious cynicism
of the government's strategy, but the editorial naturally fails to analyze
or even grasp, absent the category of the sublime, the deeper necessity
that accompanies the selling of tobacco with warnings against its dangers.

The negative aesthetic pleasure associated with the sublime logically requires the indispensable moment of menace to procure its effect. The
more vividly the abyss is opened beneath the traveler's feet, the more awesome is his satisfaction at playing with life and death and the more acute his
pleasure at defying the negativity before him. It follows from that logic that
the surgeon general's warning on every pack of American cigarettes actually serves to advertise their charms and promote their use. That strategy
has only one self-generating limitation: smokers quickly become inured
to unchanging appeals to danger, and the ante must increasingly be raised.
That may explain why legislation is pending to enlarge the warnings on
the packages and elevate their tone of alarm, all the while the trade representative is keeping up the pressure to let Asians have the right to smoke
American.

Recently a commission of the European Economic Community sur-
veyed the practice of smoking cigarettes among the citizens of its twelve
member countries.[1] The survey reveals that the country with the highest
percentage of women smokers is Denmark; the country with the lowest
is Portugal. The statistics are not an aberration: Denmark is followed by
Holland and Great Britain; Greece and Portugal are at the other end of
the scale. Question: In which of these countries would you rather have
your daughter grow up, if you hoped she would be liberated, independent, and self-sufficient? Paradoxically, it is in nations in which smoking is
most expensive that one finds the highest percentage of women smokers:
in Denmark, 45 percent of the women smoke; in Holland, 37; and in Great
Britain, 32. Sociocultural variables seem preponderant with respect to economic factors. "Is the cigarette a symbol of the equality between man and
woman?" ask the experts of the European Community. We may be allowed,
at the end of this book, to take the question rhetorically.

Other interesting results of the commission's investigation reveal the development of smoking among the young and the very young. In Greece, 59
percent of the population between the ages of fifteen and twenty-four is
tobacco-dependent. Young Spanish and French smokers reach the rate of
51 percent. Even the Portuguese, who hold the record for "nonsmoking
people," have registered a strong increase in smoking among the youngest
segment of the population, over 52 percent. They smoke in growing numbers even though the Portuguese are not allowed to smoke cigarettes with
high levels of tar; they also benefit from a total ban on cigarette advertising.

Finally, the poll taken among doctors and teachers—people who are
supposed to set a good example to society—reveals that Spanish, Italian,

and Portuguese doctors are, on the whole, the least entitled, morally, to lecture their patients on the harm of smoking. Their smoking vastly exceeds that of the general population. Can a doctor who smokes be a reputable physician? The stridency of the surgeon general's tone would seem to require the conclusion that a doctor who smokes contradicts the oath of his profession, promoting by example "disease, disability and death." Dr. Koop's tone may be intended to obscure the possibility that doctors in other societies may have criteria for judging the requirements of public health that differ from those that are officially advanced and economically exploited in America. Obesity, widespread in America, is barely known in many countries that take for granted the right to smoke.

"Slow Food" is a movement with adherents in France, Italy, Germany, Brazil, Venezuela, Switzerland, California, and even Japan. Its aim is to combat with education and example the invasion of fast food into cultures with traditional diets that are more healthy, complex, and unlinked to obesity than our own. One of the earliest supporters of "Slow Food" is Jacques Le Goff, the distinguished French historian, who is quoted as saying, "Fast Food is absolute evil, contrasted with traditional cultures of Mediterranean countries. Its success has disturbed me" (*La Republica*, November 18, 1989). Le Goff's remark makes us realize the extent to which reactions like those of Surgeon General Koop to the sale of American cigarettes abroad are culturally determined. It would probably no more occur to Dr. Koop to think that any culture could find McDonald's an absolute evil than it would to Le Goff, whose society has avidly imported American tobacco for centuries, to suppose that Marlboros were the work of the Devil.

In eleven countries, proportionally fewer smokers are found in the teaching profession than among doctors or the general public. Teachers, therefore, set better examples than doctors, but being a good example to students seems to have the effect of encouraging them to smoke in ever-larger numbers. Portugal, where only 21 percent of teachers smoke, compared to 39 percent of doctors, has registered a significant increase in the number of younger smokers. This fact may demonstrate the inverse relation between teaching and moral correction. *Caveat magister*: the best example is the worst example. The low percentage of teachers who smoke, compared even to doctors, points to the high clerical role they have increasingly assumed. That, in turn, explains the astonishing precipitation with which schools and universities in America have banned smoking from their premises under the guise of considerations of health. Students, smoking in greater numbers, are not misled; they never fail to detect the rustle of the cassock beneath admonitions coming from teachers concerning their bodies.

Moralists always want to vote cigarettes up or down; realism requires us to acknowledge that, like all drugs, they are a mixed blessing. No society has succeeded in getting along without smoking tobacco, which suggests that the practice will outlive the current wave of antitabagism, or will coexist with it as it always has. As with all drugs, one ought to resist the sort of intolerance that morally reduces these substances to their active chemical ingredients. Champagne and beer, whiskey and vodka, sake and soma, are indistinguishable in the eye of temperance—but the conditions under which they are normally consumed, the significance of their use in society, and the pleasures they procure differ widely. Similarly, tobacco in all its forms, and cigarettes in particular, cannot be judged solely on the basis of the effects of nicotine and tars. But, conversely, one must not therefore be led to believe that the harmful chemicals in cigarettes are somehow separable from the uses to which they are put. Cigarettes are bad for you, like all drugs, and that is what makes them so good to those who use them. No addict can imagine his drug without the discomfort and inconvenience that accompanies its use.

If cigarettes were not also good for you, so many good people would not have spent some part of their lives doing them uninterruptedly, often compulsively—them, or some drug or other. One thinks of the many great men and women who have died prematurely from having smoked too much: it does them an injustice to suppose that their greatness did not depend in some degree on the wisdom and pleasure and spiritual benefit they took in a habit they could not abandon. And the same could be said of others. Healthism in America has sought to make longevity the principal measure of a good life. To be a survivor is to acquire moral distinction. But another view, a dandy's perhaps, would say that living, as distinct from surviving, acquires its value from risks and sacrifices that tend to shorten life and hasten dying. A life, in that view, is judged by the suicide it commits.

The great Puritan repression began by seizing and manipulating the attribution of the word drug, defining it narrowly and abusively extending its connotations to a vast variety of substances. Since the compulsive use of drugs has been a feature of civilization from its origin, there is reason to think that it cannot, or that it should not, be eliminated. History, both universal and personal, demonstrates as well that when drugs are freely available, their use obeys cycles of excess and abstemiousness. Drugs may be necessary for the survival of civilization, perhaps even of the species,

Two Men Kissing in a Paris Café
Photo © Richard Kalvar. By permission of Magnum Photos, Inc.

but most particularly at moments of social crisis or at trying times of life. It is likely that the censors, obscurely, understand that. If their interest is not in promoting surreptitiously what they pretend to abhor, their aim is to enlarge the power of surveillance, to intensify regimentation, and to increase the principle of policing in general. Yet the reasons for smoking cigarettes are not always, are probably rarely, vital. Nevertheless, every cigarette, says Annie Leclerc, may have its secret reason, its own particular rationale. I may light a cigarette to start the day, she says, or to finish it, to find a phrase, to take a shit, to savor my coffee, to pass the time, or because I need to relax, or to concentrate, to think about this or about something else: "Piles and piles of little possible reasons can be found for our piles of cigarettes" (Leclerc 54).

In the end, of all our reasons only ashes remain—the least trace of motives that are momentarily shaped but, like them, left to vanish—and the persisting butt, the next-to-nothing-left of a cigarette that remains only to be discarded. Abandoning the butt deflates the delicate mood that the cigarette installs and restores the reality principle—stubs out the little dream that the cigarette elicited. Butts are the end, the last word or punctuation of smoking that serves to mark the close of the parenthesis the cigarette has opened. But there are good butts and bad. In France, there is a whole vocabulary of butts among clochards, the street people who are the most discriminating collectors of discarded cigarettes. A butt (mégot), for example, may be called an orphelin [an orphan] if it is too short to be smoked. A good one is called a boni, a word attested in French since the sixteenth century—not the plural of bonus, a premium or dividend that comes on top of what is normally due, but from the Latin aliquid boni, something good. When the butt is not the end of a smoke but the beginning of another, the profit seems infinite—something has been gotten for nothing: a free lunch. A good butt that can be smoked entertains the illusion that the dream of smoking, the smoking dream, can go on being consumed—with no remainder. But the illusion veils the cruel fact that every butt that is smoked in turn leaves a butt that must be discarded. In the end, the dream is stubbed out.

Notes

All translations are mine unless otherwise indicated.

INTRODUCTION

1 Gregory Bateson's decisive essay, "The Cybernetics of 'Self': A Theory of Alcoholism," in *Steps to an Ecology of the Mind* is an indispensable reference for understanding the twelve-step psychological mechanisms that AA mobilizes to accomplish therapeutic cures of addiction and habituation.

2 The word *antitabagism* is borrowed from the French word for *antitobaccoism*, which in English seems inelegant and in French refers more precisely to the general category of hatred toward tobacco, which has been a concomitant human habit since its simultaneous appearance with that of tobacco at the beginning of the sixteenth century.

3 As long as cigarettes had to be rolled by hand, they were an indulgence of the leisure class. The cigarette machine brought this indulgence to the masses. The cigarettotype was invented in the 1850s; the artisanal hand-held machine, still in commerce, "pressed" or "printed" a perfect stereotype every time. But the universalization and democratization of cigarettes had to await the genius of James B. Duke, whose exploitation of the steam-powered Bonsak machine permitted millions to be generated cheaply and well. One of the historic benefits of cigarettes is Duke University in Durham, which owes its founding to his vision and beneficence.

4 Cocteau, it appears, lit his cigarettes with a lighter, not matches; lighters produce more precise flames with an even slighter appearance of movement; they are technologically more advanced than matches and stylistically more modern. The almost invisible gesture of the thumb makes the fire appear to emerge from the precious metal as if it had been willed telepathically by its Promethean owner.

5 This appears in the preface to the catalog of an exposition on behalf of the four

hundredth anniversary of Jean Nicot's first published description of tobacco in Europe, presented by the state-owned French company SEITA (Service pour l'exploitation industrielle du tabac et des allumettes), which used to be the Régie du Tabac before its reincorporation in 1860. Recently this company has been reconstituted as a "society," changing its gender from le Service to la Société.

6 Sir J. M. Barrie, creator of Peter Pan, was a passionate admirer of Raleigh; in 1905, in My Lady Nicotine, he wrote: "When Raleigh, in honor of whom England should have changed its name, introduced tobacco into this country, the glorious Elizabethan age began. I am aware that those hateful persons called Original researchers now maintain that Raleigh was not the man, but to them I turn a deaf ear. I know, I feel, that with the introduction of tobacco England woke up from a long sleep. Suddenly a new zest had been given to life. The glory of existence became a thing to speak of. Men who had hitherto only concerned themselves with the narrow things of home put a pipe into their mouths and became philosophers. Poets and dramatists smoked until all ignoble ideas were driven from them, and into their place rushed such high thoughts as the world had not known before. Petty jealousies no longer had hold of statesmen, who smoked, and agreed to work together for the public weal. Soldiers and sailors felt when engaged with a foreign foe, that they were fighting for their pipes. The whole country was stirred by the ambition to live up to tobacco. Everyone, in short, had now a lofty ideal constantly before him" (Barrie 104–6)

7 Claude Lévi-Strauss repeats with conviction that a comfortable bourgeois of the eighteenth century lived approximately as well as a wealthy citizen of the Roman Empire (Tristes tropiques 353).

8 "I, myself, who feel singularly obliged to lie and hardly care to give certitude and authority to what I say, notice all the same, with respect to arguments at hand, that being heated either by the other's resistance or by the heat of the narration itself, I enlarge and expand my subjects by means of gestures, vigorous expression, and force of words, and also by extension and amplification, not without interest in the simple truth. . . . Lively, noisy discourse, like mine, ordinarily gets easily carried away by hyperbole" (Montaigne 239–40).

9 The cigarette and the whore are identified in this anonymous little poem:

> Au quartier de Lorette
> L'on aime au jour le jour
> Et bien plus qu'un amour
> Dure une cigarette.
> (Quoted in Rival 171)

I WHAT IS A CIGARETTE?

1 The photograph by Brassaï is entitled "Autoportrait, Boulevard Saint Jacques, 1931–32." It appears on the cover of the catalog of a recent New York exposition of Brassaï's work at the Houk Friedman Gallery on Madison Avenue.

2 See Louis Pauwels, Louange de tabac.

2 CIGARETTES ARE SUBLIME

1 In order to help the reader perceive Laforgue's parody of "Correspondances," the text of Baudelaire's most famous poem is provided below, followed by a newly published translation by James McGowan:

Correspondances

La Nature est un temple où de vivants piliers
Laissent parfois sortir de confuses paroles;
L'homme y passe à travers un forêt de symboles
Qui l'observent avec des regards familiers.

Comme de longs échos qui de loin se confondent
Dans une ténébreuse et profonder unité,
Vaste comme la nuit et comme la clarté,
Les parfums, les couleurs et les sons se répondent.

Il est des parfums frais comme des chairs d'enfants,
Doux comme les hautbois, verts comme les prairies,
—Et d'autres, corrompus, riches et triomphants,

Ayant l'expansion des choses infinies,
Comme l'ambre, le musc, le benjoin et l'encens,
Qui chantent les transports de l'esprit et des sens.
(Baudelaire, vol. 1, 11)

Nature is a temple, where the living
Columns sometimes breathe confusing speech;
Man walks within these groves of symbols, each
Of which regards him as a kindred thing.

As the long echoes, shadowy, profound,
Heard from afar, blend in a unity,
Vast as the night, as sunlight's clarity,
So perfumes, colours, sounds may correspond.

Odours there are, fresh as a baby's skin,
Mellow as oboes, green as meadow grass,
—Others corrupted, rich, triumphant, full,

Having dimensions infinitely vast,
Frankincense, musk, ambergris, benjamin,
Singing the senses' rapture, and the soul's.
(Baudelaire, The Flowers of Evil 19)

2 To Byron, however, belongs the credit for having been the first to understand the aesthetic pleasure of tobacco in connection with the eighteenth-century doctrines of the sublime, in a poem entitled "Sublime Tobacco":

> Sublime tobacco! which, from east to west,
> Cheers the Tar's labor or the Turkman's rest;
> Which on the Moslem's ottoman divides
> His hours, and rivals opium and his brides;
> Magnificent in Stamboul, but less grand,
> Though not less loved, in Wapping or the Strand;
> Divine in hookahs, glorious in a pipe,
> When tipped with amber, mellow, rich, and ripe;
> Like other charmers, wooing the caress
> More dazzlingly when daring in full dress;
> Yet thy true lovers more admire, by far,
> Thy naked beauties—Give me a cigar! (*The Island*, 1823)

3 ZENO'S PARADOX

1 The title aside, the rest of the standard translation by Beryl de Zoete (New York: Vintage Books, 1959) is deplorable, not only because of its inaccuracies, which abound, but for its failure to respect the ironic precision of Svevo's diction and syntax.

2 Roland Barthes in S/Z analyzes the uses that Balzac makes in a story of the subtle difference between S and Z.

3 This book, *Cigarettes Are Sublime*, is intended to be a piece of nuclear criticism insofar as I wish not merely to trace the aesthetic and cultural history and forms of the cigarette but also to consider them and their function now, in civilization, in relation to what has been called "the fable of total nuclear war." That is, I aim to interrogate current conceptions of cigarette smoking in light of questions concerning the survival of collective memory, such as those that the nuclear condition fosters. For Zeno, at the conclusion of the novel, the possibility of giving up smoking depends on his abandoning the idea of becoming healthy. Health, he discovers, is the condition to which the world will return after its apocalyptic destruction. Floating through the void in its nebulous form, the earth at last will be free of all parasites and disease and will have attained to the only health we can aspire to. That the wish to be healthy may be in the service of mankind's urge to destroy itself is one of the lessons of Zeno's confessions. It is a pessimistic lesson to the extent that the wish is indissociable from the developmental progress of man's machines. There is an official ideology promoting health, which may in fact be in the service of the most destructive tendencies of technology.

4 Quoted in Ellman 636. I thank Arden Reed for bringing this passage to my attention.

5 Ernest, the hero of Samuel Butler's *Way of All Flesh*, seeks moral reassurance about his habit from the fact that tobacco is not expressly forbidden in the Bible: "Tobacco had nowhere been forbidden in the Bible, but then it had not yet been

discovered, and had probably only escaped proscription for this reason. We can conceive of St. Paul or even our Lord Himself as drinking a cup of tea, but we cannot imagine either of them as smoking a cigarette, or a churchwarden. Ernest could not deny this, and admitted that Paul would almost certainly have condemned tobacco in good round terms if he had known of its existence. Was it not then taking rather a mean advantage of the Apostle to stand on his not having forbidden it? On the other hand, it was possible that God knew Paul would have forbidden smoking, and had purposely arranged the discovery of tobacco for a period at which Paul should be no longer living. This might seem rather hard on Paul, considering all he had done for Christianity, but it would be made up to him in other ways" (244).

6   To smoke like a Turk is a reference not only to the statistical prevalence of smoking in Turkey but no doubt also to the role of the Crimean War in popularizing cigarettes in Europe.

7   But instead of blaming his love of cigarettes for his incapacity to do chemistry, Zeno wonders if he does not love them precisely so that he can blame them for his incapacity. Instead of being the cause of his failure, they are an alibi for it. Who knows whether, stopping, he would have become the ideal and strong man he had hoped to be. Perhaps it was his doubt about his capacity that tied him to his vice, "since it is a convenient way to live, that of believing one is great with a latent greatness" (11). Rather than the cigarettes hindering him, he loves the cigarettes so he can find an excuse for not being what he could not in any case have been; they allow him to continue to believe in his greatness precisely to the degree that they can be blamed for preventing him from ever actually realizing it. They make possible what they make impossible.

       For a discussion of pragmatic paradoxes, which were introduced into the Anglo-Saxon philosophical literature by the Scottish logician D. J. O'Connor, see my articles, "The Future of Nuclear Criticism" and "Under Pragmatic Paradoxes."

8   The theme of time's circularity is a philosophical commonplace since Aristotle, by no means restricted to the philosophy of Zeno. Aristotle discovered the circularity of time in the very movement of time's passage, in which every instant or "now" is replaced by an identical one, exactly like the one it has replaced. For Hegel, it is not only time itself that returns but the forms of the historical Spirit that unrolls itself in time.

4   THE DEVIL IN CARMEN

1   On the eve of the Great War, in 1910, the Régie had to abandon the brand name in a dispute with a Belgian manufacturer over "Hollandaise." In 1920, Giot, professor of design and director of the Régie at the time, designed the winged helmet that still serves as its emblem. Fifteen years later it was retouched and modified by the painter Jacno.

2   Mélin de Saint-Gelais, the sixteenth-century French poet, translates the aphorism of Palladas as follows: "Toute femme est importune et cuisante, / Et seulement en deux temps est plaisante. / Le premier est de ses noces la nuit / Et le second quand on l'ensevelit" (8).

6 "L'AIR DU TEMPS"

1   In "On Fetishism," Freud insists that the fetishistic detail is more likely to figure the phallus by virtue of its metonymical contiguity, rather than any metaphorical resemblance. The fetishist often chooses his privileged objects as a function of whatever he saw last, before the traumatic encounter with the mother's sex.

2   Umberto Eco reads Rick as a "plurifilmic personality," combining the archetypes of "the Fatal Adventurer, the Self-Made Businessman (money is money), the Tough Guy from a gangster movie, Our Man in Casablanca (international intrigue), the Cynic . . . the Hemingway Hero" (205).

3   The American ego-psychology interpretation of Freudian interpretation, as the French analyst Jacques Lacan has extensively denigrated it, commits two fundamental errors: first, it forgets Freud's own insistence on the role of language in generating not only neurotic symptoms but also the conflicts from which they arise; second, it represents the human psyche, with its dynamic topography and its intersubjective logic, as if it were ontologically comparable to other "things" in the world. American ego-psychology considers language only insofar as it is a largely transparent medium for conveying and concealing mostly unconscious instinctual drives. Since this view of language is closely derived from the way one conceptualizes the nature of things (surface, depth, substance/attribute, subject/predicate), it is inevitable that the psychological subject under investigation by American ego-psychology should itself implicitly be endowed with objectifying predicates in respect to many of its most essential features. The psychological subject gets posed by ego-psychology in a way so as to determine in advance the sorts of things that can be discovered about it and the kinds of sentences that can be made describing its organization and functioning. As a consequence of this double misreading of Freud's metapsychological theories, analysts like Dr. Greenberg understand their interpretive role to consist in plunging into some ill-conceived depth of the film in order to extract a psycho-sexual content, which is brought to the surface and made manifest (in an interpretative gesture Jacques Derrida would call, following Heidegger, aletheic mimetism: the revelation of truth as its epiphanic emergence into the light out of the crypt in which it ordinarily resides). But the consequences for practical criticism, like that of Dr. Greenberg, of this theoretical error is a certain blindness to the way the Oedipal theme, dredged up from its hidden depth and exposed to the light of consciousness, may in turn prove to be only another surface masking and letting pass an even more subversive message. The Oedipal theme, rather than being the bedrock that Dr. Greenberg assumes, may be used by the film to mask another message, in this case a political one.

4   "Throughout his career Humphrey Bogart was exceptionally successful as the outsider, the dweller in marginal and dangerous milieus, exiled from love. Typically, the Bogarty protagonist has thrust closeness away and exercises eternal vigilance to survive in a hostile world. Men savagely compete with him; women seek to ensnare and exploit him. Inevitably, his deepest allegiance must be owed to his own embattled self, if he is to keep his tenuous balance on the precipice.

    "As Bogart grew in stature, the troubled idealist behind the callous facade became more accessible. One discerned an authentic decency shining through the uncaring mask. Surely the prototype of these embittered gentlemen is Rick Blaine, exiled champion of lost causes, come to an uneasy rest in pro-Vichy Casablanca, owner and sole proprieter of the nightclub where the silver screen's headiest blending of patriotic and sexual fantasy is acted out. . . .

"Rick purchases his redemption at a poignant price, a price urged on him by the limitations of his character, for we may speculate that the intimacy of an extended relationship with a woman would ultimately be unendurable to him" (Greenberg 104).

A POLEMICAL CONCLUSION

1 The results of the commission's survey, expressed in a table of percentages, are given below:

	Men	Women	Doctors	Teachers
		Percentage of Smokers		
Belgium	44	28	29	18
Denmark	46	45	38	34
Germany	43	27	25	21
Greece	61	26	39	30
Spain	53	28	45	34
France	44	29	31	16
Ireland	38	31	20	14
Italy	39	26	41	26
Holland	47	37	29	24
Portugal	46	12	39	21
Great Britain	40	32	10	13

From Il Messaggiero, September 24, 1989.

Works Cited

Alyn, Marc. *Célébration du tabac*. Au Jas du Revest-Saint-Martin, Haute Provence: Editions Robert-Morel, 1962.

Apollinaire, Guillaume. *Alcools*. Paris: Gallimard, 1920.

Banville, Théodore de. *L'âme de Paris, nouveaux souvenirs*. Paris: G. Charpentier, 1890.

Barrie, J. M. *My Lady Nicotine: A Study in Smoke*. Boston: H. M. Caldwell, 1905.

Barthes, Roland. *S/Z*. Trans. Richard Miller. New York: Hill and Wang, 1974.

———. *La chambre claire, notes sur la photographie*. Paris: Editions de l'Étoile, 1980.

Bateson, Gregory. "The Cybernetics of 'Self': A Theory of Alcoholism." In *Steps to an Ecology of the Mind*, 309–37. New York: Chandler, 1972.

Baudelaire, Charles. *The Flowers of Evil*. Trans. James McGowan, intro. Jonathan Culler. Oxford: Oxford University Press, 1993.

———. *Oeuvres complètes*. Ed. Claude Pichois. 2 vols. Paris: Gallimard, 1975.

Beauvoir, Simone de. *Adieux: A Farewell to Sartre*. Trans. Patrick O'Brian. New York: Pantheon, 1984.

Bizet, Georges. *Carmen*. Intro. and trans. Ellen H. Bleiler. New York: Dover, 1970.

Bohle, Bruce, comp. and ed. *The Home Book of American Quotations*. New York: Dodd, Mead, and Co., 1967.

Burette, Théodose. *La physiologie du fumeur*. Brussels: Dépot Central pour la Belgique, 1840.

Butler, Samuel. *The Way of All Flesh*. New York: Macmillan, 1925.

Byron, George Gordon. "The Island," Canto II, XIX. *The Poetical Works of Byron*. Boston: Houghton Mifflin Co., 1975.

Clancy, Tom. *The Cardinal of the Kremlin*. New York: Berkley, 1988.

———. *Patriot Games*. New York: Berkley, 1988.

Cochrane, Alfred. *Leviore Plecto* [Occasional Verses]. London: Longmans, Green and Co., 1896.

Cocteau, Jean. *Preface to Le tabac dans l'art, l'histoire et la vie*. Paris: Confrérie des Compagnons de Jean Nicot, 1961.

Corneille, Pierre. *Le Cid: A Translation in Rhymed Couplets.* Trans. Vincent J. Cheng. Newark: University of Delaware Press, 1987.

Doyle, Arthur Conan. *The Sign of Four.* Leipzig: Bernhard Tauchnitz, 1891.

Dye, Dale A. *Platoon.* London: Grafton, 1986.

Eco, Umberto. "Casablanca: Cult Movies and Intertextual Collage." *Substance: A Review of Theory and Literary Criticism* 14, no. 2-47 (1985): 3–12.

Ellmann, Richard. *James Joyce.* New York: Oxford University Press, 1983.

Freud, Sigmund. *Cocaine Papers.* New York: Stonehill, 1975.

——— . *The Standard Edition of the Complete Psychoanalytic Works.* Trans. and ed. James Strachey. London: Hogarth, 1958.

Gautier, Théophile. *Travels in Spain.* Trans. and ed. F. C. de Sumichrast. New York: Sproul, 1901.

Greenberg, Harvey. *The Movies on Your Mind.* New York: Saturday Review Press, 1975.

Hegel, G. W. F. *The Phenomenology of Mind.* Trans. J. B. Baillie. New York: Harper and Row, 1967.

Heidegger, Martin. *Being and Time.* Trans. John Macquarrie and Edward Robinson. New York: Harper and Row, 1962.

Hemingway, Ernest. *For Whom the Bell Tolls.* New York: Charles Scribner's Sons, 1940.

James I. *Misocapnus sive De Abusu Tobacci* [Counterblast to Tobacco]. London: R. B., 1604.

Kant, Immanuel. *The Critique of Judgment.* Oxford: Clarendon, 1978.

Klein, Richard. "The Future of Nuclear Criticism." *Yale French Studies* 77 (Spring 1990): 76–100.

——— . "Under 'Pragmatic' Paradoxes." *Yale French Studies* 66 (Spring 1984): 91–109.

Knight, Joseph. *Pipe and Pouch: The Smokers Own Book of Poetry.* Boston: Joseph Knight Co., 1895.

Koch, Howard. *Casablanca: Script and Legend.* Woodstock, N.Y.: Overlook Press, 1973.

Laforgue, Jules. *Poésies complètes.* Paris: Gallimard, 1970.

Lartigue, Jacques-Henri. *Les femmes aux cigarettes.* New York: Viking Press, 1980.

Leclerc, Annie. *Au feu du jour.* Paris: Grasset, 1979.

Lévi-Strauss, Claude. *Tristes tropiques.* Paris: Plon, 1955.

Limburg Stirum, Evrard de. *Adieu au tabac, ou du bon usage de la tentation.* Paris: Strand, 1988.

Louÿs, Pierre. *Oeuvres complètes: Contes.* Paris: Montaigne, 1930.

Mailer, Norman. *The Naked and the Dead.* London: Allan Wingate, 1949.

Mallarmé, Stéphane. *Oeuvres complètes.* Paris: Gallimard, 1945.

Mauriac, François. *Thérèse Desqueyroux.* Paris: Grasset, 1927.

Mérimée, Prosper. *Romans et nouvelles.* Vol. 2. Paris: Garnier, 1967.

——— . "Les Sorcières espagnoles." *Lettres d'Espagne.* Brussels: Complexe, 1989.

Molière. *Don Juan.* Paris: Bordas, 1965.

Montaigne, Michel de. *Essais.* Book 3. Paris: Garnier-Flammarion, 1979.

Nietzsche, Friedrich. *Briefwechsel.* Ed. Giorgio Colli and Mazzino Montinari. Berlin: Walter de Gruyter, 1981.

——— . *Le cas Wagner. Lettre de Turin, mai 1888.* In *Oeuvres complètes,* ed. Giorgio Colli and Mazzino Montinari, vol. 8. Paris: Gallimard, 1974.

Pauwels, Louis. *Louange de tabac.* Paris: M. Trinckvel, 1972.

Remarque, Erich Maria. *Im Westen nichts Neues*. Cologne: Kiepenheuer und Witsch, 1990.

Rival, Ned. *Tabac, miroir du temps*. Paris: Librairie Académique Perrin, 1981.

Saint-Gelais, Melin de. *Oeuvres complètes*. Paris: Bibliothèque Elzévirienne, 1873.

Sartre, Jean-Paul. *L'être et le néant*. Paris: Gallimard, 1943.

Sedgwick, Eve Kosofsky. "Epidemics of the Will." In *Zone 6: Incorporations*, ed. Jonathan Crary and Sanford Kwinter, 582–95. Cambridge, Mass.: MIT Press, 1992.

Styron, William. *The Long March*. London: Hamish Hamilton, 1962.

Svevo, Italo. *La coscienza de Zeno*. Rome: Arnoldo Mondadori, 1988.

———. *Ecrits intimes, essais et lettres*. Ed. and trans. Mario Fusco. Paris: Gallimard, 1973.

Vigié, Marc et Muriel. *L'herbe à Nicot: Amateurs du tabac, fermiers généraux, et contrebandiers sous l'Ancien Régime*. Paris: Fayard, 1989.

Index

Permission to quote from the following works is gratefully
acknowledged:

Ernest Hemingway, excerpts from *For Whom the Bell Tolls*. Copyright 1940
by Ernest Hemingway; renewal copyright © 1968 by Mary Hemingway.
Reprinted with the permission of Charles Scribner's Sons, an imprint of
Macmillan Publishing Company.

Jean-Paul Sartre, excerpts from *L'être et le néant* (Paris: Gallimard, 1943). ©
Editions Gallimard. Reprinted with the permission of Editions Gallimard.

Richard Klein is Professor of French at Cornell University. He is editor of
Diacritics, and has written on Nuclear Criticism and other issues of literary
theory.

Library of Congress Cataloging-in-Publication Data
Klein, Richard, 1941–
Cigarettes are sublime / Richard Klein
Includes bibliographical references and index.
ISBN 0-8223-1401-0 (cloth : acid-free paper)
1. Smoking in literature. 2. Literature, Modern—History and criticism.
3. Cigarette habit. 4. Popular culture.   I. Title.
PN56.S58K54 1993   809'.93355—dc20   93-22621 CIP